THE ENGLISH INFANT SCHOOL
AND INFORMAL EDUCATION

The Center for Urban Education, an independent nonprofit corporation, was founded in 1965. The following year it was designated a Regional Educational Laboratory under the Corporation Research Act of 1965. It is funded mainly by the United States Department of Health, Education, and Welfare through the Office of Education, but also contracts with other government agencies, state and local as well as federal, and with business firms and community agencies. The Center designs, field-tests, and disseminates alternatives to the traditional practices of formal education and citizen participation. Its headquarters are located at 105 Madison Avenue, New York, N. Y. 10016.

THE
ENGLISH INFANT SCHOOL
AND
INFORMAL EDUCATION

Lillian Weber

A CENTER FOR URBAN EDUCATION BOOK

PRENTICE-HALL, INC., Englewood Cliffs, New Jersey

For permission to reprint extracts from their publications, acknowledgment is hereby made to the following sources:

The Controller of Her Britannic Majesty's Stationery Office: From the Plowden and Hadow Reports, *Primary Education, Eveline Lowe Primary School,* and *Mathematics in Primary Schools.*

Education Development Center: From *Infant School.* Copyright © 1969 by Courtney B. Cazden.

The New Republic: From "Schools for Children," August 19, 1967, and "Teaching Children to Think," September 9, 1967, by Joseph Featherstone. Copyright © 1967 by Harrison-Blaine of New Jersey, Inc.

The New York Times: From news stories, October 23, 1966, and January 25, 1969. Copyright © 1966 and 1969, by The New York Times Company.

Saturday Review: From "Head Start to Where," by Fred Hechinger, December 18, 1965. Copyright 1965, Saturday Review, Inc.

The Urban Review, a publication of the Center for Urban Education: From "Programs, Placeboes, Panaceas," by Diane Ravitch, April 1968.

Pergamon Press Ltd.: From *Role of the Teacher in the Infant and Nursery School,* by D. E. M. Gardner and Joan E. Cass. Copyright 1965, Pergamon Press Ltd.

ISBN: (C) 0–13–281295–9
       (P) 0–13–281287–8

LIBRARY OF CONGRESS CATALOG CARD NUMBER: 71–167910

10   9   8   7   6   5   4   3   2   1

PRINTED IN THE UNITED STATES OF AMERICA

Prentice-Hall International, Inc., London
Prentice-Hall of Australia, Pty. Ltd., Sydney
Prentice-Hall of Canada, Ltd., Toronto
Prentice-Hall of India Private Limited, New Delhi
Prentice-Hall of Japan, Inc., Tokyo

CONTENTS

FOREWORD *by Dorothy E. M. Gardner* *vii*

ACKNOWLEDGMENTS *ix*

NOTES ON USAGE *xii*

INTRODUCTION: Turning to England 1

The Study, 6

part one

INFORMAL EDUCATION: The Practice
Learning Again in a Child's Way 15

chapter one

THE NURSERY SCHOOLS 17

Full-Time Nursery Schools, 18 • Scarcity and Types of Provision, 49 • Scarcity and Staffing, 54 • Solutions, 57 • The Model for the Infant School, 60

chapter 2

THE INFANT SCHOOLS 62

Some Lasting Impressions, 62 • SCHOOL SETTING: Neighborhood Schools, 66 • Staffing, 71 • ORGANIZATION FOR INFORMAL EDUCATION:

v

Class Organization and Concepts of Progression, 76 • Use of Building Space: Overflow and In-and-Outness, 81 • Plan of the Day—The Timetable, 89 • THE HEADMISTRESS AND THE TEACHER IN ACTION: The Headmistress and Communal Life of the School, 95 • Interaction and Communication, 100 • Teacher Planning, 104 • SCHOOL ENVIRONMENT AND CURRICULUM: Materials, 114 • Mathematics, 118 • Science, 122 • Reading, 126 • SUMMARY AND ESTIMATES: The Framework of Conditions, 132 • Impressions of Children's Behavior and Attitudes, 134 • Transition to the Junior School, 137 • Estimates, 142

part two

INFORMAL EDUCATION: The Entity and the Theory

chapter 3

THE INFANT SCHOOL ENTITY: Dissemination and History

147

Dissemination Through the Headmistress, 147 • The History, 160

chapter 4

THE IDEA: Rationale for Informal Education

169

Susan and Nathan Isaacs, 171

chapter 5

OTHER IDEAS: Convergence and Divergence

189

Jerome Bruner, 191 • Basil Bernstein, 197 • American Formulations, 206

chapter 6

EXTENSIONS AND REAFFIRMATION

215

SUMMARY THOUGHTS: Turning to America

232

BIBLIOGRAPHY   252
INDEX   270

FOREWORD

I hope this book will reach all those who feel concern about the education of children because to such it will prove richly rewarding.

During the year when Mrs. Weber was studying the Nursery and Infant Schools of England I had the privilege of meeting her frequently to talk over her findings. I was greatly impressed both with her awareness and understanding of current educational theory and its impact on education and also by her ability to observe and appraise the practice in the many schools she visited while in England. While never censorious she was constructively critical and no detail escaped her attention. The teachers were aware of her sympathetic interest in their work and discussed their ideas very freely with her. On our side we very much valued the knowledge she shared with us of ideals and achievements in education in the U.S.A. We found much in common—as was to be expected between two countries both inspired by a democratic philosophy of education. Differences arising from variations in historical influences and in the ways in which schools are planned and administered proved stimulating, at least where Mrs. Weber and I were concerned. We both felt we were learning from each other. I was delighted when she decided to put the results of so much careful thought and insight at the disposal of other teachers by writing this book.

DOROTHY E. M. GARDNER, O.B.E., M.A.
Formerly Head at the Department of Child Development, University of London Institute of Education

ACKNOWLEDGMENTS

Of the many who have helped me, my thanks first go to my family for their cheerful acceptance of my total preoccupation and for their unwavering conviction that I would prove equal to my self-imposed task.

Then I thank Spuyten Duyvil Pre-School, to whom I owe the means of carrying out the preliminary study and whatever I brought to it that helped me see and select.

I thank the heads of English schools and Mrs. G. M. Goldsworthy, Miss Nora Goddard of the ILEA, Miss Marianne Parry of Bristol, and Mr. R. D. Chapman of Birmingham, who arranged many of my visits, answered questions, and made me welcome.

Mr. E. R. Wastnedge of the Nuffield Junior Science Project generously shared with me the thinking of the project as it was being formulated and made it possible for me to participate in the workshops that introduce teachers to the new approach. Miss Alice Murton of the Froebel Foundation discussed with me the serious analytic work of the Foundation. Miss Mary Puddephat and many others of the Rachel McMillan College gave me an intimate view of teacher training and helped make my last three months in England good ones. Miss Peggy Jones introduced me to NNEB courses and to the National Campaign for Nursery Education. Mr. K. Pickett of North Western Polytechnic College helped me see many of the special services for children I would not otherwise have seen.

I owe thanks to many who, after my return from England, supplied the bits of information I needed for correct presentation, and who read and commented on sections of the manuscript. Miss Betty Grubb of the Rachel McMillan Nursery School, Mrs. E. M. Obsorn of the National Campaign for Nursery Education, Miss Daphne Wiseman and Miss Mary Anthony from the Department of Education and Science, Mrs. Eileen Maloney of B.B.C., and Mrs. Moira McKenzie of the Bousfield School in London were especially helpful.

During the preparation of his report on American education for the Carnegie Corporation, *Crisis in the Classroom,* I was happy to share my findings and analysis with Charles E. Silberman, and in the long interval before the publication of this volume, his frequent expressions of confidence were a welcome support.

I thank Vera Galanter for her intelligent assistance in typing and in details of preparation. Nancy Korman patiently helped type and categorize the mountain of raw material I accumulated in London. Others, Frances Clark, D. Maltpress, Ethel McGee, patiently assisted with typing earlier versions; and Marguerite Joba, Myra Segal, Sue Perscheta, Madeline Smith have also helped.

In a special category are my thanks to Miss Dorothy E. M. Gardner for her encouragement to come to England to see, and for her patience in allowing me to set the problem in my own way, to learn in a child's way so that I thought I had really "discovered." How easy it would have been to cut it all short with answers, to refer me to the "proper" book that did indeed have many of the answers. In some ways it was the example in herself of detailed observation and empathy for children, her own ability to see with a child's eyes, that gave me clues to definitions of "informal" education. I am grateful for this contact with her humane, disciplined, always inquiring mind.

To the late Mr. Nathan Isaacs I owe more than can be expressed here —a beginning grasp of the theoretical base from which English infant school method follows as necessary and inevitable.

The study, developed and prepared in consultation with D. E. M. Gardner, was submitted to the Institute of Education, University of London, December 1967. It was accepted with permission to publish and prepared for publication 1968–69.

I am indebted to Ruth Dropkin, Senior Editor of the Center for Urban Education, and to Arthur Tobier of the Cambridge Institute, whose confidence in the manuscript sustained me and who brought patience, experience, and insight to the editorial task. Initial contractual arrangements were made through Mr. Joseph Lederer, Publications Director of the Center for Urban Education.

LILLIAN WEBER

THE ENGLISH INFANT SCHOOL
AND INFORMAL EDUCATION

NOTES ON USAGE

1. Spelling throughout the book follows American conventions except where, as in a title of an English book or quotation from an English source, the original spelling is used. Use of English school terms follows conventions of the Plowden Report, e.g., "infant school" instead of "infants' school."

2. The term "state" education is used for what is called public in the U.S., to avoid confusion with the English usage of "public." It refers to free and publicly funded schools. The equivalent Plowden usage for free schools is: "maintained" by Local Education Authority and "supervised" by the Department of Education and Science.

3. "Plowden" is the common designation of the report, *Children and their Primary Schools*, issued in 1967 by the Central Advisory Council for Education of England, Lady Bridget Plowden, chairman.

4. "Hadow" is the common designation of the report *Infant and Nursery Schools*, issued in 1933 by the Consultative Committee of the Board of Education on Infant and Nursery Schools in England.

5. NNEB are the initials that identify an assistant who has passed the examination given after a two-year training period by the National Nursery Examination Board.

6. HMSO (Her Majesty's Stationery Office) is the official government publication distribution agency in Great Britain.

7. HMI (Her Majesty's Inspectors) are the national, politically independent inspectors of education, responsible only to Her Majesty.

8. LEA is the abbreviation for Local Education Authority; ILEA, for the Inner London Education Authority.

9. "8/60" refers to the circular issued by the Department of Education and Science in 1960 closing off further expansion of nursery education and setting the size of the total nursery school enrollment at the figure of 1957.

10. New Towns are new cities that have been deliberately planned to curb the uncontrolled growth of the old cities; most of these were developed during the post-World War II period.

11. The Nuffield Foundation in England is a research foundation. In the field of education it has sponsored experimental and innovative approaches, particularly in science and math.

12. Complete references for those sources not listed in the Bibliography are given in the footnotes.

INTRODUCTION
Turning to England

Why did I turn to England and what made me undertake, during 1965–66, the study reported in the following chapters? What was it that concerned me about our preschool education, and what guides to solutions did I think I would find in England?

As an American nursery school teacher and director, I was aware of how few children were being served by private or cooperative nursery education or even day care. I was convinced that we needed a vast expansion of preschool education, and equally convinced that the "quick" education that was being planned at that time could only offer a poor solution.

It had not been clear to me that "good" education could exist under the conditions usually found in the public sector until I discovered that England had what I considered to be "good" education, even with large classes, and that *it provided this in the state framework.* After initial skepticism, I became intensely interested, and determined to see it with my own eyes. And indeed, everything I saw in the English nursery schools was relevant to American problems. As a result of what I saw in English *infant* schools—their support of the continuity of a child's prior-to-school or

1

nursery school experience—my focus widened from the relatively narrower concern for preschools to a broader one: the investigation of possibilities for such continuity in our own public schools.

While American educators are still concerned with expanding preschool education, they now strive for more than that. The major focus of current efforts has shifted sharply, not only as a result of the inadequacy of the solutions offered in the name of preschool compensatory education, but also in light of the questions raised by that experience. The present focus in public education is on establishing *continuity* between preschool and the early grades, and on challenging the "usual" or traditional—in short, it is on *changed* education.

My introduction to English school practice for young children took place at the International Summer School of the Nursery School Association of Great Britain and Northern Ireland at Vassar College, in 1963.[1] What I heard and saw of public preschool education seemed to share the premises of the nursery school education I knew. I had come to the conference expecting no startling disclosures and, along with the other American participants who represented the private or, as in my case, the parent-cooperative sector of nursery school education, responded initially to what was familiar in the English setting: the responsive, individualized communication that made up the school day, and the look of the movement in the classroom. I basked in the superficial "sameness."

The special relevance of the English system to American concerns had indeed escaped me, but soon my attention focused on the essential *difference* between American and English schools: the English schools with their large groups were part of a system of state education. And though their "best" and our "best" looked very similar in action, still *our* "best" related to the few and small private or demonstration schools. Public education that looked as *good* as private education seemed well worth investigating.

At the time of the Vassar meeting, a national discussion on public preschool education was getting underway. The discussion had been stimulated by research confirming the importance and possibly critical character of early childhood learning.[2] Descriptions of poor school facilities and learning disability in the depressed areas of the cities added the note of urgency.[3] Moreover, the discussion reflected the forces put into motion by the civil

---

[1] Its VIIIth meeting at Poughkeepsie, N.Y., in 1963, was the first to be held in America.

[2] Benjamin S. Bloom, *Stability and Change in Human Characteristics* (New York: John Wiley & Sons, Inc., 1964).

[3] "The Great Cities School Improvement Study," Ford Foundation Project (mimeo.) 1960; *Youth in the Ghetto* (New York: Harlem Youth Opportunities Unlimited [HARYOU], 1964); Frank Riessman, *The Culturally Deprived Child* (New York: Harper and Row, 1962).

rights movement—forces that demanded not merely a description of problems, but *solutions*.

America had at that time no publicly funded education for young children—or so little of it that it served only a small fraction of the children who needed it. Care for children of poor and working mothers, limited to certain big cities, was in small supply, having been cut back rather than expanded after World War II. Most of whatever education existed was used by the middle class.[4] Even among the few excellent and expensive private schools physical arrangements for nursery schools were often makeshift. Most private and cooperative schools had to bend circumstances in churches, settlement houses, and even apartments, to implement their ideas of good living for children. The demonstration schools for teacher-training programs at universities and colleges could not be characterized as makeshift but there were, and are still, few of these. While day care services in some cities were provided in premises planned for such use, in most places only minimal building and health standards were enforced. Licensing based on educational standards, including those of qualification, was still a battle being fought, and standards were characteristically uneven. This state of affairs compounded the problem of scarcity.

With the forces of the integration movement baring the facts of poor educational facilities and mobilizing public opinion, great pressure was exerted for improving schools and revising educational perspectives. Concentration on early childhood, where there was little already existing structure, seemed to offer least trouble; on this level racial integration was least resisted. The enormous variation in nursery school standards and the lack of articulation between nursery education and the education that followed, however, turned the new program planners away from the private nursery schools. A really wide extension of nursery education within the public institutional framework was the obvious next step. And so, Operation Head Start was born.

Federal funding followed the avalanche of public pressure, supporting preschools both within the public school organizational structure and outside it, where in fact the federal guidelines introduced a new standardization. The first eight-week program of Head Start in the summer of 1965, and the year-round programs that grew from this, have, of course, made history. Over a half-million children attended Head Start that summer, in

[4] Samuel Schloss, *Enrollment of 3-, 4-, and 5-Year Olds in Nursery Schools and Kindergartens, October 1964* (Washington, D.C., National Center for Educational Statistics, June 1965). In 1964 the percentage of children enrolled in nursery school and kindergarten for each age was as follows: age 3, 4.3%; age 4, 14.9%; age 5, 58.1%, and of this group only 44.3% were actually in public kindergartens. The statistics did not indicate how many of the nursery schools were licensed or measured up to the various state department of education standards.

classes whose size was set at 15. When I left for England in August 1965, public preschool education was no longer "on the brink" but underway.

In that first winter of Head Start, however, it was plain that what had been possible at the outset could not be sustained without some serious thought for permanence. Though many year-round Head Start programs exist within the present building and space limitations, capital outlays are not part of the federal program. Despite much talk, there is still no funding for new buildings, which would represent real acceptance and institutionalization of Head Start programs. In fact, funding for Head Start is still precariously on a year-to-year basis and has not become an accepted part of regular school business and planning.[5]

Head Start's limitations were not only related to disappointments in funding, they were built in by the very nature of the program's definition: *compensatory education for the disadvantaged child in preparation for attendance at the regular school*.[6] The narrowness of definition even made itself felt in the character of training received by Head Start teachers and assistants.[7] In response to the emphasis implied in Head Start, the pro-

[5] No school system, not even that of New York City, seems financially able or has sufficient staff to undertake what is involved in a permanent overall extension of preschool education. At this writing, the 7 states Peet reported in 1965 as having no public school kindergartens still have none ("Why Not Enough Public School Kindergartens?" *Young Children*, Nov. 1965). In October 1968, Berson listed 17 states as providing no state aid for kindergartens ("Early Childhood Education," *American Education*, Oct. 1968). In 1970, 30% of children of kindergarten age in New York State were not in kindergartens, public or private, according to Commissioner Nyquist ("The State's Responsibility," see Bibliography). The original bulletin announcing Head Start noted that 1 million deprived children entered school every year; yet as of July 1970, only 258,000 children were reported in year-round programs; from the 560,000 of the first summer, Head Start registration was down to 472,931 in the summer of 1968, as recorded by the Office of Economic Opportunity.

[6] One reflection of this narrow focus was the appearance, in the years following the introduction of Head Start, of article after article belittling the usefulness of nursery school to any other than the disadvantaged child. It was not until 1967 that the position paper on prekindergarten education issued by the New York Board of Regents countered this trend by calling for free public education for *all* four-year-olds on a voluntary basis by 1970–74: *Prekindergarten Education* (Albany: State Education Department, Dec., 1967); budgetary and organizational implementation of this proposal, have not yet been made, however.

[7] One of the new elements Head Start injected into traditional systems was the addition of assistants. (Such staffing, in fact, has implications for further change still only partially realized.) The assistants, for the most part parents, were recruited from the community as one phase of the federal anti-poverty program and given an emergency training designed to fit the demands of Head Start. Training courses were soon extended but at this writing only a few community colleges project a full two-year program planned with a wide educational focus, and only a few programs are being offered for a sequence beyond this, that is, career development in which assistant can become teacher. See G. Bowman and G. Klopf, *New Careers and Roles in the American School* (1968) and *Teacher Education in a Social Context* (1967) (New York: Bank Street College of Education); also, F. Riessman and A. Pearl, *New Careers for the Poor* (New York: The Free Press, 1965).

grams had to offer not only training but retraining, based on material elaborating the differences in the deprived, and on a new educational approach thought to be necessary. Special programs and institutes proliferated, rallying the small number of qualified teachers from the private sector for training tasks. Inevitably there was dilution as qualified personnel were spread thin. The situation demanded heroic efforts, and quick training was stressed; institutes often were conducted in an atmosphere of "emergency."

When the early assessments of Head Start indicated the necessity of continuity to bridge the gap between preschool and the next level in public school, it became clear that the usual school organization did not provide the needed continuity, and the focus of discussion shifted to changes in the organization of the public elementary school. Fred Hechinger, summing up that first summer, discussed Kenneth Clark's warning:

> . . . compensatory education . . . is no substitute for change in the structure of education itself. Merely giving such children an opportunity to begin slightly ahead of the class is of little use if the regular school is not, at the same time, made relevant for them.[8]

Clark predicted a very limited short-term benefit unless there was consistent followup. *The New York Times* (October 23, 1966) reported studies indicating that the educational advantages of the Head Start program tended to disappear as a child moved on through the later grades and that

> either because of poor teaching or because of an uninspired curriculum in the public school, the pre-school child's thirst for knowledge went largely unquenched and the other advantages of pre-schooling rapidly dissipated.

A report by the Westinghouse Learning Corporation and Ohio State University (released April 13, 1969) also confirmed that the gains were rapidly dissipated.

The case for continuity was argued in even stronger terms in the *Urban Review*:

> If compensatory education were recognized for what it is, quality education, the absurdity of a limited one-, two-, or three-year program, particularly at the pre-school or elementary school level, would be apparent. After all, of what value to the student is temporary quality education? . . . Only sustained quality education makes a difference.[9]

[8] Fred Hechinger, "Head Start to Where?" *Saturday Review*, December 18, 1965, p. 60. See also Hechinger, *Pre-School Education Today* (New York: Doubleday & Co., 1966); Pines, *Revolution in Learning* (New York: Harper & Row, 1966); Grey, Miller, and Forester, *Before First Grade* (New York: Teachers College Press, 1966); Robison and Spodek, *New Directions in the Kindergarten* (New York: Teachers College Press, 1965).
[9] Diane Ravitch, "Programs, Placeboes, Panaceas," *Urban Review*, April 1968, Vol. 2, No. 5, 11.

The discussion mounted, but few proposals for developing this continuity were actually made. It is only since 1967, and on the most limited scale as "pilot projects," that continuity and Follow Through programs began to be developed, starting with kindergarten and adding a grade each year. Even though plans were made for 37,000 participants in 1969–70, double the number accommodated in 1968, the limited scale was plain.[10] Nevertheless, the arena has moved from publicly funded preschool education to the changes necessary for continuity. With no improvement seen from compensatory programs as long as traditional schooling was the next step, the focus was now on the public school organization itself. Finally, we have faced the problem of making our schools "good" schools that can assure continuity of experience for a child.

In America, this problem seems overwhelming to those who despair of the possibility for change within the huge public school organization; all public school solutions seem to threaten loss of the human dimension. But both the English infant school and its model, the English nursery school, are examples of state education that *have changed* and that possess human dimension; and so they are examples for us of a genuine possibility for change within our own public schools.

THE STUDY

The study reported in this book of a group of English nursery and infant schools is based on observations made from September 1965 to May 1966 as part of a year-and-a-half stay. Part One presents descriptions of the practice of informal education; Part Two summarizes the spread of this practice in England, its history and theory. As illustration, or as a case study, this report on informal education is meant to be freely interpreted and freely applied.

Data

The study repeats little of the tons of reportage that already exist on the current and projected status of preschool programs in the United States. American ideas are considered only as they affected the reexamination of English ideas.

Neither is this study meant to duplicate the descriptions of informal education that abound in English educational literature. The most extensive of such descriptions appears in *Children and Their Primary Schools*,

[10] "Follow Through Programs, 1969–70," *American Education*, Vol. 5, November 1969, 26–27.

the Plowden Committee report published in 1967 by the Central Advisory Council for Education.

By observing somewhat analogous situations in the industrial cities of England, I sought relevant answers to the problems of present preschool expansion in the United States and to the needs of children in the deteriorated areas of our cities. Eventually I narrowed my visits to London, Birmingham, and Bristol.

In planning this study, I had to match focus to possibilities. I first aimed at getting some idea of general organization, administration, and standards, but soon discarded the administrative survey and retained only enough information on administrative and supervisory standards to add pertinence to my observations. Though I left statistical evaluation of "good" or "bad" infant schools for English consideration, my visits to schools were at first conceived as a test with these questions in mind: What was the size of the classroom? How was it grouped? What was its schedule? What was the teacher's planning? Was the atmosphere responsive? Did it foster communication? I also considered long revisits to try to estimate a child's development, a child's progress in the learning of skills. At that point, I was thinking of the efficiency of the system, not of the system itself as the focus of interest.

Eventually I discarded the testing point of view, while still observing from the perspective of many of these questions. I directed my attention on all visits and revisits to absorbing as much as possible of the many different ways through which the responsive relationship of children and teachers was developed and the supporting conditions of the development. This framework for informal relationships was the real center of my observing; my notes on how skills were learned were intertwined with and incidental to this central framework.

Clearly I could not attempt to describe the *complete* functioning of any single informal school. I had to concentrate on and select only those factors to which I thought "informal" could be applied as the categorizing word. I did not, therefore, see or even note *all* the conditions in the schools visited. My plan was simply to observe those conditions that made possible education meaningful to me as an American nursery school teacher and that might be useful in our plans for preschool expansion and continuity for the whole age range of early childhood education (3–8 years).

Before leaving in December 1966, I had visited 56 schools in England, of which 53 were state schools. However, the study is based on the analysis of observations made in 47 state schools—17 nursery schools, 12 infant schools, 10 infant schools with nursery classes, 7 combined infant-junior (JMI) schools, and 1 junior school. (Junior school, the level following the infant school, serves children 7+–11+.)

Twenty-four of the schools were in London, 7 in Birmingham, 10 in

Bristol; 4 were New Town schools and 2 were suburban schools. The one junior school, in Bristol, was included because of its explorations into continuity of method from the infant school to the junior school. In the summer of 1969 I visited additional junior schools, all examples of the spread of this continuity of method, but these schools are not directly included in the analysis.

Schools were visited from before 9:00 A.M. until their closing at 4:00 P.M., for a minimum of one day each. Six schools were revisited. I lived next door to one nursery school and was able to observe it frequently and at length. I visited one infant school for a month, during which I studied patterns of children's and teachers' movement, in preparation for the production of the visual supplement to this study.

How were the schools picked? In London, Mrs. G. M. Goldsworthy, then Inspector of Nursery Schools for the Inner London Education Authority (ILEA), gave me a list of all nursery schools in her authority, leaving me free to visit any I chose. The infant school and nursery school heads or teachers I had been writing to since meeting them in 1963 also furnished me with leads and referrals for my first visits as soon as they understood I wanted schools in poor city areas. A couple of schools were referred to me by the University of London, Institute of Education, Child Development Department. My visits to Bristol and Birmingham were organized through the University of London, with the cooperation of the Inspectors of Infant Education in both Bristol and Birmingham. Except for the visits organized by the University of London, all others were arranged between the heads and myself, and in every case the freedom of the school was given me—for that day I was part of the life of the school.

At times I veered from this major plan of school visiting to sample other services for infants and children up to 8 years old, to substantiate an idea I had that the informal concept in education was not an isolated one but part of a generalized public attitude towards children. Visits were made to infant welfare stations where I saw toddler groups, to play centers, to adventure playgrounds, to play groups, to residential nurseries, and to day nurseries.

At the Vassar Conference in 1963, I had speculated that the assistant (the "NNEB," qualified by the National Nursery Examination Board), was very probably an important factor, making possible more informal relationships, even with large groups. I directed my observation to the functioning of these assistants in all the schools studied, and also visited five technological colleges that had programs for the training of nursery assistants, in particular, North Western Polytechnic. (Even before coming to England I had explored the possible significance of such programs as career training and recommended their incorporation into the New York City community colleges.)

I visited three teachers colleges and had prolonged contact with one of them at the very end of my stay when I was able to live in the Rachel McMillan College Annex residence for three months, as Warden (graduate/resident available to students and responsible for parietal rules). In this way I was in close touch with students, was able to visit lecture rooms and to see students during the period of student practice. These observations contributed some insight into the training of the teacher and into the dissemination of the "idea." Dorothy Gardner's seminar on teaching teachers, in the spring of 1966, added much to my understanding. Since I was registered at the University of London, attending child development lectures and participating in research seminars, I was in continuous discussion with students who were heads or prospective heads of schools.

Of profound significance to me was hearing Nathan Isaacs lecture and later having a long discussion with him shortly before his death in 1966. My participation in a Nuffield Junior Science Project Training Course was essential to my understanding of the English response to a child's "own question"; throughout my stay in England I was able to maintain contact with members of the Nuffield team. I was carried farther into the English analysis of the child's thinking at the Oxford Session of the Nursery School Association's International Summer School, July 1966. I became immersed in the English educational world, wading my way through the detail of discussion, observation, and reading. On Miss Gardner's advice I held off reading the English educational literature until my direct observations had given me a frame of reference and until I had made a tentative structure of "significance." The wisdom of that advice became clear to me when I found in much of what I read discussions of some of the aspects I had "discovered" in my hard work of observation. My reading and analysis confirmed and expanded in logical sequence what, in rough form, I had already found through observation.

My return to the United States and the subsequent delay in completing the writing of the study because of my immediate assumption of teaching duties at City College had significant effects on it. For one, all speculation about the Plowden Report with which the English educational circles were rife had to be updated in terms of the actual recommendations released in January 1967. Through correspondence, reading of English periodicals, discussion with English visitors, attendance at conferences, and finally, a revisit in the summer of 1969, I followed the effect of the Plowden Report on English education.

In addition, the visual supplement to this study, the movie, *Infants School*,[11] was shown widely. Questions that were asked raised points ob-

---

[11] Directed and filmed by Peter Theobald, and distributed by the Education Development Center, Newton, Mass.

vious to me when I was swimming along in the English milieu but which now had to be explained more specifically.

My own development of projects—clustering classrooms that open their doors to the corridor, with the whole considered as common living space—emphasized the need for great descriptive detail.[12] In all these ways the study has been extended, but it is still based primarily on observations made in England.

Definition of "Informal" Education

Over the course of a year and a half in the English schools, I gradually fathomed that the conditions I saw were themselves the mechanisms for deep change in the traditional school pattern. Particularly striking was the fact that these mechanisms and this change were widely spread without any visible official enforcement or prescription, and so the history and the techniques of this dissemination became part of my study.

When I went to England to observe the functioning of "informal" education, I had not yet questioned its definition. My preliminary notion of informal education was as the kind of teacher-child relationship and classroom organization stressing greater individualization with which I was already familiar. This view was to remain, but observations in the infant schools led to a detailed consideration of the meaning of "informal" and to an extension of definition.

It soon became clear that the definition or the idea itself was *one* of the conditions influencing the infant school's total function. So the theoretical basis for the practice I saw and tried to describe became an integral part of this study; the reexamination of my preconceptions, those premises I had taken for granted as "common," became intertwined with it. As my understanding of "informal" was extended, the study changed, even in the focus of its observation. Thus this report is, among other things, a step by step account—from "seeing" to reexamination to redefinition—of my understanding of the English idea of informal education.

As I visited schools, observed, and read, a more complete definition of "informal" took shape for me. It was a word I found more often in speech than in the literature, but all of those using it seemed to be quite clear as to what they were defining and of their reference. In the literature "formal" was usually used to express the opposite of activity methods. For my purposes I have continued to use the word "informal," as I first heard it, as contrasted with "formal." As time passed, "informal" came to have a broader meaning for me than the description of methods, as in activity or

[12] I am grateful to the School of Education, City College, and particularly to Prof. Marian Brooks, for their prompt support of these projects I designed for a number of Harlem schools.

discovery methods—and broader, too, than the description of experiments and experimental schools.

Informal, as I understand it, refers to the setting, the arrangements, the teacher-child and child-child relationships that maintain, restimulate if necessary, and extend what is considered to be the most intense form of learning, the already existing child's way of learning through play and through the experiences he seeks out for himself.

The active force of such learning is considered to be curiosity, interest, and the needs of a child's own search for definition and relevance. The school setting or environment must be rich enough to foster and maintain this curiosity; it must be free enough to allow and even to help each individual follow the path indicated by his curiosity. Entwined with the experience gained through a child's own use of the school environment is the learning of skills, because skills are needed in the process. *How* a child would learn in the school setting was also individual—he would learn in his *own* way, at his *own* pace, exploring his *own* interests, for his *own* purposes.

Understanding and examining this formulation of informal education occupied me throughout my stay in England. As my appreciative response grew, so also did my perception of differences between American and English schools; and my response grew because what I saw and understood seemed even more relevant, not less, to the discussion underway in the United States.

part one

INFORMAL EDUCATION
The Practice

Learning Again
in a Child's Way

Like many Americans, I had been exposed mainly to English literature, rooted in the English scene. I had assumed a comfortable understanding, a familiarity that, it turned out, had little connection with reality. Only after going to England did its place names, events, customs—even food—have meaning for me. All this is commonplace, the very reason for travel. But the strong shock all travelers feel on exposure to the firsthand gave me new insights on education. For the very act of seeing immediately catapulted me into a state of deep personal awareness of the learning process and so to receptivity to all definitions of informal education.

Placed into a context of utter unfamiliarity, my vision at first blurred and became dependent. I had to ask the bus driver to call out the stops, etc. Then I became almost painfully aware of signs, train tickets, idiom, movement, different patterns of streets, of traffic. Eyes intent, ears pricked up, I was unable to take for granted the smallest point. I began to realize what a great deal of detailed experience is needed before a pattern is seen. Immersed in strangeness, my own learning, my ability to make correct deductions was not very quick. Detail had to accumulate. And I was ready—

15

in my situation of having no clues—to accept *anything* as possible, even things for which I could find only absurd or magical explanations. The meaning of small experiences, how they "fit," would strike me hours or even weeks later.

I remember my first bruising on the unfamiliar. On my first night in London I started to check out possibilities for long-term housing and boarded a bus. No driver in sight, only an attendant pulling a cord, the bus was swerving its way through traffic. "Is that the driver?" I asked a passenger, pointing to the attendant. "Is it all right?" A woman leaned over and patted my knee, "Not to worry, love." That night I wrote home, in all seriousness, "The English are so clever, they even have a new kind of automated bus." The next day I *saw* the front cab construction of the bus and its driver, but I still thought the other one had been driverless, an experiment. A couple of weeks later, I woke up convulsed with laughter, my long-established basic distrust of magic reasserting itself. But at the same time, I was startled that this could have happened to me, an adult with lots of framework in which to fit new experience, and happen in England where so much was warmly familiar.

I give this apparently irrelevant illustration because it was a salutary beginning for an investigation of informal education. My sense of disorientation quickly receded, and I could learn and expand and correct. Another person, depending on his unique bent and background, would have different disorientations and different disconnections. But it was, perhaps, this vulnerability, the sudden realization of unfamiliarity, the sense of disconnection, that made me more open to new meanings in "simple" formulations, to differences that were important. I could see the differences because the blur was not total; some of my background in education and in child development did stand me in good stead.

At first I saw the small differences of use, of function, of condition, which I expected and to which my attention was directed. Later, because I was a sufficiently experienced teacher from a background sufficiently similar, I could be critical, even see and weigh degrees of difference. There was *enough* difference to force the seeing with new eyes, to force the slight shift, the reordering, to prevent me from treating differences as only an addition of facts and information, and to permit me to learn again in a child's way but feel with an adult's awareness that I was learning. The process was part and parcel of my rethinking, redefining my understanding, because it was an idea and a system supportive of a child's way of learning that I was seeing.

chapter 1

THE NURSERY SCHOOLS

Their status in state education first stirred my interest in the English nursery schools. Here I hoped to find clues to solutions of American problems in public education for the early childhood years.[1] My observations focused on answers to these questions: Why were the nursery schools considered so important in spite of being so few in number? What was the national importance of their high standard? Why were they treasured as models for the infant school? Did their large groupings, 30 children to each qualified teacher, work? Did individualized nursery education as I knew it exist with these groups? If it did, what were the conditions that made it possible? What did it look like?

Overall, the impression I took away of English state nursery education was that absolutely everything had been provided and thought through

[1] In all, I visited 17 nursery schools: 4 full-time, 7 full-time/part-time, 6 part-time; 13 were in London, 2 in Bristol, 2 in suburbs. I later visited 10 *nursery classes* located in infant schools. Of these, 4 were full-time, 1 full-time/part-time, 5 part-time; 6 were in London, 2 in Birmingham, 1 in Bristol, and 1 in a New Town.

for the maintenance of healthful school living, for the support of emotional adjustment, and for the stimulation of intellectual response. Though there were classes of 30 children, these had been planned for in space, in staffing, and in equipment, so that the natural pace of a child's development was in no way impeded. The excellence of the planned structure of English nursery education came through clearly; the serenity of the school atmosphere was remarkable.

FULL-TIME NURSERY SCHOOLS

Setting and Intake

The location of the nursery school was almost always in the poor working-class areas. Identification of the areas as "poor" was sometimes difficult because of the "high-rise" apartment house complexes ("Council estates" which correspond to our public housing projects for low-income tenants) that had replaced the slums bombed out during World War II. Even though the new housing was much less drab than what it replaced, it was still considered "poor," since it was constructed to relocate a predominantly working-class population.

It was not only because the poor were housed in these new apartments or "flats" that nursery schools were established in those neighborhoods. English educators view living in high-rise flats as "deprivation." They recognize that such housing provides a less natural way of living for children because it separates children from the natural materials of learning, the natural environment that helps children begin to develop understanding of process and causality. Living in these buildings is considered a hardship for children. The hardship is more than the hardship of poverty. It is the hardship of urbanization. The nursery school, according to English planners, would help children overcome this hardship.

Admission was often from a much wider area than the school neighborhood. Sometimes this occurred because an old stabilized population had outgrown the need and left vacancies in the nursery school register. More often, admissions were based on selective judgments about need. With nursery schools in short supply, the waiting list for admission was very, very long. Recommendations by the health visitor (a trained nurse with additional public health and social work qualifications) or by the doctor usually gave definite precedence to children or parents in need, and need might be poverty, illness, large families, bad living conditions (including high-rise housing), or other problems.

The relatively small number of immigrant children in the nursery schools seemed to be largely the result of the failure to expand provision of nursery schools. Also, the immigrants, new to the community, either had not put themselves on the waiting list or were last on the waiting list. If a headmistress could not respond to an application from immigrants, she immediately put the younger child of the family on the list. Where immigrants did manage to get into housing estates, their number in the schools increased. Once in the school, immigrant children were easily accepted and included in the program.

The attention given by the Plowden Report to "educational priority" areas, which are analogous to our inner-city areas, reflects the prevailing view of the importance of nursery education for an immigrant child. Plowden urged a policy of positive discrimination and advocated active persuasion to enroll all children in need of nursery education.

Information on the children's economic background that I culled from the heads' listing of parent occupations indicated that even though the local area was no longer the only one served, the bulk of intake was working class. Nevertheless, since many headmistresses used the waiting list as their main guide, it could happen that enterprising parents of any class who had registered their children very early could conceivably be rewarded by admission. But the schools had been set up with the intent of serving those most in need, and for the most part still largely served the poor. There were fatherless children, children whose fathers were in jail, children whose mothers were in hospitals. There were children who were described as very, very poor. None of this, however, seemed to declare them "different." Certainly, the children's poverty did not stand as a barrier blocking the teacher's understanding. Some of the heads still resided in the neighborhood of the school. They had shared war experiences with their older neighbors, and were known to have lived with children from just these backgrounds during the wartime evacuation. The teachers, too, seemed deeply aware of and full of empathy with the burdens and the conditions of the children's lives.

The School Building

The concern for the loss of human dimension in the urban environment helped shape the physical design of the English nursery school. Each school was a planned oasis of beauty. Such planning provided immediate access to the outdoors, so that indoor and outdoor play could go on simultaneously. It provided for a garden. Above all, the building plan offered space for all the richness and variety of equipment as well as the means to arrange this equipment in areas that were suitable and inviting.

The building itself was a one-story structure. Windowed doors opened out onto paved bays under a slight overhang and led to the garden. Each group of 30 children had a large room. Additional rooms were set aside for staff use, the headmistress's office, and a medical office. Most schools had kitchens. A number of schools maintained laundries that were used by several schools jointly. Usually a wide corridor connected all these facilities.

The washroom and toilet areas were spacious. They were filled with children-sized sinks, six to a group of 30, and children-sized toilets, five to a group of 30. In some of the older nursery schools (pre-World War II vintage), the washroom had a large tub, placed originally to allow the teacher to stand while bathing the children. Redesigned with benches around it and a shelf for accessories, the tub now served for expanded water play. Large window walls divided these facilities from the classrooms to permit the teacher a quick look-in for checking the whereabouts or needs of pupils. Each child had a locker for his plastic cup, comb, wash cloth (flannel) and a towel, and sometimes even toothbrush. Each item was marked with a picture symbol—a ship, ball, train, etc.—special to that child.

With present-day central delivery lunch service, use of the kitchens for lunches is no longer necessary. But the kitchen still served as the area for children's cooking projects. Widespread use of paper goods is beginning to make laundries less essential, though the full-time schools, equipped as they are with linens for cots, blankets, and often coveralls or smocks for the children, still required laundry services.

All these linens were also marked with a child's special symbol. Seeing all the personal items in washrooms, lockers, and on cots, I was impressed with the work entailed in marking and keeping track of them, thinking that in a typical American setup and with our staffing, we would find such effort very hard. Certainly we do use more paper goods, but the amount and detail of what we provide, even in our day care centers, are not as great as in the English nursery schools.

Each school had a cloakroom or a rack in a special space in its entry way or in a space in the entry way of each classroom. Just as with us, cubbies were divided with a bottom shelf, serving as a seat as well as for storage of extra shoes (usually soft slippers) or Wellingtons (boots), and with a top shelf for extra clothing and personal possessions, again all with picture symbols special to each child.

The Garden

The school garden was usually marked by a luxuriance that offered a multitude of uses. Levels and areas were planned to create spaces for small groupings. Some did this with encircling paths and plantings for privacy and protection. There were various places to climb and objects to climb on. There might be a small pool with steps leading down to it and edged with flowers. Often, steps and seats were situated all over. The landscaping varied from school to school. In one, an unusual area featured a large sea net spread over four posts and a stone seat circle. One garden used the bent-over branch of a tree as a climber, and big trees or full-branched shrubs were especially prized as additions to the flower-planting areas. There were areas for digging, areas with cut-down stumps covered with mosses, fungi, and peeling bark, and even in a few cases, a high-grass, meadowlike area. In some gardens a hill had been constructed, grown over with wild flowers. Animals such as rabbits and guinea pigs could be brought out to pens in the garden. Finally, there were the paved areas, just outside the window-doors, with standard nursery outdoor equipment, where children could ride tricycles and scooters, play with ropes and sticks, or enjoy a rope swing. In good weather, these areas were used for lunch service and for naps on cots after lunch. An overhang made possible the outdoor use of easels and work-benches. An interesting and important aside: in London, the school gardens are maintained by the Parks Department and repairs are taken care of by agencies of the London City Council.

Some Typical Schools

In one school in London, children moved about independently, at ease, comfortable in their surroundings. I saw a corner lovely with green growing things, a whole window of this in fact. In the corridor a windowed bay was filled with a sofa, two easy chairs, a bottle garden, and two children were curled up on the sofa looking at books. Children arrived in twos and threes over a period of an hour or even longer. I began to see this gradual arrival as a factor in the creation of the ease of movement. They went over to a favorite corner, fingered some things, greeted the teacher. Stopping to say a word to this one or that, they gradually got to the corner where some milk was set out, drank their milk, and then went back to play with whatever attracted them.

I saw mothers help undress their children as they arrived in this gradual way. They chatted with the head, chatted with the teacher, left the school in the same gradual way, in twos or threes, as they arrived. In one school, I noted that four mothers stayed on through the morning, sitting in the midst of all that was going on, calmly knitting. A pram was outside with a baby sleeping in it. Nobody seemed to be in any kind of rush.

I saw three different kinds of sand: dry coarse sand, damped-down sand, and a very, very fine sand. In addition to the sand, clay and dough were laid out, easels were set up for four, and an arrangement of block accessories on the floor invited children to start at block building.

Musical instruments were hanging on a rack near the piano. There was a book corner, a housekeeping corner (usually called the Wendy house in England) that was extremely well furnished, with a closet filled with dress-up clothes hanging ready to use for dramatizations. Outside there were mice, hamsters, guinea pigs and rabbits—and a workbench.

In another London school the long, wide corridor had a slide in it, a book corner with child-sized upholstered chairs, and interesting plant arrangements. Even so, it was not crowded. Each area was attractive, inviting. Children were using all this and with nothing hectic about their use.

In one of the classrooms three or four mothers were sitting right in the midst of things with their children. The window-doors were open. Children went to some of the things outdoors, left those, and came back to some of the things indoors. They went in and out and in again. The planning of the day was obviously different from ours. Until lunch time the day had no periods of *all* being in and of *all* being out. This simultaneous in-and-outness in use of the rich environment struck me immediately. Perhaps this was the key to the planning for the 30.

In another classroom one young staff member, holding up a jar with some sprouted beans, was talking quietly about the growth of seeds with a child sitting near the nature table; another staff person was near the animals, holding a guinea pig in her lap. The first woman turned out to be an NNEB, the other was an NNEB student.

The headmistress moved in the midst of everything. Even when she returned to her office, she found two children there, doing a puzzle on the floor. Almost every moment a child appeared to tell her something or to look for a minute at her collection of tiny treasures—mementoes from her summer trips perhaps—that were *meant* to be looked at, wondered at, fingered, talked about in quiet, calming conversation. Indeed, every head's office was an oasis of calm in the midst of the general activity, a place of flowers, a few lovely books, puzzles, and nearly always one or two children.

One morning I met the health visitor who had stopped in at the head's office before going on to the medical room. She reported to that school every Monday, making herself available to the mothers and inquiring of the staff if there were any problems. She moved through the school, talking to children, now and then passing a word with the teacher. Everyone, not only the staff but the children as well, was quite at ease about talking with each other and talking with me.

Indeed, there was no forced or pressured sense about anything. The ease of the teachers with the children was enormous. One memorable vignette: I saw a child take some dress-up clothes and start dancing around, saying she was a bride. A teacher promptly sat down right in the midst of all the other activities and played a couple of bars of "The Wedding March." Three or four children joined her; they all sang for a moment and then went back to their own play.

Through the glass wall of one of the classrooms I had a view of the washroom, and watched children use the facilities as needed. I saw them washing with their flannels, carefully combing their hair, and admiring their efforts in the many child-height mirrors.

At lunch, teachers and children sat and conversed in groups of approximately eight at tables that were covered with colorful cloths, with a nosegay of real flowers in the middle. Before rest time, cots were set up in little groups to prevent too much disturbance, and with awareness that some children did not want the rest. Some children had games on their cots, some played quietly in the Wendy house, some rested for only a short while. A good many cots were put outside on the paved bays and under the overhang; these were largely for the sleeping children.

Awakening gradually, the children resumed play gradually. Outdoors, in addition to the standard equipment there were piles of ammunition boxes (discards from World War II) used as large block building material, boards, ladders, wheelbarrows, and commando nets for climbing. Children helped take care of the animals outside, the rabbits and the guinea pigs. Also outside were the easels and the workbenches—all in the setting of a garden filled with flowers, bushes, trees. Even the paved areas were made more interesting with a lovely bit of planting encircled by an old tire or a brick trim. A gardenlike effect was duplicated indoors with the flowers and the lushness of the large "woods" garden on the window ledge. Here in a very large hollow tile all sorts of mosses, wild flowers, and tree seedlings would grow. It was clear that much attention had been given to detail, to attractiveness, to variety that could stimulate on many levels.

In a somewhat different setting a nursery school located in a house was planned inside and out for young children's use. This school had one large room and a smaller room, with the children using both at the same time. In the large room the teacher had put out dough on one table, manipulative games and puzzles at two other sets of tables. The workbench was in this room, and there was space for tables, screens, etc., to be put together for dramatic play. The tables themselves were on a kind of stand where both the table top and the stand could be used for large block building. One long wall was entirely lined with cupboards for storage of blocks. In the smaller room there were doll beds and carriages for house play and the sandbox, paint, and games.

There was, of course, a good bit of setting up to be done, because the environment was not entirely prepared for the children's immediate use. This was apparently a conscious and calculated decision. Both the pace of arrival and the tempo of the unfolding life of the school were adjusted to ensure involvement of the children in setting up for their own activities and for their school. Certainly the children knew how to help; they got out more things as they wanted them, although some material had been put out by the teacher.

Children, escorted by parents, arrived very gradually starting at 8:30;

at 9:30 children were still coming. There was no particular fuss over any child. No issues were forced. One very timid little girl came with a grandmother. The grandmother stayed awhile, chatted with the teacher, with her grandchild, with the other children. The teacher then brought over a little doll and a puzzle and talked with the girl: "Can you do this? You do a bit and then I'll see it." Then she continued helping some other children with the color cone. After a while the grandmother left. The headmistress, seated on a low ledge, half inside, half outside the window-door, was reading a book with a boy. One little girl walked in with a dog. At one table a child was very carefully attaching all the builder-men together; another was doing a puzzle. "Have you ever tried this one?" asked the teacher. "See if you can find the piece left out." In the smaller room children were painting at a table, and a shy little boy after first watching joined them. He finished and held up his work. "I've done it!"

A Rainy Day

The extra rooms, the staff room, and the headmistress's office, as well as the corridor, seemed always to be in use, but until the first rainy day I had not fathomed the importance of their use. On that day I saw three children sitting on the rug in the head's room, playing a card game: "A spade, a club," one child said. Two other children were sitting in an easy chair looking at a book together. Four children were in the staff room with an NNEB, having a story read to them. Another group had been allowed to take housekeeping things to that room for a more private game, and another couple were in the corner playing a special house game.

The corridor allowed for an indoor in-and-outness, for overflow and outlet. In it children were using wheel toys, running about, and talking with each other. In this school the large tank was in the corridor and the children could use tubing, funnels, pourers, and containers of all sizes for water play.

I was struck by how easily the English accepted not only their bad weather but water play in that bad weather. Seated on a rocking-horse a child watched the water play, offering a remark in that direction now and then. Suddenly, a line of prams swung into view, manned by the housekeepers, all dressed in hats, trailing skirts and carrying pocketbooks.

Over in a corridor corner three little girls were seated on little chairs looking at books, and a boy was "reading" to them. In this corner were a few upholstered easy chairs, pillows, fresh flowers, a lovely drape of material, an interesting shell on a low shelf and some intriguing arrangements of a bit of sea glass and a piece of blue glass on a low table close by—all available for fingering by the children.

On this particular rainy day I was visiting a school where the situation might well have seemed especially difficult. It was a school in a housing project in London, a part-time school. Since the rooms were larger than average it had been decided to increase the register of each class to 40 and also to adjust the number of NNEBs. (The usual ratio was one NNEB and one NNEB student to each group of 30.) Each room was now staffed with a teacher, two NNEBs, one student from a teacher training college, and one NNEB student. Yet even with the larger register there existed the same atmosphere of serenity, the same absence of confusion, and the same planning to produce good living for the children as existed with smaller registers.

Five children were at one table with scissors, paper and paste, and boxes of scrap material. Dough for four children was set out at another table. Two corners had been set up for puzzles, and at one of these four children were busy at work. Chalk, colored and white, a slate, and paper were laid out at another table. The dress-up corner, right next to the housekeeping corner, was in use. A raised platform across one end of the room, like a stage, was the block area. Three children were building with great concentration. In another corner was another housekeeping area with a hospital section quite near this, with a large quantity and variety of "doctor things." In addition to a housekeeping corner, a corner in almost every room was set up as a hospital. Almost always a helper was nearby, joining now and then with a word or two to keep it going; the conversation was very specific about real illness even in the hypothetical situations of the playing.

Of course there was a book corner with flowers on the table and easy chairs. In fact, every room in the nursery schools seemed to have one large upholstered chair or a rocking chair. Powder paint and water cups were set out on a tray beside a table. Next to a window I saw the usual nature table and near the door another table with interesting "junk." The teacher was greeting children as they came in, saying "hello" to their parents. Some children went to a game of magnetic fish played on the water table, now covered for this temporary purpose. Some went to the sand table.

In the other room the sand table was covered with a farm board that created a farm setting to encourage play with mini-farm figures. There were cover boards also with settings for miniature car or miniature train play. In this way particular pieces of equipment could have different uses. On the raised stage platform in the room three children were playing "office" and one boy, using very large tinkertoylike pieces, was quietly adding to a large construction. Another was sitting "reading" to a friend. A mother was helping a child with dough; two other mothers were talking to each other. The teacher joined some finger painters, while at another table a student helped some children, drawing with wax candles and then covering this with thin color. The wax resist was extremely popular; six children were at it, others wanted it. An assistant came over to help. At 9:40 five mothers were still in the room.

In the first room two boys were at the powder paints, two children at an easel, and four were using dough. A couple of children were playing with the instruments at a music table. An assistant joined the boys at the powder paints. The teacher was talking to a child who had brought in two very large leaves. Then she spoke to another child who wanted help in buttoning her dress. She seemed somehow to be all over the room, going to all the children, in all the corners.

Later, in visits to nursery classes held in infant schools, I had the same impression of enormous flexibility. In one such nursery class, which was full-time to meet the needs of teachers' children, an effort had been made to reproduce some of the stimulation missing for these children who were away from home all day. The teacher was reading with a child on one arm of a large upholstered chair and another stretched lolling across the top. Two pillowed armchairs crowded with children had been drawn near. An NNEB sat at a sewing machine, with a child "feeding" the machine as it seamed. At a full-sized stove, a small group was cooking. There was all the usual rich equipment of the nursery school, but it was somehow less sterilized and less simplified, creating a warm, stimulating atmosphere with all the overlapping complexity of home.

Other full-time nursery classes served other special needs—needs of working parents, of parents whose trip to school was overlong, or partial-hearing children. In one for such children, specific help was given at certain periods of the day; at other times of the day they could join other classes or groups, could mix with the infant school children. I recall seeing an infant child turn fully to the nursery child and speak with him, with obvious mouthing. The child answered and the first child patted him, smiled, and said, "You said it nicely. You heard me." The imitation of the teacher's way was perfect!

Standards

In spite of small differences between the nursery schools visited, the uniformity of standards was impressive. Moreover, the standards appeared to be far in excess of our own middle-class nursery schools.

CLEANLINESS AND HEALTH. In addition to the planned buildings already described, the cleanliness was characteristically of a very high standard. The English maintenance of cleanliness was more pervasive, compared to the American. In fact, it seemed impossible to duplicate with our kind of staffing. For example, it was taken for granted that before a child went home and back to his mother, he was "neatened up." At that time, he washed up, combed his hair, and then enjoyed a quiet kind of period for a bit. Such neatening up and quieting may of course have made for much better and easier school-home transitions. Some schools, it seemed to me, had almost too many procedures, almost too much cleanliness.

The emphasis on cleanliness was an aspect of the overall emphasis on health. There are historic reasons for this significant feature of English schools. The nursery schools had started in poor areas and were intended for poor children whose need for this kind of care was often extreme. The health program was a way of combatting the high disease rate of an economically deprived population. The glorious sturdiness and zest of the children now in these schools, with intake listed as "poor," is a tribute to the success of the national health program of which this is a part. As already noted, the nursery schools had close contact with the health service which sent health visitors once a week. Heads told me about dental visits and medical visits, and there was also the regular help of a speech therapist. The teachers could arrange for additional visits of the speech therapist and other special help for children of slow speech. At one London school I was told that any child not progressing was tested by an audiologist. In effect, services of all kinds were available.

MATERIALS IN ENVIRONMENT. There was nothing unplanned about the English settings. Rich provision of equipment was standard. Parents contributed and helped in making things, perhaps especially the costumes. The ingenuity of the headmistress in getting donations of all sorts and in foraging was just as important as it is for American heads of nursery schools. The funds could be spent by the headmistress in any way she wished and of course this made for some differences. One school, for instance, might seem to concentrate on enormous variety in art materials. Another might offer more provision for hospital play and for office play. Still another could have a lovelier garden and a large number of animals, and provide more opportunity for children to garden. Or a school might have lots of block play or lots of music. All these variations indicate slight differences in emphasis or use of equipment.

Clocks, numbers, letters were available for children to use if they wanted them. Toys that required a great deal of use of hands and fingers were very popular with the children. An American, Lochhead, observing these schools in 1928–29, commented on the amount of manipulative apparatus, Montessori apparatus, and the lesser amount of large muscle equipment.[2] I saw a great deal of manipulative equipment but it was used in free ways, not at all in sequential Montessori-like ways. And I have already noted that large muscle and dramatic play equipment was in very good supply, very much used, and used in a free in-and-out way and in combination, one material with another.

[2] Jewell Lochhead, *The Education of Young Children in England.*

Assembling, cutting, and pasting of all sorts of shapes and kinds of boxes and discard junk material are perhaps more characteristic of English than of American schools, although these activities are becoming more prevalent in our nursery schools, day care centers, and Head Start groups.

Along with the basic standard equipment, there were all kinds of improvised materials, in and outdoors, and unique ways of using materials. The teachers revealed enormous ingenuity in figuring out ways of a child using a material or a piece of equipment without interference with other children's use of other materials. For instance, in many schools I saw a blanket tacked to the top of the workbench, which quite effectively dulled the sound of the hammer and allowed its use at all times.

What was particularly striking was the willingness on the part of the teachers to construct an environment that would help children make ready use of it, even to the point of moving a great deal of equipment, if necessary. Teachers revealed also an impressive lack of grudging about leaving things out for use and a great readiness to be flexible. Rooms seemed to be changed around quite often, and teachers said they made a point of this. It was quite clear that the teachers were aware of the necessity to create stimuli. Corners were arranged to be stimulating: "what makes sounds" corners, corners that had all kinds of "blue" together, including even the word "blue," or a table that held only round things. Such corner arrangements clearly reflected the teacher's effort to bring in interesting things that would provoke and stimulate questions. Then there were corners that were just extremely inviting, with flowers and easy chairs, things which made it very pleasant to sit and look at books. And children *were* looking at books in every book corner. Assistants and teachers were sitting and reading to children, much more often than only at the story period. The corners and the areas fostered the conversation that was going on all the time. An adult sitting down in an area immediately became the center of a conversational group. Often I saw a teacher with three or four children gathered near her to help clean the cage, and to feed, hold, pet, and converse about the ways of the animals.

One possible exception to English high standards in equipment was the block area. The supply as well as the planning for use of the blocks (called "bricks" in England) were often weak. Breaking down of others' block building was more or less accepted, and I wondered if this sometimes reflected the English teachers' low opinion of block building as a form of play and of intellectual exploration. There was often very little provision, such as shelves, for putting away blocks in an orderly fashion. In many cases blocks were dumped into boxes with little sense of precaution, indicating not too much experience with them. Judging from the condition of the blocks in many schools, they had not been sanded, shellacked, and waxed every year as is customary in many American nursery schools.

In many schools, a blanket on the floor protected children from the cold floor but made block building difficult if not impossible. The easy and casual English attitudes about weather and clothing were not consistent. Though they were relaxed about these for in-and-out play outdoors, they were concerned indoors about drafts along the floor.

Despite the generally low level of block play, I did see schools with a large supply of blocks where the level of block play was quite good. Some had made building easier by putting a stiff rug rather than a blanket on the floor to create at least a smooth, steady surface. There seemed to be no interference with the use of tables, chairs, and so on, as improvised props, and there were a great many accessories for block play.

In-and-Out Use

The easy in-and-out use planned for in nursery buildings, and even provided in houses remodelled for nursery school use, was endlessly surprising and delightful to me.

This in-and-outness, now part of English educational philosophy, has a long history. It was originally a response to health needs. The Hadow Report notes that a 1905 report by the Committee of Inspectors, which criticized the dull, repetitive tasks given the under-5s, enunciated the open air principle. Many reports followed, recommending as much open-air activity as possible; one specifically outlined arrangements for in-and-outness to dilute the impact of the common cold.

In 1907 medical inspectors, confronting the high incidence of physical defects in the five-year-old children in infant school, changed their minds about their criticism of school for the under-5s. They began to consider the bad educational practice as an argument for improving conditions for the under-5s, not for abandoning their education. They defined such education as *nursery* education.

In 1914 at her school in Deptford, Margaret McMillan experimented with open-air sheds in gardens, thus building in-and-outness into her structure. Nursery schools, in her view, should be open shelters set in garden playgrounds. Here poor children would be helped toward a better life and better health, a good way of growing up.

The use of the outdoors now has come to be a way of easing the pressure of large numbers and a way of allowing greater access to the rich supply of equipment. Old lorries, old cabs, old rowboats, and even commando nets, enrich the standard equipment outdoors but far more equipment serves the double category of in-and-out use than a single in *or* out use.

The fashions of English children's clothing make it easy to use the in-and-outness that was part of every school's arrangement. Shoes are easy to take off, for frequent barefootedness, for feeling sand outdoors, or feeling grass, for dancing, for activities in the dress-up corner, for resting. Very few children had to bother teachers with tying shoelaces or knots; they wore sandals they could buckle themselves. Children did not wear snow pants, and the anoraks or ski jackets were easily slipped on, with only a bit of help needed from the teachers. Children did not have to struggle putting boots on *over* shoes; Wellingtons are easy since they slip on over socks. When the Wellingtons were discarded indoors, the child often stepped into soft slippers. When I thought of the amount of clothing we used in the winter time, in-and-outness seemed less possible for us, but on the other hand, we had not set up the situation which would allow for in-and-outness when it *was* possible, in our long fall and long spring.

English weather does not have our northern United States' bad winters; the winter temperature average in London is approximately 40 degrees. Even conceding the milder winters, however, it was obvious that there was great ease about the weather. If it had been raining during the morning but had stopped in the afternoon, the children went out. Wet ground or wet grass did not seem to matter, though a number of children did have Wellingtons along with them. Cold, gray days were certainly no impediment to use of the outdoors. Children, their legs bare, ran out in such weather and right after the rain. In the spring, I saw the outdoors used for sleeping and for lunch as well as playing. There was no hesitation about this if the weather was not absolutely forbidding. I certainly was taken aback to see children sleeping outdoors on February 1, but it was a pleasant, warm day!

The teachers had no reluctance about moving almost any kind of equipment for use outdoors. At the same time, there was duplication indoors of the outdoor sand and water. Bathing naked in outdoor pools or spray was started quite early, as soon as there was a warm, sunny day. The children and mothers seemed to expect this. Use of the outdoors was facilitated by the shelter of windbreaks and overhangs, so that even on a rainy day, if mild, some outdoor activity such as painting, or perhaps the workbench, could continue. Thus, whenever it was possible, the outdoors had *everything*: painting, clay, finger painting, woodwork, the animals. This made it quite possible for small groups to work in and out. The large window doors—the rooms are on the same level as the outdoors—made it very easy to set up this outside playground.

On a bad, rainy day the principle of in-and-outness was extended to the many extra areas of the indoors: the headmistress's office, the staff room, the corridors, the entry ways, the sink area. Every bit of leeway the building allowed was used to create overflow in-and-out indoor areas for the most complete and flexible use of the environment.

Gradual Procedures

The gradual arrival and the gradual departure of children were basic procedures of each nursery school, marked by a wholehearted and relaxed acceptance on the part of staff.

Gradual arrival extended over a period of time as long as an hour and a half in the morning. Children arrived in ones and twos, escorted by a parent. Each child received a personal greeting and undivided attention for those first few minutes, and was helped to get started. The headmistress as well as the teachers had time to talk to every parent, to catch up on family business and news, which they could then help the children share during the day. This could take place again at the end of the day, during the period of *gradual leaving*. Some children left early because their adjustment was still new. Some left because they were tired, overstimulated, etc., and when they were called for, the teacher and the mother talked again. In this way the teachers and the headmistress came to know a great deal about the children's lives.

Gradual admission, and other measures for helping children separate from their mothers without too much stress, are accepted procedures in all English nursery schools and nursery classes. Every school I visited, at any date, had some mothers present.

Having devoted time and study to the problems of gradual admission I was very conscious of the difference in the English schools.[3] It was a difference not in technique but in the actual formation of the registered group. In my own experience as nursery school director, that process had not been as gradual because of the private and therefore minimal and precarious budgeting that framed our work. Our teachers, first of all, were paid from the beginning of the school year. Secondly, we could not ask a mother to delay the starting point for her child until, say, November 15— even though that date might be best for both the school and the child— and still expect payment of the tuition from the opening date of school. We had to work out solutions for the reduction of tension within this limitation. It was accepted that the time needed for a particular child's adjustment was undefined but, under the pressure of private budgeting, the period of planned gradualism was quite short, with a premium on accomplishing a separation adjustment as quickly as possible.

In England, with state education, the criteria could be the needs of a child, the situation within the school, and the pace proper for both. The

[3] Lillian Weber, "Study of Development of Adjustment Practices" (New York: Bank Street College of Education, May 1959). (Unpublished Master's Thesis). This study describes gradual admission and mixed-age or family grouping in an American nursery school.

starting of a child in school and his adjustment to it could be stretched out appropriately. This was one of the factors accounting for the school's notably serene atmosphere, the lack of hecticness or sense of forlornness on the part of the children. By placing their gradual admission on an almost one-by-one rather than a group basis, the school eased the strain of admission and created an atmosphere of welcome and generosity. With no more than a couple of new children being admitted at any one point, the admission period could sometimes last several months. Children were permitted to visit during the term before their actual admission, and the mother was encouraged to join the group with her child for short periods whenever convenient. The actual process of gradually shortening the stay of mother with child in a school was similar to ours, though it was allowed to extend over a longer time than in American nursery schools.

Gradual procedures involve cooperation on the part of the *parent*. Their successful operation presupposes that the school has helped the parent understand the needs of her child enough to go along with necessary adjustments. The warm, informal relationship between parents and teachers is built up during the prolonged contacts of gradual admission. After all, the mothers were all there in this settling-in period. Since there are no car pools the mothers brought the children and called for them. The few words of immediate response to parent need could occur right in the midst of all the children's activities. Obviously, "catching up" on family business resulted in support for the parent as well as for her child. Thus, at the same time that parents are asked to understand children's needs their own needs and adjustments are understood and appreciated in a nonjudgmental way by the staff. Parents' values are respected, as illustrated by sending a child home "neatened." Policy on full-time or part-time arrangements was guided by an awareness of how hard travel could be for a parent with several children. In general, nursery school provision was thought of as a response to parents' as well as to children's needs.

Because of this atmosphere of warmth and acceptance parents stopped in any time of day to ask questions. I saw applicant parents welcomed warmly, shown around the school, and the question of whether there was a place for their children discussed. No secretary created a barrier to protect heads from interruption, or insisted that an appointment be arranged for another time. There was an occasional meeting over a problem, usually over a cup of tea, and at times convenient for parents. Aside from attending the group meetings held once a term (three terms a year), mothers came in simply because the school was the center of social services. The head, together with the health visitor, seemed to accept the role of emergency troubleshooter for any social service needed. The fact that the health visitors were there once a week and the fact that the mother was present with her child when the health examination took place created close contact.

Parents sitting around helped with the jumble sales, and prepared and repaired all sorts of materials. Altogether, the inclusion of parents is conducted in the most relaxed and most supportive way. The parents feel it is their school.

The nursery school relationship to parents, however, was not quite what Margaret McMillan had visualized when she included a parent room in the Rachel McMillan Nursery School in Deptford in 1914. She had thought of adult education, of cooperative community responsibility. Nor was the present-day relationship quite in the style of the intensive and very personal conferences of our good private schools. Perhaps it is better than these, though less than the McMillan idea. The teachers and headmistress shared the experiences of the neighborhood, were fully aware of the problems of the parents and empathetic to them.

Whether the educational program of the nursery school itself was sufficiently explained, whether parent understanding was drawn on so that carry-over of the ways of the nursery school to the home could be ensured, I do not know. Whether the nursery school thought of itself as an agency of change or of adult education, of community service or of further involvement of the parent in the working of the nursery school, I do not know. The Plowden Report, however, calls on the nursery school to be just this—especially in the areas of high educational priority. It considers that the nursery school with its present close and warm parent-teacher relationship has a base from which to expand its educational role with parents and community.

Family (Mixed-Age) Grouping

The degree of flexible adaptation to child and parent needs was related to the *form* of school organization. All English literature about nursery schools *assumes family (mixed-age) grouping*. Almost all the nursery schools (and nursery classes) I visited were family grouped.

Family grouping as part of the structure of gradual admission helped diminish the intensity of the stress of new admission by allowing the teacher time for a substantial amount of individual support for newcomers. Children joined an already settled group, one already enjoying the nursery school and thus proclaiming the safety of such a school. This kind of grouping was also used to give a child a chance for a changed role or "place" in the group. Instead of a young 3 going on to be the young 4 in the 4s, he could be the older second-year child to the new young 3s and therefore try his hand at a new relationship. Gardner describes how this works:

The younger and older children are encouraged to play together during part of the day, because the little ones learn much from the older and because their presence leads the older ones to help them. But it is realised, too, that the little ones need quiet and leisure and close contact with the grownups for part of the time, and that the older ones need opportunities for more boisterous play and for intellectual experiments which would be hampered by the constant presence of the little ones. The four-year-old is a long way from the two-year-old in intellectual achievement, and becomes disheartened if his elaborate buildings are destroyed and his imaginative play too often interrupted, just as the two-year-old can become distressed by the older child's interference or help which he does not desire.[4]

Family grouping provided for such variation of need and use. There was a story group for children at an older level and a story group for children at a younger level. The different kinds of materials could be used with different degrees of skill. But access to materials was open, and it was the child who selected from materials and determined the level and kind of use right for him at that moment.

Family-grouping organization in the nursery school was clearly a long-established practice. During wartime, 3–5s were mixed. In 1937 in *The Children's Play Centre*, Gardner spoke of mixed ages in the play center and of its enormous significance for informal education and the training of teachers in a wide range of possible child behavior. And still earlier, the Hadow Report mentioned mixed-age groupings.

Relationships: Children and Teachers

Planned buildings permitting in-and-outness, standards of health and cleanliness, standards for equipment and for gradualism in procedures —what were these all for? Did these add up to a use by teachers and children that was familiar? What did the teacher do? Was it in any way different?

The aims were familiar: to enable, facilitate, and promote a child's growth in his own way. All arrangements were designed so that a child could do the things he was interested in at his own pace. He was to be able to tell about these. He was to be able to get response.

All nursery schools were full of encouragement of communication, full of the spontaneous conversation of the children, full of adults who were appreciative of what children had done and responsive to their attempts to talk about it. As a visitor I was included in all this conversation; all adults were included. The teachers expected children to approach me and expected me to respond. Clearly, the "word" was valued. A child was

[4] D. E. M. Gardner, *Education Under Eight*, p. 18.

bound to know that the adults cared about what he had to say and would listen in response to *his* interests, not just to what could be used to reinforce the teacher's purposes.

Talking was *easy*, whether between two adults, a child and an adult, or two children, and except at the short group period, always individual. Everywhere I saw adults stopping and talking with this child or that one about his building, or a puzzle, or the construction. A child was encouraged by this immediate personal response to ask questions, to chat. Every lunch table was set up in a small grouping to encourage conversation, and with prior knowledge by the teacher of many details of the children's lives, so that conversation could be supported.

In this setting, many immigrant children extended their language. Those with no English had fewer problems learning the language. The ease of conversation in the nursery schools was particularly significant in view of the evidence that these schools served the poor. Conversation was assumed possible and, in fact, a need of children of this age, no matter what their background.

I sought for the same gradualism I had found in procedures of a child's admission, his arrival and leaving, in the procedures for organized group formation. Acceptance of a child's pace and interest, support for a child's natural growth in his own way, basic to the concept of informal education, would demand this. Gradual formation of the group, with some respect for and some interest in what a child was engaged in at that moment, would allow for relaxed transition, an atmosphere of interaction and back-and-forth flow of ideas even at the times when the teacher was leading the group. But occasionally an inconsistency was apparent—a break in modality between play and routines. Although the *general* atmosphere was *always* free and respectful of a child's purposes, routines were sometimes imposed on the children. It was possible, in other words, to allow free play and still be quite directive, allowing no interplay during any organized period.

Most English nursery schools seemed to respect a child's needs for gradualism, even in such organized periods. In most schools the teacher sat down and, very gradually, the children joined. For some routines even a child's joining was voluntary. Where there was voluntary formation, this indicated respect for differences. Certain things, like lunch, were never voluntary, though great adjustments were made for choice and appetite. Children had access to the toilet and washroom whenever needed, and the facilities, as already noted, were so good that independence and relaxation about routines were very possible. Children washed up before lunch and as they finished their play. Resting schedules might be adjusted to need and differences, resulting in great variation. In almost every nursery school there were adjustments for those who slept heavily, those who needed a catnap, those who didn't sleep. In one London school, where children had manipulative games on trays on their cots, the time on cots gave each child a chance for a kind of withdrawing from the group. At many other nursery schools some cots were outdoors, some indoors, and some children played quietly at putting a puzzle together in the head's office.

Joining a music period might be voluntary but usually was not. Nursery rhymes were used a great deal, partly because they were traditional, partly because the teachers felt that speech is clarified with nursery rhymes and singing, partly because the children liked the rhymes enormously. Dancing was most often free and easy without suggested movements. The children listened to the music and their movements followed from the listening instead of any set patterns of teacher suggestion. Whether or not joining a story was voluntary depended on whether it was an "extra" story during the period of free play, or it was a scheduled event like a music period. In fact, most often storytelling was arranged for a cozy small group.

More than anything, natural growth implies *movement*. A child must be able to move to what he wants to do and to move at his own pace. Such movement was characteristic of all the nursery schools.

It was just this movement of children and of teachers to children, all doing different things, that made knowledge of individual children *easier*, not harder. Children were not blurred into a composite of uniform action. They stood out by the differences of their movements and behavior. I was easily able to sort out children as individuals even after a fairly short period of observation. It was obvious over and over that the teacher differentiated in all kinds of particulars on each child. In answer to a question one teacher said, "Oh, I put that out because Pamela seemed to like that so much yesterday."

I could not really answer for the depth of records on individual children. Heads told me that records were kept but I did not, on the nursery school level, investigate this further. It was obvious that the movement of headmistress, teacher, and NNEB was planned on the basis of what they knew of an individual child. Their free movement among the children was certainly not totally in response to the momentary scene. It reflected a great deal of knowledge of individual children, a good bit of feeling with, thinking about, and planning for individual children.

The teacher's role, however, could be one passively allowing of movement. She could be easily available and responsive to children who approached her. She could provide the varied equipment they needed and accept their varied purposes. But teachers and heads were also actively moving *to* the children all the time and without waiting for a child to approach. A teacher would sit down near animals, hold a guinea pig in her lap, and of course children gathered around. Teachers were busy in a gardening corner, and teachers were singing with children. There was the occasional bit of story implementation of activity, the occasional incidental enrichment with music. Teachers joined children who were painting, writing down exactly what each child said about his painting. Teachers were quick to latch on to the many incidental counting, number, size, and weight experiences, emphasizing their interest in them. The counting of children, of chairs, of buttons on clothes, the commenting on weight of boxes or of guinea pigs, was part of the life of the school. Incidental teaching and new words to fit what was going on were offered all the time and very easily, as part of the teacher's expression of interest in anything a child was doing.

Small Grouping

Teachers revealed varying degrees of skill with small grouping but I observed small grouping in all schools. With small grouping the teacher sometimes reinforced a child's purposes, sometimes attracted children not engaged in their own activity to an activity she searched out, suggested, and organized.

Teachers sat down at a particular table of art materials or of cooking materials. They set out some new game or some new tools and materials at the workbench. They set up a special activity in the midst of free play and joined it and in this way created a voluntary small grouping. A teacher joined a particular child and by her joining attracted others to support him. Small grouping, thus, is a *special* aspect of the teacher's or head's helpful movement to children in the environment. The teacher joins the free play, using herself as a center to support further development or play in one area. She no longer makes a sharp line of demarcation, free play versus routines, free play versus teacher-directed and controlled activities.

Small grouping was one of the ways in which the teacher responded to the great variations in children, planning differentially for special interests and needs. The teachers tried to be supportive and responsive to any growth already started and to anticipate, to stimulate, and to encourage new development. Their great faith in development and in growth was by no means a *passive* one. When the English teacher joined the play in the ways described, on the whole it was with the intent to *implement* a child's purposes. I saw no pressure for predetermined goals. An English concern I heard discussed again and again was that the teacher guard against having her actions reflect *her* interest, not a child's, and in so doing cut across a child's purposes in his play instead of furthering these. Teacher sensitivity was tested by whether, after having started a child in an activity, the teacher could allow the child to take over, or indeed, if he found it meaningless, to drop it altogether. On the whole, the English teacher with her trust in development was less of an interventionist than her American counterpart.

The English Teacher's Way

A number of small differences added up to what is worth noting as "the English teacher's way." There was tremendous physical closeness of teacher and small child. Children were easily picked up, easily comforted. There was not a great deal of discussion about it: teacher reaction was quickly and immediately physical in response to need. If a child was hurt, or if a child was asking for comfort, he was just comforted without more ado. It seemed to me that the English nursery school teacher had a generous and easy acceptance of the children wherever and whatever they were, an unquestioning, affectionate way.

In addition to the "immediacy" of physical response, I noted even more particularly the phrases that were used and that were certainly different. The English teacher seemed to be consistently polite. If she walked in front of a child or brushed against him, she immediately said, "Sorry." If a child was what we call "ornery," the teacher just mildly said that he was being "awkward."

The English teacher says, "Clever boy," to the English child who, finishing a puzzle, says, "I've done it." Most often a child saying, "I've done it," noted his own achievement and the teacher simply smiled. But accomplishment was certainly recognized. Success with even the smallest task was noted and praise freely given. Yet what was noted represented the teacher's sensitivity to the child's success with things he had himself chosen and pursued at his own pace. What was noted was his own response. The success represented his own solutions and the teacher's praise was not a judgment of his success on a scale of prescribed achievement. Thus, the teacher's response had nothing to do with any obligation to take the child through an already determined pace of change.

Some teachers speaking to me used the words "bright" and "dim" very matter-of-factly. Taking their use as serious judgment, I thought that in a comparable situation an American teacher would have said "not an early developer." Actually their equivalent for that was "immature" more often than "dim." Their use of this expression "dim" did not seem to mean less acceptance of a concept of development. They claimed that most often they too were commenting on the development of the moment. They pointed over and over again with pleasure to a child who was beginning to function better, and they did all they could to assist this. They would say, "Oh, he's a bit dim but he has time to come along, doesn't he?" or "I'd thought he was dim last year but he's getting on now."

Rather than an immediate intervention to produce "catching-up," the teachers provided a highly stimulating setting and then were willing to *wait* for a sign of interest which they would then reinforce. Typically, this teacher behavior was not just patience but also courtesy. It was based on respect and interest in the children. A teacher once said about a child who was cutting up a catalogue, "Oh, look, he wasn't ready to do that before." Apparently cutting was a new thing for him and the catalogue was brought in as incentive. The teacher kept putting the question to him every now and then very lightly. "Well, what do you want to shop for? What would you need next?" In answer to these questions the child did continue cutting and with great pleasure.

It seemed to me that all the schools lived longer than we might with children who seemed quite slow or disturbed in development.[5] The teachers accepted the possibility of real difference openly and matter-of-factly. In no case did I see a teacher acting remote or being anything but helpful to a child who seemed different.

The English teacher characteristically expressed herself in the form of suggestion: "We'll help her, won't we?" The suggestion created the atmosphere of expectation of helpfulness, but there was no dwelling on such expectation or any pressure for responsibility. Such suggestion, it seemed to me, was a way of speaking influenced or perhaps created by English culture: lecturers at the University of London would say, "Research shows us, doesn't it?" Bus drivers gave directions, "You'd find it at the top of the street, wouldn't you?" It was a way of *telling* that sounded like only *reminding*. It was a way of drawing listener and speaker into agreement, into mutual discussion, perhaps into thinking together. It assumed that the other person could think and could cope. It was more of a nudge or a gentle prod, than a bludgeon. Sometimes when I did *not* agree, I found this atmosphere made my assertion of my own viewpoint more difficult, or at least more careful. Most of the time, it was a pleasant way, distinctly different from our positive statements.

The use of the helpful kind of question was very typical: A child would say he had broken something, to which the teacher might respond,

---

[5] A report by Bernard Coard (*New York Times*, May 12, 1971) points to errors in placement of immigrant children as ESN (Educationally Sub-Normal), but the decision to place a child in special education was usually made only after the entire period of nursery and infant school growth. Plowden recommended that the term "slow learners" be substituted for ESN. The vast majority of slow learners do remain in ordinary primary schools, mixing profitably with other children for many of the informal activities, their special needs met within the school. An Act transferring responsibility for children previously deemed ineducable from the Health to the Education Dept. was passed July 1970. Some separate provision under shared health and education authority will remain, but the new formulations are based on the needs of borderline children. *Children and their Primary Schools* (Plowden), p. 304.

"Is it something we can mend with cellotape?" or sometimes, "It's something we can fix with cellotape, isn't it?" A child might bring in a truck from the garden. The teacher asked, "Could you take it out there?" or "Is there more room there?" A child might take a chair out to the garden. "That chair is an indoor chair; will you want to take it back? No? I'll put it back then."

Also characteristic of teacher expression was a smoothing kind of phrasing. A child throwing sand was asked, "You do know about these, don't you?" and the teacher would show the child a strainer. Stopping near a puzzle, a teacher would say, "Have you tried this one?" or "You did find the pieces that were left out, didn't you?"

The teacher operated on the expectation that children would help each other. She frequently suggested that one ask help of another. "Young ones" or "new ones" were spoken of as such quite openly, with the expectation that help would be volunteered by the others.

In many schools, I saw a few handicapped children, children with hearing difficulties, slightly spastic children, a child who apparently had been referred with a diagnosis of autism, and children who might possibly be, according to the head, "educationally subnormal." Having one or two of such children in a group was commonplace and seemed to be fully and openly accepted by the headmistress and teachers, by the other parents, and by the other children. These children were ones to whom others would be helpful, with open acknowledgment of the handicap. This built-in helpfulness was induced by the fact that English nursery schools were family grouped and, therefore, younger children were always present. Helpfulness was further supported by the patterns of arrival and leaving and of gradual admission. When mothers came, babies also came, and at the time when parents were sitting around during the "settling in" period, babies were always present.

Listening was highly encouraged. The teacher had an expectation of being listened to, and perhaps this was an adult expectation from the home. But how *little* the children had to listen *to*, and how often the teacher stopped to listen to the children! They were considered individuals saying important things. Certainly they were talked *at* minimally.

No great fuss seemed to be made about pickup of objects. The teacher or NNEBs, as they moved about during play, might pick up what needed picking up to prevent clutter that could confuse the play. They matter-of-factly included *any* child in this process if he was nearby. They assumed he expected and liked to be included. Thus, without much righteousness about pickup, there was a great deal of self-help as well as staff help in the children's use of their school. Very little lecturing of the children of any sort was going on. Children acted as individuals and were treated so. They did not have to toe the mark in any set kind of fashion like little soldiers.

The open acceptance of difference or of variation was true also of aggression. A child who was disruptive was just lifted up and held in the teacher's arms during the story. There was no measuring of affection, no peremptory standard or demand for absolute immediate function from the children. There seemed very little of our apprehensiveness about aggression and very little determined organization by the teacher to cope with it. But, of course, there *was* aggression. I saw an occasional hit, occasional interference, certainly a breaking down of block building. The teacher might ask sympathetically, "Can you fix your building?" Often the teacher would very openly explain the reason for this aggressive act to the other child or children. Usually the response would be an accepting one by the children that "he's new," "he's young," "he's younger," or "he's feeling bad" or "awkward." There was very little intervention about aggression, very little expectation of real hurt. Most of the time the aggression was passed off as a momentary thing with the expectation that a child who was being bothered could cope with it and that a child who was doing the bothering would reestablish himself in a moment. Occasionally, there was a word of reassurance, but there was far less discussion of aggression than might have been expected. This was true of social as well as physical impacts. A child was not shielded from experience through the teacher's immediate intervention; he was assumed to be capable of establishing his own equilibrium. This does not mean that social or physical aggression was approved or not stopped if dangerous, or that help was not rendered to a child who was bothered or not coping. What it does mean is that aggression was handled in a nonjudgmental, bypassing, matter-of-fact way.

While on the whole there was a very low level of disturbance and a low level of teacher intervention on ordinary aggression, there was also a very low toleration of any real disturbance, of any "unsettledness," as being part of an expected norm. The teacher, within this setting, had a definite sensitivity to what *she* considered "unsettled." This did not make her reject a troubled child. It indicated her sensitized notice of these children as needing help, as needing watching or observation, as behaving in a way that was outside the norm. Children who were pointed out as troubled or awkward did seem to stand out, but I was not at all sure they would have stood out in an American group, perhaps because we expect more children of that age to be rather unstabilized.

Perhaps, just as the teachers' expectation of being listened to was part of the atmosphere that produced listening, so too their expectation that aggression would be momentary was part of the unfocused mildness of much of the aggression observed. Their uneasiness with and nonacceptance of a real disturbance led to a quicker notice of this, precisely because it was not within their norm of expectation.

There was much less apprehensiveness about accidents. This accompanied both the low-keyed response to ordinary aggression and the shock at any real hurt. There was very little expectation that playing with sticks or use of the workbenches or playground equipment was particularly dangerous. Teachers did not regard the children or the environment as dangerous. In general, they did not hover over the children while they used equipment and were tremendously easy in situations where American teachers might take great care. They did not expect a teacher to be outside to supervise the in-and-outness. The window-doors, with the glass going all the way down to the bottom, facilitated supervision, of course. Certainly the watchful eye of the teacher was on the in-and-outness. She herself was going in and out all the time, but not because of worry or the need to supervise *everything* at all times. Even with good staffing, had the teacher felt she had to see everything all the time, she could not have allowed as much free movement.

Clearly some trust of children was involved. There was a general acceptance that experience and exploration were necessary and good and that children needed to test the limits of their ability to cope. Use of the environment was not avoided or prevented for fear of possible accidents, unless clearly and obviously dangerous. Some risk was taken and accepted as part of the educational experience. And because this general acceptance was shared by parents and Local Education Authorities (LEAs), fear of legal suit was much less prevalent than in the United States. The teacher was expected to use the same "reasonable care" as the parent, and no more. This did not make accidents common. Accustomed as they were to free access and frequent use, the children seemed to have gotten past the hecticness that often accompanies the appearance of new equipment. They seemed to know what they could do safely. Indeed, the tale was that the accident rate went up when well-meaning exchange teachers, unused to such free use, "hovered."

There was little worry about visitors. Teachers did not think of the school scene as one that must on no account be disturbed. The presence of mothers and babies made no one nervous. Because of the teacher shortage, in many places teachers were allowed to bring their own younger children along with them, and teachers were working in classes with their own children—a situation that did not seem to create any disturbance at all.

This respectful, unobtrusive, helpful, and suggestive way was *the* way of the English teacher. Its recognition of individuality meant accepting rather than intervening. This led me to question our habit of insisting on the direct impact of teacher on child and between teacher and child. We sometimes do this even to the point of breaking up twosomes which seem to serve the function of evasion of this kind of direct contact. English teachers accepted such "inseparables" and assumed the relationship had function and meaning for the children. As part of their awareness of a child, they usually joined him or the "twosome" on his terms.

Summing up my observations of teachers, they had not only a good deal of confidence in children but also solid knowledge of growth and development. Furthermore, they adjusted their ways very flexibly to the level and variations of a child's development and accepted that a child needed time for his development. They conveyed an atmosphere of generosity and giving and yet great adultness.

Overwhelmingly I identified what I saw in the English schools as within and exceeding my definition of good nursery living. *Most* of the schools were glowing in atmosphere and reflected a uniformly high standard of operation. The few schools that had a lesser degree of beauty and richness of atmosphere, it often turned out, had a lesser investment in and development of the environment by the headmistress, teachers, or gardener. Some few schools might have allowed procedures for cleanliness to take precedence over children's use for their own purposes. In a very few schools one could see too clearly the machinery of what had produced the beauty so that what was happening seemed an imposition rather than the result of imagination or improvisation.

Despite these small differences between schools, my impressions led to one conclusion: Even with their large groups, informal education, good early childhood education, functioned in the English state nursery schools. The buildings designed for in-and-out use and the planning that had produced a qualitatively different gradualism helped make this possible. But the teacher utilized the buildings, the teacher planned. The staffing of the schools, so vital to their successful function, is described in detail in the section that follows.

Staffing and Training

The overwhelming fact was that the English teacher worked with large groups. Though it is true that certain small and subtle cultural emphases may help produce the more serene living that characterizes English schools, it is also true that by themselves these differences do not account for her success with large groups. Rather, it was the special planning for in-and-outness, for gradualism, the special planning to ease all stressful situations and to match the needs of a child's growth that supported her. A key part of that planning was the number and the training of staff in a school. The teacher's ease with a group of 30 children certainly hinged in large measure on the use and quality of the total school staff.

Every school had a headmistress. The staffing proportion was usually one teacher to 30 children, with one NNEB and one student NNEB.

Occasionally the ratio was one teacher to 40 children, with two NNEBs plus two student NNEBs. The amount of trained assistance given by the NNEBs was a significant element in the effective functioning of these large groups.

In addition every school had Parks Department help for the playground and garden. The LEAs provided help on building repair and maintenance. Schools also had cleaner help, kitchen help if lunch was served, and laundry help if there was a laundry. If the school was of any size the headmistress had clerical help.

In most schools I saw students from training colleges engaged in a variety of chores. There were precollege students serving as aides, reinforcing their educational background before starting their training. Of unusual interest was the use of the secondary school girls, not only for the help they could give but also for stimulating in them vocational aims for work with small children. Finally, parents found many ways to be an extra source of help, doing such things as sewing to refurbish the dress-up clothes or helping with jumble sales.

Not only is the ratio of staffing to children spelled out but every member of the staff has a status spelled out by local and national education authorities. Staff standards, including pay scale, are officially determined. Staff amenities are spelled out just as clearly. Included in the planning of every school is a staff room, as well as time for morning coffee and for afternoon tea.

Nursery teachers and heads and primary teachers and heads have equalized qualifications and have long had an equalized professional status. More than any other factor, the pay scale parity between those who teach in nursery and in infant schools underscores their equalized professional status. The two groups, including as members many heads of schools, enjoy an easy and fruitful association in one professional organization— the Nursery Association.

It was clear to me that the horror expressed in America of 30 children to a teacher had to be modified by the actualities of staffing in the English schools. It is important to understand factors inherent in the levels of staffing and in the standards of education programs that frame selection and differentiation between levels. (Chapter 3 further relates teacher education to the teacher's understanding of the ideas of informal education.)

The Headmistress

How the staff functioned was largely a reflection of the tone set by the headmistress. She was the mainspring; through the example of her own activity, she set the standard of relationships—of teachers to other teachers and to student teachers, to parents, and to children. In ways that reminded me of the work of directors in many of our own nursery schools, the headmistress *expected* to work actively with children. Supporting in different ways each teacher's different development, she helped them work together to make possible the children's use of the school. The children could use all parts of the school because the work of the headmistress tied together all its parts.

Obviously the care taken in selection of the head is an important determinant of the atmosphere and function of the school. The procedures in the selection of the headmistress are common to both nursery and infant schools. A teacher who has taught a certain number of years very often has taken an advanced course at one of the Institutes; she applies for the position of deputy headmistress. She may be put on an approved list after a series of observations and interviews by and with the LEA inspector. She next applies for promotion to headmistress. The inspections and interviews are repeated at intervals, and in this way she is assessed. If she is accepted for the promotion list there are more interviews. The teacher aspiring for a headship applies for an advertised post and is interviewed by the school's Board of Managers which, together with the LEA, make the actual appointment. (This was described to me as a role of the Board in London schools and not the general rule.)

As a politically responsible body elected by the local parties and representing the local people, the Board of Managers assists the headmistress with the administration of certain funds and consults with her at her request. Such an association also serves as pressure for and support of school standards. It is important to separate national and local function in this account of the appointment of the headmistress. The setting of qualifications, standards, and the inspectorial system are national functions, but the Board of Managers and the LEAs have a clear role in choosing the headmistress and in support of her freedom, and there is unusual reconciliation of local and national function.

I was impressed by the very great care taken in the selection of these heads. The long involved procedure is certainly justifiable in view of their great freedom. The head will set the path of education in her school. There are of course a number of possible safeguarding procedures: A head who has had a long absence must pass a medical examination. She can be visited at any time; the local authorities have inspectors who can come at any time and seem to come quite often; Her Majesty's Inspectors (HMIs), responsible only to Her Majesty, can also come at any time, though their general inspection is scheduled to be held once every ten years. There are also regularly scheduled, extremely thorough inspections which may involve subject specialists and last several days. Such inspection may be held whenever it seems warranted or when the Board of Managers raises questions. But as in America, after appointment, removal is difficult. Therefore, initial selection is particularly important and not only is great care exercised to keep the quality of choice high but maintenance of that quality by supporting professional growth in the headmistress has come to be considered an aspect of the inspectorial function as important as inspection itself.

Teacher Education

The head had first been educated as a teacher. Since nursery education is under the umbrella of the state and is recognized as part of the national education system, teacher education is officially evaluated and ends in qualification by the Department of Education and Science after the probationary year. But the Department of Education and Science qualification is given *after* recommendation by the Institute of Education of the university where the teacher was educated and examined, and much of the responsibility for teacher education has been delegated to these Institutes. Thus, the criteria for qualification and the standard for evaluation, which are accepted rather than imposed by the state, developed and continue to develop within the functioning world of English nursery education in which Institutes and Teachers Colleges are closely related to the schools. Though the enormous variations found in American teacher qualification and training standards are nonexistent, variation and experimentation in teacher education and in ways of assessment are encouraged.

The nursery school teacher has some training on the level that precedes her area of concentration and on the infant school level that follows. Infant school teachers in turn also have worked on the nursery level and on the succeeding junior school level. Such training has created a base for continuity of nursery school methods into the infant school. In periods of restriction of nursery school provision, limited job openings often meant that a teacher with nursery training concentration taught on the infant school level, to the profit of the infant school. But limited job opportunities also led to a decrease in the college offerings in this special concentration area, very much as it had in our own colleges prior to the expansion of the Head Start programs. Because of these limitations infant teachers may have been trained more on infant-junior levels than on nursery-infant levels. Implementation of the Plowden Report will increase the college offerings in the nursery area.

Following her sixth form in secondary school, the student who is accepted at a college of education embarks on a three-year course of study of the field as an integrated unity of theory and practice rather than as separate subjects. The course is divided into three general areas—child study, practice, and a main course or area of individual exploration. The bulk of work is in the study of child development. In addition, practice is scheduled for *each* of the student's three years, and is the core of the training.

Pressure for higher standards, often interpreted academically and traditionally as additional and "stiffer" courses, exists in English teachers colleges, just as in ours. The new Bachelor's Degree program adds a fourth year to the college education program. Starting after the sixth form (comparable to the first two years in our colleges), this program provides for a longer training than American programs, which have extended their requirements to a five-year training. The Plowden Report is a source of further discussion of ways for improving teacher training, for improving the contact of schools with teachers colleges, for improving and maintaining teacher supply.

The NNEB

A description of the selection of the head and the training of the teacher is an important preface to the description of the training of the NNEB. The specific differences in training must be weighed in the light of the present trend to make greater use of the NNEB.

From the beginning of my stay I observed closely NNEB training programs because of my concern with our training programs for assistants in our preschool expansion. I observed NNEBs in all the nursery schools visited, NNEBs working with teachers in Bristol infant schools, and NNEBs in charge of a nursery class in Birmingham.

The NNEB begins a two-year training at the end of her fifth form in secondary school, at age 15 or 16. Her courses at the technological college focus on three areas: (1) the physical and social development of small children, (2) their mental and emotional development, and (3) her own further education. Two days a week, or 14 hours, are given over to lectures on the health, development, and education of children up to age 8; the topics are mainly on the adjustments of children in situations without the mother, on play, on speech. Other lectures at the college help the NNEB student with "further education," i.e., courses in liberal arts areas. Three days a week are spent first in nursery school and then either in a residential home or in a day nursery center. NNEBs usually have had experience with babies so that they can do residential home or day nursery work. Summing up, the NNEB training represents a professionalization of the assistant by providing a qualification that is nationally recognized, interchangeable from job to job, and kept up to the standard of the National Nursery Examination Board.

Although some girls had been admitted to teacher training colleges from every NNEB college I visited, the entry standards are on the whole considerably lower than those for teacher training college. Some girls, still unclear about their career aims or unable for family reasons to go further at that time, had chosen NNEB training as good general training and had become more ambitious in "midstream." Some of these went on to teacher training college, some to nurses' training. Others had used the education opportunities of the NNEB work to improve their standing. Thus, even on the level of the advanced courses at the Institutes of Education, there were a few who had started as NNEBs. It was generally felt that all who could qualify should be encouraged to go on to teacher training colleges.

Considering the group as a whole, the working NNEB has had her training at a younger age, has not been to sixth form, and may not have passed the relevant examinations. The practical work requirement, three days a week, cannot be equated with the experience of supervised practice teaching, even if NNEBs may be placed only in schools that have been approved. Most important, the amount of education that she receives, two days a week at the college during the whole of her two-year course, is far less than that of a teacher in academic content, in ways of introducing and extending use of skills, and in general understanding of children, although it is definitely superior to that usually given our aides and assistants.

The NNEB assisted with all the physical needs of a child, sat with small groups of children, conversed with them, and helped in welcoming them. I thought these assistants contributed greatly to the school life in the warmth of their relationships with the children and in the smoothness they gave to the background mechanics of classroom routines. It was they, for example, who made it possible to maintain, complete with labels and markings, the children's supply of personal belongings like combs, flannels, etc. Their major orientation, which probably reflects the focus of their training, was clearly a more body-conscious way with children than was the teacher's way. Warm and pleasant, easing and helping as the NNEBs were, they were only gradually becoming more involved in conversation with the children. I thought they could be guided in learning techniques of sustaining conversation. Nevertheless, the degree of skill and sensitivity the NNEBs revealed in their responsive approach to children was most impressive.

With serious appreciation of the NNEBs' already important role with children, English educators are evaluating current NNEB courses and are revising them with a more educational focus. This ongoing development is aimed at making NNEB training the foundation for real assistantship to the teacher, and is in response to the discussion initiated by the Plowden Report and its recommendations of additional uses and responsibilities for NNEBs. The new National Nursery Examination Board syllabus allows for a flexible exploration of new content. One suggested implementation of this new flexibility focuses on art, the family, and nature study.[6] Further it suggests two years in English studies on the theme of the Ages of Man as seen by poets, painters, and novelists. Much that is described in this course, if pursued in any depth, would be valuable for *any* teacher education.

SCARCITY AND TYPES OF PROVISION

Admission to full-time nursery schools was extremely limited, and other types of schooling and care developed. The organization of the full-time nursery schools most carefully worked out the adjustment to the natural rhythm of the children's day. The full day not only eased the hardship of travel to the widely dispersed nursery schools, it also lessened some of the difficulties for children living in crowded housing and in large families. Working-class parents were eager enough for this kind of schooling for their children that they would undertake long travel, without car pools. As the heads pointed out, if a mother had many other children, less than a full day might hardly be worth so much travel. Part-time nursery schools did not solve the problem for working-class mothers.

Part-Time Nursery Schools

The part-time schools were opened in 1952 as a response to the burgeoning need for expansion. By aiming to meet the demand without regard for economic need, the part-time schools are departing from the definition of the nursery school as an institution concerned mainly with serving the working-class child. Since the change to part-time doubled the supply, the trend, particularly evident in London, is very strongly to the establishment of more and more part-time schools. The Plowden recommendation for a nationwide expansion that is largely a part-time provision confirms this trend.

Part-time nursery schools were often converted full-time schools and so inherited the setting of the full-time schools. They had the same buildings and the same standards of cleanliness and equipment, but differences arose from the possibilities for use of these facilities. Part-time schools met children's needs but without the leeway in scheduling permitted by the full-time schools, without the extra nooks and crannies to fill in the extra moments of wondering and looking.

In part-time schools the pressure to get another session underway

---

[6] Described in the *Froebel Journal*, June 1968, by Catherine Lee of the Oxford College of Further Education.

made more difficult the leisurely, gradual leaving often observed in full-time schools. Another session had to get started, another group of children was arriving, the room had to be straightened and prepared. Inevitably then, gradual arrival in a part-time setting was not as relaxed because everyone tended to feel they should make the most of the three hours, to have a full program. Yet even if not easily accomplished in part-time schools, gradual arrival was characteristic of *all* of them, and arrangements were made to fit the special needs of individual children.

The pressures of the part-time group are familiar to American teachers and parents. In many of *our* nursery schools, so many of which are part-time, arrival is hectic and leaving is hectic. The teacher or head in our setting is often besieged in this all-at-once way by intense demands for immediate attention. Very often this is because children come and go in car pools. Probably the long day setting of our day care centers has the greatest possibilities for the kind of flexibility characteristic of full-time English nursery schools.

Nursery Classes

The other big expansion, in addition to the turning of full-time nursery schools into part-time double-session schools, was the opening up of more and more nursery classes within the infant schools. By exploiting a major loophole of Circular 8/60 (see Notes on Usage), a nursery class could be created if, by placing six teachers' children, it returned six teachers to teaching jobs. The six children might not be working-class but the rest of the roster might well be of this background.

On the whole the new English nursery classes are part-time except where special need dictates full-time organization. Full-time classes exist to serve only children with special needs.

Nursery classes often seemed to have better physical conditions than other classes in the infant schools in which they were housed. They were bright, well equipped, and well staffed. The toilet and sink facilities were equal in adequacy to those of the nursery schools. The same training for teachers was required, and the teachers worked in the manner of the nursery school teachers.

Although location of nursery classes in buildings housing infant or primary schools could have given the children an even greater sense of a *whole* school, of the complexity of space and great flexibility of many areas, it failed to do so. Since the nursery class was but one class in a relatively big school, it was confined to its one area of the school. It did not have the use of the extra space furnished by corridor, staff room, head's office, and garden. This "enclosing" into a single classroom meant a loss of space for "corners," for extra enrichment, or for easy expansion of activities. Though every nursery classroom still provided for in-and-outness (walls were broken through if necessary in many instances), the in-and-outness was only to a very small and enclosed part of the school playground.

Housing the nursery class in the infant school could also have extended the use of family or mixed-age grouping whereby children of nursery age would know slightly older children, but again, this did not happen. A child could have learned to know the teachers of his older brothers or sisters. Without the pain of learning a new building, a new way of getting to school, he could have moved into new relationships. But, as a single class within a larger school, the nursery class did not have contact with other classes. The life of the several groups housed under one roof in the infant school flowed around it without including it. The loveliness of the nursery classroom was "protected" from the more rowdy infant school, with loss to both infant school and nursery class. In effect, the nursery class was *in* the infant school without being part *of* it, because there was no real blending of nursery class and infant school informalities.

The policy of "protection" operated so that no pressure from the infant school could be imposed on the nursery class. The infant school was not quite trusted to have reformed the dulling routine and restriction of movement that had at an earlier period characterized its organization.[7] (See section on History, chapter 3.) The three-year-olds and four-year-olds were not to be swallowed up in the pace of infant school life. The fact that change had occurred, the fact that there might no longer be anything against which to protect the nursery class, was not yet acknowledged. Without arguing against separateness, given the present linked nursery class and infant school arrangement, we might argue for a greater realization of the possibilities in that link for easier transition.

These shortcomings in the nursery class were discussed in the Hadow Report, which recommended at least *some* continuation of the nursery school as a separate organization because in this way the nursery school could best develop as a model and most fruitfully contribute to the rest of state education. This view is less forcefully presented in the Plowden Report which found less need to make this point after the thirty years of nursery school development since Hadow's recommendations. But the nursery school as a separate unit was and is still prized because it fosters for the nursery school child the fullest and most relaxed use of the whole school environment.

[7] This separation of nursery and infant school organization is discussed in the *Hadow Report* (1931, 1933).

Day Nurseries

The small number of full-time nursery schools is clearly insufficient for the working mothers who need care for their children all day long, and those who need care for children *under* nursery age are not served at all. Day nurseries that include babies and toddlers were a response to the needs of working women, first in the Depression of the 1930s and then in wartime (World War II). After the great increase during World War II, English day nurseries experienced the same cutbacks as did the nursery schools.[8] In an attempt to positively discourage women with children under 2 from working outside the home, fees were charged for day nursery care.[9] The result was that:

> For the children who are found places in nursery schools and nursery classes because of various social priorities . . . whether their mothers are at work or not, the school place is, of course, free just as it is for all children in maintained nursery schools and nursery classes, since these are provided as part of the educational services. For exactly similar children who are found places in day nurseries, a fee is officially chargeable and, even if the fee is waived or reduced as it sometimes is, this can only be done after careful enquiry into the financial circumstances of the family. The extraordinary anomalous position therefore occurs—and examples are not difficult to come by—that one child recommended for day care may not be able to have that care in a local day nursery because a fee is charged which the mother cannot or is reluctant to pay, whilst another child, recommended for day care by the same doctor, will be granted a priority place in a nursery school without fee and without a means test.[10]

Ironically, the somewhat punitive language of the circular on charges for day care reflected the thought that the day nurseries would gradually be absorbed by the nursery schools and come under their umbrella. This was the vision of the Education Act of 1944. But this has not been realized, and there is a void just at the time when a great need has been created by the great numbers of working parents in England. The inclusion of day nurseries under the state standards will not enormously increase the supply of nursery education, though it may improve the standard of the day nurseries—and concern about the standard for day nurseries and for nursery education is part of the concern for expansion.

The day nursery can offer fairly wide enrichment and can provide

[8] Between 1952 and 1955, 259 nurseries were closed. Only 448 day nurseries, providing places for 21,396 children under 5, remained open by 1965. Simon Yudkin, 0–5, *A Report on the Care of Pre-School Children* (a discussion based on Ministry of Health Circular 221/45, 1945), p. 26.
[9] *Ibid.*, p. 26.
[10] *Ibid.*, p. 34.

quite a pleasant way of handling children. The buildings are planned for children's care in somewhat the same way as are the nursery school buildings. The sanitary and health provisions are high, and the Ministry of Health is the responsible department. NNEBs with some additional course training are in charge instead of trained teachers. It is said that the NNEB warden or the SRN (State Registered Nurse) can secure the same equipment for the children on request from the LEAs. If the day nurseries seem pleasant and planned but not as glowing as the nursery schools, this is attributed to a lack of push and know-how on the part of their heads. The focus of the present struggle for supervision of all day nurseries by the Department of Education and Science is aimed at raising the quality of the teaching staff to a point where it can consistently produce stimulating environments for children. This is intended by Plowden's recommendations for a single education standard for all children of nursery school age.

Play Groups

Even with the part-time groups and nursery classes, the problem of the enormous demand and the short supply of government-maintained nursery education remains. The day nurseries do not help the middle-class working mother, and the long waiting lists for the government-maintained nursery schools, part-time or full-time, make placement for such a mother unlikely. But middle-class mothers and those not exactly middle-class are more and more interested in provision for their children. Other solutions, such as the play groups, are being tried.

All over England play groups are starting up, very much as in the United States, because of the shortage of facilities for many groups in the population who now value nursery education or for those who work and need nursery care for their children. The groups that use play schools in England expect to pay very little, whether or not they are middle-class. Understandably, the presence of excellent free nursery education creates pressure to produce more of the same. High fees are resented, and the government is frequently criticized for lack of provision. In some cases, play groups are partially subsidized by the community in ways that allow fees and are acceptable to the government.

The play groups, however, do not in any way match the standard of the state-maintained nursery schools, nor could they do so without the most enormous additional expenditures. For that matter even our own very high-priced private schools do not succeed in matching the planned buildings and the planned environment of the English state nursery schools.

Many parents, aware of the poor standard of their play groups, are anxious to secure licensing and inspection by the Department of Education and Science as well as training courses for leaders. In fact, some of the recruits for courses for mature women leading to teacher qualification come from the play group parents. Many of these parents would like, however, to retain the participation in the control of the school that has been part of their play group experience. They enjoy also "getting together," breaking up their previous homebound isolation.

The involvement of parents in play groups is different from the parent-teacher relationships in the nursery schools. It is closer to the relationships in our cooperatives. The parents often teach in the school and are actually responsible for the care of the children. Probably application of standards to play groups is resisted for fear that this involvement will be diminished when qualified teachers and state financing are introduced. Many play groups would like to retain voluntary status. But even maintaining their voluntary status, some development of standardization and a higher standard seems possible, so that the best of them may come under the state umbrella if nursery education is expanded.

SCARCITY AND STAFFING

In the battles currently raging around the means of providing more nursery services in England, a number of solutions propose different uses of staff. The Plowden Committee recommended that with ultimate responsibility remaining in the hands of the qualified teacher the main day-to-day care should be given over to the NNEB. The number of children in each group would be reduced to 20, with the adult/child ratio one trained NNEB to every 10 children. There would be one qualified teacher for 60 full-time places.

No one challenges the use of helpers, which has an old history in the English nursery school. The Hadow Report includes a whole section on such use, differentiating very clearly between helper and teacher. In *Education Under Eight*, Gardner describes the wartime practice of placing the nursery school in the charge of a hospital-trained nurse so that children under 2 could be safely accepted, while the educational activities of the children, ages 2–5, were in the charge of a woman given a short course of training and supervised where possible by a qualified nursery school teacher. After the war when the NNEB role was defined for the nursery school, the nurse continued in charge at day nurseries which took small babies. The continuation was tolerated because it was thought that such staffing would soon be phased out as the day nurseries were absorbed into the overall expansion envisioned in the 1944 Education Act. But this overall expansion did not happen, and the Plowden recommendation for a unified and equalized day nursery and nursery school service and a changed role for the NNEB is meant to heal the breach of this long separation and meet the needs for expanded provision.

It can be argued about this Plowden recommendation that placing NNEBs in charge of nursery school groups imposes the day nursery standard on the nursery schools rather than vice versa. I think this is not the case. The Health Authority closely supervises the health and welfare features of the present day nurseries, but the orientation of this supervision is less educational than is that of the education authority which, of course, also recognizes health and welfare requirements. The Plowden recommendation would put day nurseries (for children over 3), play groups, etc., all under the supervision of the LEAs and subject to inspection by the HMI. *All* nursery groups would come under the ultimate supervision of a qualified teacher, as described. There is some implication in the proposal that children in day nurseries would be shifted for part of the day to nearby nursery schools, the whole to be considered a nursery center. This would represent a *lifting* of the day nursery standard.

Some welcomed this lifting of standard to supervision under the Department of Education and Science and did not seem to be critical of the proposals for revised use of the NNEB.[11] But the Nursery School Association *was* critical of this proposed use of the NNEB in place of the teacher, and with reason. Even though the ultimate responsibility would continue to rest with a trained teacher, and the size of grouping would be reduced from 30 to 20, there would undeniably be a dilution of supervision with the proposed ratio of one qualified teacher to 60, or one teacher to three groupings.

The question of dilution is not easily dismissed as an academic exercise. English nursery school teachers regard dilution not only defensively but as a major threat to the high standards of teacher education and of professionalization that have produced such flexible, responsive nursery education.

Gardner discusses the "mixed feelings" of the nursery school teacher:

> While they will welcome the recommendation that, even in these difficult times, there should be a large expansion of nursery school education they may very well feel that the price suggested for this is too high and that what would happen would be perhaps enlightened 'child minding' but not nursery schools. . . .[12]

Her comments on the dilution of the training of the teacher herself, the one who supposedly must take overall responsibility for the assistants, seem particularly important:

[11] *Ibid.*, p. 28.
[12] D. E. M. Gardner, "The Plowden Report on 'Children and their Primary Schools'," *Froebel Journal*, January 1968, p. 6.

. . . whether the teachers themselves would gain the necessary knowledge and wisdom to be able to function through other people would be doubtful if their own training on the practical side was not given in close association with trained teachers but in nursery units, and if after being trained they had no experience of day to day conducting a group of their own and no trained colleagues with whom to exchange ideas.[13]

The Plowden Committee did not specifically suggest that nursery schools should remain as centers sustaining the quality of nursery education, but this seems to have been its intent.[14] Gardner suggests that the training of the teacher is lowered if the quality of nursery schools is lowered, and urges their retention in their present form as training centers.

Nursery school teachers . . . are shocked that the Report does not even recommend that nursery schools with the present required quota of one trained teacher to every thirty children should be retained as training centres for those who under the Plowden suggestions would have the day to day care of the children (though admittedly with 'ultimate supervision' from a trained teacher).[15]

Dilution of standards is permissible only within the framework of a genuine shortage of teachers. Challenging the Plowden Committee's acceptance of statements about teacher shortage as "fact," [16] the National Campaign for Nursery Education felt that maximum efforts have not yet been made to bring teachers back to the profession; that many teachers would be willing to return to work on the part-time basis possible in a part-time, double-session school; that they wanted to teach nursery school and not infant school; that teachers, who for family reasons were not mobile, were available for nursery school placement if easing of the present figure of fixed provision allowed such placement.[17]

It was my impression that many measures had been taken to remedy the teacher shortage. There was already some use of part-time teachers. Evening courses for mature women, however, were fewer than in the United States. Slow retraining, as is possible for American women with home responsibilities, is not the pattern in England. Income or tax adjustments to make return to work more attractive do not exist. And even if

[13] *Ibid.*, p. 7.
[14] When I was in England during the summer of 1969, Lady Plowden indicated that the Committee had always assumed that side by side with the growth of the nursery groups, the nursery schools would continue.
[15] Gardner, "Plowden Report," p. 7.
[16] The National Campaign pointed to its 1967 survey in which 66 LEAs (one-third of the total investigated) responded to a questionnaire with information that they were not handicapped by a shortage of teachers. National Campaign for Nursery Education, *Newsletter*, No. 2, 1970.
[17] Reference is to Circular 8/60. (See Notes on Usage)

all inducements were used, there might still not be enough teachers to staff the proposed expansion.

While the Plowden recommendation of one qualified teacher supervisor to two or three units in different areas does seem a serious dilution of the vital standard of close supervision, grouping of the units together would at least assure a constant supervision from the responsible supervisor. Gardner suggests two trained teachers for four "units" (the term used in the Plowden Report) or, in effect, a lesser dilution of the present standard, with one qualified teacher to 40 children, instead of the present one to 30.[18] The threat might be less if the dilution could be considered temporary, until the time of adequate teacher provision—and perhaps all this has been considered and weighed. The decision is still to be made on the very important question of expansion and the price of such expansion.[19]

SOLUTIONS

The present facilities for children under primary school age—within and outside of the structure of state nursery education—present a clear picture of scarcity. The problems of expansion and the eagerness to find solutions are also clear. Everybody now wants more nursery provision *for everybody.* Nursery school education can no longer be planned for as services for the poor. The Plowden Report response is to plan for overall expansion.

In urging the assumption of the state's responsibility for all children ages 3–5, the Report proposes to reverse the trend that resulted in the decline of state education for that age group, a trend described in the section on history (see chapter 3). The 1944 Education Act plan for nursery schools for all who would want or need them was also an attempt to reverse this decline. But its implementation was halted by the troubled economics and the great rise in population of the post-World War II period.

In 1960 total nursery school enrollment was fixed at the figure of 1957 in a Circular that became known as 8/60. It is still the determining factor in stemming expansion efforts, though there has been progress in easing its restrictions, as, for example, in recent funding that would increase the number of spaces for nursery school children by one-fifth; money will also

[18] Gardner, "Plowden Report," p. 7.
[19] E. M. Osborn, "The London Nursery Plan," National Campaign for Nursery Education, *Newsletter*, No. 1, 1970. The ILEA London Nursery Plan has suggested that the realization of all the possibilities discussed in Plowden for increase in staffing would allow for supervision of *all* classes by a qualified teacher.

be spent on day nurseries.[20] Success in procuring this appropriation is attributed, at least in part, to the National Campaign for Nursery Education, representing the combined effort of professional organizations and parent groups. In a historic demonstration (May 21, 1968), now repeated every year, working-class and middle-class parents presented a petition to the Secretary of State for Education and Science. They set up a nursery group in Parliament Square, and mothers and children from all over the country drew their representatives, their M.P.s, out of session to answer their questions. In response, the Department of Education and Science conducted a survey on parental demand for nursery schools, and reported to the House of Commons that the government was considering relaxing 8/60 in some areas. It seems clear that there is a desire to scrap Circular 8/60 and that there is now a real chance that it will be greatly modified.

The expansion now recommended by Plowden is as follows: a 50 percent jump for three-year-olds, based on an estimate that the demand for space for 3s would come from only 50 percent of the parents, and an equal jump in full-time nursery provision in priority areas. For the nation as a whole, the recommendation is for a 15 percent increase in full-time nursery education for the 3s, 85 percent for the 4–5s, but 100 percent for this age group in priority areas.

The timetable for these plans is similar to that of the New York State Board of Regents plan—1970–1974. With genuine nursery school provision now offered to so small a percentage of the eligible population, implementation of the space provisions of the 1944 Act is still the focus of campaigning. In that Act, sites in housing estates and elsewhere were designated for future buildings of nursery schools and were to be held for that purpose. Many local areas have retained some of that space, pending the removal of Circular 8/60.[21]

The pressure that resulted in the Plowden proposal for overall expansion came not from any single group but from a large segment of the population, convinced that all children can benefit from nursery education. The Plowden proposal received a great push from women in the trade union movement who demanded better and more educational day nursery facilities, more supervision of child-care, and the extension of nursery schools. It gained strength from the middle-class mothers involved in the

[20] £25 million were released July 1968 for a four-year housing, education, and welfare program, with the major part to go for education.
[21] 3,000+ sites in 162 LEAs were designated for nursery schools in the 1947 Development Plan. Though some of these have been taken for other purposes and a good number used as playgrounds pending their use for schools, a large number remain available for school use. Eirene White, "The Under-Fives in Present Day Society," in White et al, *The Forgotten Two Million.*

play groups. Pressure for nursery education has come also from industry, which recognizes its usefulness for their women workers.

Though not as marked as in the United States, there is national interest in special provision for the deprived and for those who might have difficulties in their further schooling. The Plowden Report, for example, makes specific proposals for full-time and immediate expansion of such provision. There seems to be no question that nursery education would be the best way of quick language learning for immigrant children. The Save the Children Fund, for example, has organized special volunteer groups to serve immigrant children who have not been included in state nursery schools.

Play provision exists not only because of need but because of what seems to be a component of English culture, namely, a wholesome respect for the importance of play in a child's growth. This is evidenced by the increase in the number of play centers, of adventure playgrounds, of One O'clock Clubs, and of supervised play groups, all for children under 5, and all partially under the umbrella of the state or at least the Parks Department. The Health Visitors' Infant Welfare Stations, toddlers clubs or toddlers play groups with mothers' clubs all are part of the state services for children up to age 8. Unstructured play, attention to a child's purposes, nurturance, and spontaneity are the stated aims of play centers, of the Parks Department in its adventure playgrounds, and of the LEAs. Such a universal feeling for play both influenced and was in turn influenced by the nursery school movement and the development of informality in infant schools. The Plowden Report is testimony to this. So too is the suggestion that, in the interim before the expansion of government-maintained provision, LEAs support play groups run by nonprofit associations. So too is the recommendation for inspection by education authorities of all voluntary groups. So too is the demand for enormous expansion of nursery education.

The major problem of nursery schools in England today remains the very small provision. All the English agree that:

> The only permanent solution lies in the implementation of the 1944 Education Act, making State Nursery Education available as an educational right to those children under five who seek it.[22]

The Plowden Report's revolutionary recommendation for nursery schools across the board is the logical response.

In their current national discussion, English educators are concerned equally about the *kind* and the *extent* of the expansion they seek. While

[22] Ena Abraham, "Young Children in High Flats," *Froebel Journal*, June 1967, p. 6.

they may consider a plan concentrating on part-time schools, they are at the same time aware of possible losses in gradualism. They may be expanding nursery classes, at the same time acknowledging their narrowed function. They recognize further that difference in nursery organization may also affect the potential for transition to, and influence on, the next level of primary education—the infant school. But none of these dilemmas is considered insoluble.

THE MODEL FOR THE INFANT SCHOOL

The Plowden recommendation that one full year of nursery school be an expectation for all children before entrance to infant school would result in increasingly close relationships between infant and nursery schools down the line.

That the nursery school has had and continues to have a strong influence on the infant school has been insufficiently evaluated. The Hadow Report had supported the separate nursery school as a *model* for the infant school. Even within the Plowden proposals for changes in staffing, as Gardner points out, preservation of some model may be a necessity for education of the teachers who will have overall supervision of the NNEB.[23]

The full-time nursery school represents the touchstone of adequacy or inadequacy for evaluating all other efforts in nursery education. It also constitutes an unquestioned standard as the model for expansion. Despite the fact that it serves so few, the full-time nursery school has enormous significance as such a model, as an influence on the infant school, and as the cornerstone for growth and change on the next level.

The influence of the full-time nursery school stems not only from the training of teachers and of the NNEB, from the planned buildings that allowed in-and-outness, and from the planned environment, but also from what happens *in* the schools: arrangements that are a precondition to informality and provide for the human dimension. This standard of *function* has created in the nursery schools an atmosphere of serenity, ease, and responsiveness to individual children—even with their groups of 30. Without advocating that number, the schools accepted that number and met the challenge. They worked out the conditions that would allow them to work in the way they believed right, that would permit relationships supportive of each child's adjustments and growth. And this standard of function has guided adaptations in the infant school.

It is a standard that is no longer related to the poor. It relates to *all*

[23] Gardner, "Plowden Report," p. 7.

children. Only the conditions of scarcity maintain the orientation of the state nursery school to the working class.

It is clear that while the exigencies of the national economic and political scene produced compromises within nursery education, the standard itself was never in question. The true significance of the Plowden Report is that the value of nursery education for *all* children is accepted and that the high standard of the full-time nursery school is what is wanted for day nurseries, for play groups, for the deprived child, for all children. It is deeply significant that the Plowden Report accepts as the aim of education the support of natural growth; that experience and play are described as essential ways of learning for children at all levels—nursery school, infant school, junior school—in fact, all primary education. The Plowden recommendations, though they may suggest modifications that threaten the model, still represent the success of that model.

chapter 2

THE INFANT SCHOOLS

The nursery school, as described, became the acknowledged model for those changes in the two-year infant school that guaranteed continuity of experience for children, ages 5–7. In my study of the conditions that made possible this continuity, the provocative and significant discovery was that "model" did not mean replication, "continuity" did not mean repetition. The infant schools were interesting far beyond the model.

SOME LASTING IMPRESSIONS

. . . An old stone building, a wall, a bare playground, but with large tubs for planting. Inside, suddenly all is light, movement, color. The first impression is of lovely things on the eye level of five-year-olds, in corners that invite use and lingering—flowers and potted plants, easy chairs, books, paintings, shelves filled with china, a length of soft patterned fabric, a lovely bit of sea glass in the midst of an arrangement of blue pottery. The blue pottery is just one part of a total pattern of beauty—all for seeing and touching and arranging into new compositions. There are precious things, lovely things, colorful things where children can see them and handle them or, seated around a small table, enjoy quiet reading near them. Some of the corners display musical instruments, all laid out for children to see, to handle, to use. In fact, in all the corners all the objects seem to be set out with confidence that the children will handle beautiful things carefully and with respect. And also on view are things the children themselves have made with clay and wood, with paint and paper, with shells and stones.

An environment bursting with invitation, bursting with all the things children are producing right then and there. In the entry way is a paint table and three children at work painting. The hall itself is large, with five doors opening out on it. Six children are there, painting a large sheet, barefoot so they can get in on the painting. The teacher is right in there with them, offering them material. Three children are at a workbench. A couple are selling cakes they had made, making sales and change with real money. Another couple sit at a table writing; still another, quietly reading. Through an open door one catches a glimpse of three girls using weights, weighing flour, making some cakes; of others in a housekeeping corner; of two children building blocks on the floor; of a boy arranging number trays of nails, buttons and conkers (our American horse chestnuts); of another measuring with knotted string on the floor.

All over the classroom wall—under paintings, on shelves, in front of clay figures, attached to woodwork—are words. "I used three pieces wood." "My boat is 11 and ¾ inches long." "This girl has a red dress." "It is a man." A little boy dictates to the teacher and watches while the teacher writes. Another writes his own sentence and asks for a word. A couple of children are absorbed at a water trolley with tubing, and with all shapes and sizes of plastic bottles, funnels, strainers, and a really fine collection of measuring cups. In the library are eight children, each one at his own task, which seems to be phonetics. The teacher helps each one separately in whatever way he needs. All during the day, groups or individuals, after asking permission, use the library, but book corners are in every room as well as in the corridor and in the big hall, often with easy chairs grouped around them and flowers on the table.

The classroom does not contain the class. The children spill all over in little groups going to use things in various areas of the room and hall. The teacher is not behind a desk but moving to all these children. The headmistress is in the midst of it all, too, knowing everyone, helping wherever needed. Talk is going on all the time. Words for activities are being sought all the time. The children seem to know just what they want to do, where to get material, how to go about it. The children move with self-assurance, *using* their school.

. . . In another infant school, also an old building, drab and gray, in one step I am in a gymnasium-sized room—the central hall—with five rooms leading off from it. I stop a child to ask for the headmistress. He takes me up to a lady in the center of a group around a workbench. They are cutting lino-prints. Another group nearby is printing for a book they are designing. Another is printing fabric. Two little girls are drawing thick wool threads through a standing pegboard, following a design they have drawn on the pegboard with colored chalk.

The room is full of activity. In one corner, two girls are marking what, on inquiry, I discover to be the register! Children collect milk money and sell snacks, using real money. Children are going in and out of a supply room that contains pieces of wood, different kinds of paper, thread and fabrics, buttons, boxes, animal supplies, wheels, paint—all sorted and labeled. A sign advertises: "Animal Grooming in Room C," and the cost; "Animal Food," and the cost. One little girl is weighing an amount of animal food. While a boy is giving out a circular describing the offerings of this animal clinic, another is making a sign needed for this. At a table six children and a teacher are cooking. An older child is helping a sewing group, and another is helping a child to read. Over in one corner two children are writing. Three little girls are walking about, holding and fondling guinea pigs, "loving them," they tell me. There seem to be no groups of more than six.

Even the old building poses no limits to possibilities of use. I begin to see that the use of the big hall and the corridor permits the break-through from classroom to use of *all* the school areas, thus creating a new unity of school life. Classroom doors are open to corridors or hall where children can go to acting boxes, to workbench, to musical instruments, to library corner. No child moves as part of a class; he moves as an individual to things he chooses to do and the teacher and the headmistress move to help him do these things. The classroom, the class, the teacher behind the desk—all are metamorphosed, all are changed.

Each classroom contains the standard equipment of blackboard, chairs, and tables. Though there are enough chairs to construct a large circle if desired, it is usually a few chairs around a number area, around a book corner, around an interest table, around a table covered with junk material or with clay, or around a table for children sitting writing. A good deal of empty space is left for block building, for floor projects, for all sorts of use. Children sit on the floor for storytelling, for group teaching, for a group reading. Children can always be seen writing, sprawled comfortably on the floor.

. . . There seems to be a plan of the day but few fixed periods. The fixed points tend to be the Morning Service, Music and Movement, and

Physical Education (P.E.). These last two are class activities held in the big hall, and even these often break up into small groups where individual children may show their skill or make their own use of some of the P.E. apparatus. Sometimes children from the class having P.E. or Movement do not join with their class; sometimes children from other classes continue whatever they are doing in the big hall around the edges of the P.E. activity or of the Music and Movement. Sometimes P.E. and Movement are the same activity.

At lunch, another fixed part of the day, there are eight children and a teacher or a "dinner-lady" at each table. Conversation is expected; a service that is orderly is expected, and some effort is made to make it attractive.

. . . There seems to be no syllabus controlling what work has to be covered nor at what time. The children come in one by one and start doing things. At any number of points in the day, an astonishing amount of writing is going on, an astonishing amount of measuring, of weighing, or exploration of shape and size. Writing and reading seem to be simultaneous, and standards of spelling seem to be relaxed. Children are not at all worried about whether they are right or not; they try. There seem to be no prescribed standards of achievement. A child is not competing. He is busy increasing his own growth.

. . . The growth of skills is entwined with this life. In the free, self-chosen movement of children through all areas of the school, in the movement of teachers and headmistress to children to help them in their activities, skills are not precluded; rather the activities seem to foster skills, giving the children something to talk about and something to write about. The intense involvement of children in the running of the school—through errands, collecting of milk money and dinner money, marking of the register, helping prepare material—itself becomes a steady stream keeping fresh and vital the ways and means of communication.

. . . The headmistress in this old school tries "to have something in the environment which will fire off the child." This interest, she says, "must then be kept going." The notebooks the teachers keep of some of the casual conversations with children indicate a possible interest, a starting point they can follow up. As I sit near a child fingering the shape-board and talk with him about it, the teacher looks up and suggests, "He isn't up to that yet. He's just looking," and tells me at what point he is and encourages me to become even more involved. I am free to talk to the children: children read to me, show me their books, ask me questions—always as individuals, not as a class instigated by the teacher.

. . . Teachers take time to read poetry, and children have favorite poems and ask for these during almost every one of my visits. Children create poetry. Poems, their own as well as their favorites, are written large on display boards next to paintings or in other places. Poetry is also part of the Morning Service.

. . . The headmistress seems to know every child, to know things about a child: that his grandmother is sick; that his dog had run away; that he is going with his daddy on holiday; that he has an "aunty" in Australia. If, in a rare moment, the headmistress sits down and talks to me in her office, situated sometimes on a half-floor above the central hall and from which she can see all that is going on, children are soon knocking, asking would she like to see their building, their painting, their junk invention, or read their poem or story. There seems to be complete free access to the headmistress. A word or two to this one or that one is part of her progress through the school. Incidental learning flows from her. A small sample: A child tells her, "I want to be a teacher in this school when I grow up." The time of growing up is calculated. The head asks how old would she (the head) be then, and would she then still be the head? "Oh no, my granny is that old and she has the rheumatism." The children write her notes, receive answers, write back. I recall a child asking the headmistress was she aware that he is this height? Her answer is prompt: No, she appreciates knowing that he is that height, and is he aware that she is this height? In quick response he writes, telling her how much taller she is. Whenever the school calls itself "informal," there is this spontaneity of communciation.

SCHOOL SETTING

NEIGHBORHOOD SCHOOLS

In contrast with the wide area intake of the nursery schools, the match of school to area was more generally the picture in the infant schools. Children in the infant schools, on the whole, went to neighborhood schools.[1]

English urban neighborhoods, which often reflected a mix of economic circumstances, were generally composed of small one-family row

[1] Of the 30 infant schools visited, in 16 the children were poor or working class; in 9 they were of mixed economic background; in 5 they were of professional parents' background. Immigrant children were enrolled in 14 of these schools; they made up 30–84% of the infant school population in Birmingham.

houses, often drab and deteriorated, larger detached houses, and Council estates. In the New Towns, the new and well-kept row houses did not necessarily indicate middle-class background as comparable housing in the city might suggest. New Towns had a planned economic mixture, but were predominantly working class. Council housing estates, where working-class families had been relocated from the small row houses, were as new and well-kept as the New Town houses, yet they were for the most part, more sterile living areas than the old working-class areas. As in some of American subsidized housing, the estates tended to foster a type of segregation in that poorer and poorer workers had come to be concentrated there. An earlier mixture of working-class people—some skilled, some unskilled—seemed to have been lost. Those who were able to do so tended to move to suburban housing.

Home address was only one of the indicators of a child's economic and social background. Information about parent occupations, the number of free lunches, and health and welfare statistics—all gained usually from the headmistress herself—revealed that more than half of the sample population was solidly working class in background, and only five schools had a concentration of children from professional middle-class background.

However, the matching of area and background of children with their schools is not the absolute equation in England that it is in America when we refer to "neighborhood schools." For example, the Plowden Report affirms the *principle* of choice:

> . . . we are sure that parents must be given some choice whenever this is possible and they should have information on which to base it. They are more likely to support a school they have freely chosen, and to give it the loyalty which is so essential if their children are to do the same. Whenever a school is unpopular that should be an indication to the authority to find out why and make it better.[2]

Freedom of choice may be nominal where there is only one school available or where "one favored school would burst its walls without some form of zoning."[3] Wherever possible, however, some degree of parental choice did operate.

Comparisons of schools in old, poor urban areas with those in new, middle-class suburban areas led to the conclusion that neither poor area nor poor children could be matched with a judgment of the neighborhood school as inferior.

[2] Plowden, p. 44.
[3] *Ibid.*, p. 44.

School Buildings

Nor was there a consistent match between working-class or poor area with new or old school buildings. Whether buildings were new or old depended upon the postwar pattern of relocation and redevelopment. Housing Estates and New Towns of course had new buildings. The poverty areas, which often were awaiting redevelopment, had old schools more consistently than areas of middle-class housing. By "old" is meant construction at the turn of the century. Some old school buildings in England look new because they reflect renovations based on the new thinking in planning; such buildings had been renewed with an eye for color, light, and movement, and an awareness of the need for facilitating in-and-outness. Some had even added a garden. Some old schools were three-story structures in which the infant grades were all located on the ground floor. More often the old buildings, which were surprisingly intimate, were small and one story. Playgrounds were asphalt and bare, though occasionally a row of old trees had been left, or an edge of unasphalted ground had been prepared for growing flowers. The gardens of the nursery schools, missing in the old infant buildings, were features of the new infant schools. Outdoor toilets remained in the old schools though supplemented by indoor toilets, and they were valued for the playtime period. An overhang usually existed, which was used by mothers when waiting for children, or for some dramatic play by the children. New buildings frequently had extensive grounds, flagstoned terraces outside of each classroom, and courtyards. A number of London infant schools had swimming pools (baths).[4]

In contrast with the nursery schools, almost all of which had buildings planned for use by that age level, the infant schools had buildings antedating their use for informal education. Where these old buildings had been revamped to permit the new use, they were highly influenced by the nursery school model. For easier in-and-out access to the play yard new openings were sometimes made even in the old walls. Ingenuity and a willingness to bend circumstances and to experiment produced the effect of light, color and openness despite the bare asphalt schoolyards and the heavy gray stone or faded red brick façades.

Types of Infant Schools

The main types of infant school organization were the following:

(1) Units under their own heads and in their own buildings—these

[4] London County Council, *Evidence by the London County Council to the Central Advisory Council for Education*, 1964.

are separate from the preceding level of education or from the one that follows.

(2) Such units with the addition of a nursery class. Under the present trend more and more infant schools will contain nursery classes even though these are not part of compulsory education. Though it shares housing and head with the infant school, the nursery class (already described on pp. 50, 51) for the most part functions separately and retains its separate identity.

(3) Independent infant schools sharing a building with a junior school—these infant schools usually occupied the ground level rooms. The clear separation of organization even in the shared building was underlined by such accommodations as separate exits and a separation wall.

(4) Infant departments or sub-units of a primary or junior-mixed-infant (JMI) school, sharing a common head and occasionally housed in a separate building—if the junior school was still a formal one, it tended to have an inhibiting effect on informal education in the infant department and on the ease of transition between the two levels.[5]

Funding

The national government, which supplies 60 percent of the funds for England's infant schools through grants-in-aid to the LEAs, sets national standards for the minimum cost of buildings and teacher salary scales. The LEAs, which provide the remaining 40 percent of required funds through property taxes, determine their application. Because of variations in local property tax bases, this arrangement has resulted in inequities that were largely offset by the Local Government Act of 1966, providing proportionately larger government grants to poorer localities. The Urban Aid Programme for Educational Priority Areas (1968) was a further move toward equalization. The headmistress receives a per capita alloment for usable goods which she disburses according to her own judgment.[6]

School and Class Size

Schools were quite small, compared to those in American cities, with registers that ranged from 185 to 350. The small size was as true for

[5] This study is based on observations of 12 infant schools, 10 infant schools with nursery classes, 7 JMI schools, 1 junior school.
[6] Claire Hardesty, "Education and Finance—Who Pays for What?" National Campaign for Nursery Education, *Newsletter*, No. 4, Summer 1969, and National Union of Teachers, *The Financing of Education*, London, 1964.

London as for any other city, and this seemed to be the purposeful conception of English educators. The Plowden Report recommends 240 as the optimum size for the infant school (300 to 450 for the junior school),[7] a size considered "small enough for children to move freely about the the building without anxiety,"[8] and small enough for the school to unify this movement.

The actual range was wide but average class size was 30.7; average pupil-teacher ratio, 28.5:1. According to the Plowden Report, 14 percent of the children were in classes of 26–30; 24 percent in classes of 31–35; 35 percent in classes of 36–40; and 17 percent in classes over 40.[9] (The Report recommends that class size be reduced to 30, with classes for the youngest children to have the smallest registers. Since its publication, preferential staffing for priority areas is achieving the ratio of 25:1.)

English educators concede the argument for a smaller pupil-teacher ratio; they do not deny the hardships in large classes for teachers and for children. Though they point to the inconclusive research on appropriate class size, they fight for smaller classes. In the face of prolonged teacher shortages they have accepted the large class, but they have not permitted this acceptance to undercut their commitment to acknowledge each child as individual and different. One headmistress, expressing this English commitment, described the prewar reality of screwed-down desks.

> I've even done this work in a classroom with stepping and with sloping desks . . . there's nothing that people can say we can't manage.[10]

And about war time:

> In the classroom I had, at a school which was bombed, we had tables— adult tables, teachers' tables, and teachers' chairs. . . from here, there, and everywhere. I can't describe the furniture. And yet, we managed to do just this. With very little material. We were painting on newspapers— using anything. But it can still be done.[11]

The commitment was strong enough to override *all* circumstances, including those of classrooms crowded with children and furniture.

English educators, while coping with but not defending large class size, take a definite stand in defense of small schools. (Here, too, research on size is questioned; it is not clear that an economy is realized from in-

---

[7] Plowden, p. 172.
[8] *Ibid.*, p. 167.
[9] *Ibid.*, p. 280.
[10] Courtney B. Cazden and S. M. Williams, *Infant School*, p. 1. "Stepping" refers to the steps to which children's desks were screwed down, all rising from the teacher's desk at the center.
[11] *Ibid.*, p. 2.

creasing building capacity.) They maintain that the small school makes possible the unique English achievement of commitment to a child's individual ways of learning even within large classes. The small school mitigates the disadvantages of the large class by lending itself readily to a key adjustment of informal education: *the overflow from the classroom to the use of the whole small building.* The traditional class-school separation disappears into a "use of the whole school." (Thus, the significant impact of the large class is different in England's small schools than in American schools. In the United States the necessities of behavior in the schools are defined by their mammoth size, and even the smallest classes—the Head Start groups with a teacher-child ratio of 1:15—are not permitted free movement and use of the building.)

In addition to school size, the factors that tend to minimize the disadvantages of large classes include the numbers, the use, and the quality of staff. An assessment of staff roles not only sheds considerable light on the real meaning of class size in English infant schools, but also explains in large measure how the schools could respond to children's needs.

STAFFING

The effect of multiple staff, of a number of adults working together, was a striking facet of the infant schools I visited. It could be attributed in part to the *movement* of staff out of their classrooms *to* what children were doing, individually or in small groups. Classroom doors were open, and movement and mixing of staff as well as children in their use of the whole school was easy and encouraged. There was no encapsulated classroom.

In the open school, teachers could work most readily with other teachers as well as with extra staff; they could work where needed. All staff seemed to share the prevailing attitude of accepting and helping children's purposes. All seemed to function quite well in the midst of noise, movement, and a great deal of material and equipment.

The Headmistress

The headmistress for the most part selected her own staff from referrals made by the LEA. She determined their deployment, making it possible for them to work where *needed*. She could experiment with different staff combinations of varying levels of experience and training, thus making certain that the impact on children of inexperienced, probationary, or unqualified teachers and of aides or precollege help was a positive one.

The training of the teacher (described in chapter 3) was certainly important, but thanks to the headmistress no class was totally dependent on that teacher and her training. Through her own participation, and by fostering the interchanges possible in the open school, the headmistress could ensure that the teacher's education was a continuous one. The headmistress was par excellence the *extra staff*, as well as the demonstration teacher working with this child or that, lending a hand here or there. The open school, created by the breakthrough of the closed classroom, enabled the headmistress to assume the special role that was the keystone of staffing in the infant school. (See pp. 44–46 for a full description of the training of the headmistress and pp. 95–97 on the communal life of the school for a fuller description of her role.)

Teachers

The teacher's role and function are noted elsewhere in this volume (see particularly, The English Teacher's Way in chapter 1 and Teacher Planning in this chapter). This section deals with the issue of teacher supply. A great deal of thought is reflected in the Plowden proposals to increase the supply of qualified teachers and to make better use of the present supply. Plowden's discussion of quota teachers distinguishes between "mobile" and "immobile" (family-tied) teachers, and suggests the assignment of immobile teachers to schools near their homes in order to release mobile teachers for priority areas. Plowden notes that where the inclusion of immobile teachers' children (younger than the age group of the class) was the only way to get these teachers back to the classroom, it was easily arranged and seemed to work without difficulty. Plowden also considers the provision of housing for teachers; it explores the use of part-time teachers in ingenious combinations with full-time teachers. (One suggestion was a joint assignment of one full-time teacher with two part-time teachers for two classes.) As already mentioned, the open school and the open-door classroom that have gradually evolved in infant schools facilitate such experimentation. Further use of part-time teachers is proposed through children's part-time schooling up to two terms before full-time entry. To protect its recommendations on class size, Plowden suggests that for staffing purposes part-time children be counted as full-time, and part-time teachers be used for "specialist" subjects, remedial work, relieving heads and deputy heads, working with small groups, and support of young teachers who have large classes. Finally, teams of experienced and inexperienced teachers are urged to take parallel classes and work together.

.5 Remedial Teachers

For assistance with actual teaching, a .5 remedial teacher (.5 meaning half-time) was employed as a special reading teacher. A .5 teacher might also help in the library, or take a class for a short period, thus releasing a teacher for close work with a small group in reading, or carry on the experimental mathematics work, or even function as a part-time accompanist.

Unqualified Teachers

A teacher who was called "unqualified" might not have passed her final assessment or completed her training. Her status is somewhat analogous to that of "permanent substitutes" in American schools but she was rarely in charge of a class. The unqualified teachers were usually used to give special support to individual children or groups. The pressures of the teacher shortage threaten an increased use of the unqualified teacher, a development the Plowden Report does not support. Plowden suggests, in fact, that unqualified teachers be employed on a daily basis for a particular emergency only.

NNEBs and Infant Helpers

In a number of schools, qualified NNEBs were used, as in the nursery school (see pp. 47–49), as part of a policy of help to individual children within the large class. In Bristol, for instance, this use of the NNEB was made more possible by that city's general teamwork and unity of approach in the field of child care. In Birmingham the use of the NNEB was part of the effort to cope with the greater needs of children who were immigrants. In general, the NNEB served as an extra hand, helping the teacher in every way possible to relate more closely to the children.

The NNEB role thus was in line with Plowden's proposal: the NNEB would release the teacher to give far more specific and relevant help to a child or to a small group of children. Many teachers had feared that the Report would suggest use of the NNEB to replace the teacher. They feared—and Plowden did in fact propose it for nursery school—that such assistants would be given some additional intensive training and either employed in place of teachers or under teachers' supervision to take over a group in a way they have not yet done.

Infant helpers had duties akin to those of NNEBs though they were not as much a part of the classroom as the NNEB in the nursery school. However, these infant helpers were enormously helpful to the younger infant school children, especially in all sorts of physical ways: they could fix a hurt or scraped knee; they could help with washing up. They also assisted with replenishing the great variety of classroom supplies.

Plowden proposes to extend the NNEB training and qualifications to infant helpers and in this way to equate their roles. The three possible roles of the infant helpers envisaged by the Plowden Committee are:

1. As an extra pair of hands, to (a) help with use of visual aids; (b) accompany teachers and children on out-of-school expeditions; (c) help in and outside the classroom in preparation and maintenance of materials and equipment.
2. Contributing special skills—within school hours or in club sessions after school—such as help in needlework, arts and crafts, gardening, swimming, drama, music, and library.
3. Supervising children after school while waiting for parents.[12]

Such an explicit outline seemed intended to dispel the fear of teacher displacement. In the schools I visited, the distribution of infant helpers was a couple to a school. The proposal is for a distinct increase—one NNEB for two classes.

Student Help

Additional help in most schools came from students doing their practice teaching. (This is described in chapter 1, p. 44, and in chapter 3, p. 150.) Students in training for NNEB qualification, precollege students, and secondary school girls also contributed valuable service to the schools.

A word on precollege help. From conversations with many of the girls who were awaiting college placement and who meant later to undertake full teacher training in the Rachel McMillan Teachers College, it was clear they valued highly their chance to give this precollege help as a way of confirming their vocational choice.

The secondary school girls helped as part of the secondary schools' program to develop vocational goals as well as interest in children's growth for the eventual parental role these girls might have. They were welcomed and were very helpful with the children for the hour or so of their stay.

The School Keeper

The school keeper, who was a resident on the grounds in a cottage set aside for his use, often took great pride in stretching to the utmost the facilities of the school in support of informal education. His work was appreciatively noted as most important by all heads. The children knew him and often would turn to him for direct help with a problem. In some areas the courses offered for school keepers on changes in primary education towards informality featured leading educators. School keepers seemed anxious to do all they could to support modern methods.

[12] Plowden, p. 330.

Dinner Helpers

In the attempt to have at least one adult at each lunch table of about eight children, the dinner help (in addition to teachers) sat with children at the tables in the big hall. Because the big hall was in full use until the last minute before lunch, a cooperative effort of children and staff was needed to make space for lunch. The dinner help set the tables, sometimes with the assistance of the junior children or some infant children. They functioned in the manner of the teachers—sitting with children at the table, saying the blessing, sustaining the conversation, helping with the difficulties of eating, and indicating the order of clearing. After lunch, the dinner help gave teachers a chance for a few minutes (usually a half-hour) of relaxation over coffee, by supervising the playgrounds, or on wet days, by supervising indoor games. A supply of games was kept especially for this purpose.

Welfare Helpers

Welfare helpers appeared to be a kind of volunteer lay social workers. They visited homes if it became necessary to inquire into a child's absence or if need had to be established and assistance arranged. Their work was useful to the teacher as well as supportive to the job of the health visitor. They were often assigned to escort children to the dental clinics during school hours.

Professional Services

Since special help could be called on, professionals from a variety of fields might be seen about the school. The health visitor came once a month. A doctor examined the children at least once during their infant school years and for necessary checkups. Audiologists, speech therapists, cerebral palsy therapists—all were available upon request. School psychologists came into the school to observe and to investigate the causes of some difficulties; sometimes children were called out of their group for conversation with them.

Clerical Help

Part-time clerical help was used because office work was very unobtrusive and deliberately kept so by the headmistress, who was determined to maintain her primary role as educator, and who viewed her administrative activities as secondary in importance to her participation in the life of the school.

ORGANIZATION FOR INFORMAL EDUCATION

Several organizational adaptations consciously fostered informal education in the infant school. These adaptations—in how the class was organized, in the use of building space, and in the plan of the day or timetable—all supported the direction toward informality.

CLASS ORGANIZATION AND CONCEPTS OF PROGRESSION

Examined and reexamined, class organization is still undergoing analysis and evaluation. Though the trend is to family grouping, age grouping was the dominant form in the majority of the schools. It was not, however, a static form; within it lay variety in structure, depending on how progression within the infant school was viewed. But whether age or family grouped, the infant school was conceived as a basic, unstandardized unit, with growth for a child over the entire two-year period, with use of all parts of the school, and with no retardation at any point along the way.

In "one-directional progression," the progress of a child was conceptualized as a one-way street with no stops, no diversions, no bypasses, and no indulging of old skills while new ones were being acquired. Where this view prevailed, the sense of the infant school as an ungraded sequence, responsive to varying paces of development, was lost. All children moved with their age group. Although one-directional progression never meant retarding, it might mean that a child, though being lost to the pace of the class, was "carried along" even though no longer learning. The normal "regressions" and "backward steps," the time for growth in one's way and at one's own pace, the chances for repeated encounters with the rich environment, all might be eliminated and no longer permitted, so that a child's "unevenness" of development remained unrecognized. The setting changed for each class and some of the more fluid and flexible provisions of environment were no longer available for older children. Thus, the steps necessary in integration and for the continuous flow of a child's learning process might be blocked.

On the other hand, where progression meant that the same child might be at one point in one skill, at another point in another, or at the beginning in still another skill, such schools, even though age grouped, conceived of progression for each child individually and so developed a sense of ungraded sequence. Materials available for five-year-olds were still available for seven-year-olds. Teachers in these schools did not rate children by a *grade standard* of performance but planned for the progression of each child; they observed and recorded what step he was at in that progression and considered the step he might be taking next. In an age-grouped school, the 5s were said to be in a readiness setting for reading; the 6s, of course, moved ahead, with many at the beginning stage. In the 7s' classroom some phonics and word-building cards could usually be seen; here most children were reading and those who were still at the beginning were accepted as such. Where there was free use of the whole school, even if age grouped, there was at least some mixing of all children, and the school called itself a family school even when it was not family grouped for each class.

The Reception Class

The function of the reception class was to provide for the first and youngest of the age groupings. In family-grouped schools it was not part of the system at all, though from the name (new to an American observer) it would serve to stand for a short-period sorting-out class, funneling children into family grouping. In some instances it was used in this way for immigrant children.

The teacher in the reception class was supposed to focus on beginnings, on "readiness" for skills. Reading readiness materials were around, and a few children went beyond this readiness and used actual reading materials. Children who had been in schools more than one term sometimes made a slight beginning in reading and writing and in work on number. The teachers supported this slight beginning by writing words under anything a child had made and by encouraging copying or matching of the words. Gardner, in a lecture at the Institute of Education, indicated that some thirty years ago there had been a more relaxed interpretation of "not offering reading until they're ready" than exists today when it is hard to find a five-year-old group where the teacher is not encouraging some beginning of reading with one child or another.

In a few cases the reception class was the class where play was accepted and where children became accustomed to school rules and then went along in the more or less distinct one-directional progression. In such places, the relationship of the reception class to the rest of the school was analogous to that of kindergarten classes to the first grade in America, though not quite as discontinuous. In such schools the richness of environment typical of infant schools existed largely for the reception class and not for the classes that followed.

In the majority of cases the reception class provided the extra support needed by 5s and rising 5s. It was a class of beginnings, but its modes of teacher-child relationships and its encouragement of play continued throughout infant school.

Gradual Admission

Practically no schools would have all new children on the same day in an all newly-formed class. The reception class admission was held three times a year: in January, at Easter, and in September, thus adding new entrants to an already formed group. This process to some extent created both gradual admission and family grouping in that class, if a child stayed in it three terms. If this did not happen—for example, if the reception class, because of the pressure of numbers, passed children on after one term—then the children might have the difficult situation of several teachers in one year. But even so, schools made other adjustments to promote gradual admission; stretching the admission period over a couple of days or weeks, usually a fortnight; allowing five-year-olds to join any day in the term before they became 5; and accepting rising 5s on a half-day basis for six weeks. Some schools tried to mitigate stress by having the children go through the infant school with the same teacher.

Gradual admission, with the aim of easing children's first school entry, is so important to the English that it could not escape comment by the Plowden Committee. The Report devotes much space to a discussion of gradual admission within a three-term entry. It also discusses ways of protecting arrangements for gradual admission within the single entry and the raised age of entry proposed as a way of increasing the supply of teachers.[13] With raised age of entry and single entry the rising 5s would be kept out of the infant school and would be provided a year of nursery school prior to admission to the infant school, but this year would be with the less qualified NNEB. Gardner, concerned that such a year would give a child a less valuable educational experience, has suggested that the NNEB could be used more profitably as an aide to a teacher heading a nursery class in an infant school.[14]

Plowden points out that when there is only one yearly intake, there will be a greater need for staggering admission over a longer time. Praising the arrangements some heads already had made with parents, the Report recommends: (1) visits by mothers and children before admission

---

[13] *Ibid.*, p. 139. Plowden proposed raising the age of entry to the September following the child's 5th birthday. This would reduce the number of children and release staff for nursery expansion. The plan for single entry would similarly release staff by putting an end to the practice of "holding on" to teachers for the possible influx of registration in the second and third term.

[14] D. E. M. Gardner, "The Plowden Report on 'Children and Their Primary Schools'," *The Froebel Journal*, January 1968, p. 6.

where mothers are encouraged to stay with their children while the children are anxious, certainly during the first few days at school; (2) joint meetings of nursery and infant school staffs and meetings of these staffs with heads and with parents to plan an eased admission; (3) attendance of young children at school functions, such as the Morning Service (described on p. 98); (4) admission over a period of a half-term; and (5) flexibility in adjustment to an individual child. Thus, if a child is not ready at the point of statutory entry, nursery school can be prolonged for a term, or half-day attendance at infant school may be prolonged from the suggested two terms before full attendance, with the decision left to parents in consultation with the headmistress. Flexibility also may lower the age of entry as well as delay this. But all this presupposes that part-time nursery education will be available for those who want it one year before compulsory school education. Until single entry can be operative, Plowden proposes a twice-yearly entry.

The issues relating to age of admission, nursery education, half-day infant education, and the supply of teachers are all connected; and in the resolution of these issues, gains for some aspects may mean losses for others. For example, in the period since Plowden, proposals to meet the increased demand for nursery education have tended to favor the half-day infant education and the delay of full-time compulsory attendance, which would in effect release teachers for the nursery expansion. Theoretically, with a concomitant enormous increase of nursery education, a child would have more half-time nursery education and half-time infant school experience, too. Nevertheless, the fear is expressed that some children, perhaps even those most in need, will not take advantage of the voluntary half-day offering and therefore will have a shortened or a curtailed infant school experience.

In the midst of teacher shortage, the contradictory pulls for nursery education versus infant education continue. Change of age requirements for compulsory full-time attendance, however, necessitates an Act of Parliament and, in the meantime, the argument continues.

Prior to the publication of the Plowden Report, half-day infant school, as long as needed for new children, was advocated, provided it did not become a fixed policy for all children, age 5. Opposition to this policy was based on the possible erosion of play and flexible infant school curriculum if half-day were to become standard. Gardner pointed to the possibility that with only a half-day there might be pressure to maximize the use of this time for "learning," and the real richness of the day would be lost. Since many mothers work, the half-day would not protect many children from pressures, but would certainly deprive them of play. All these arguments were recognized by the Plowden Committee in its recommendation for a policy of individual easing, not a fixed half-day policy for all children. There is specific injunction against use of this for a more pressured learning; there is also specific reminder that anxious children need the play offered by the infant school.

Family or Mixed-Age Grouping

Family grouping is a form of gradual admission in that a small number of new children join an already formed group. A not too uncommon pattern is that of children coming for one-half day (following a spring visit and a spring interview with the mother), gradually increasing their attendance, and sometimes, after a month, staying for lunch. In family grouping the five-year-old increases his participation as he is ready and wants this.

The mixed-age grouping inherent in family grouping diluted the impact of admission for new children.[15] The younger, new arrivals could see the comfortable adjustment of the older children in their use of the school, which showed that this was a safe place in which to be, and so the adjustment of the new ones was helped. Helpfulness was elicited from those older and more familiar with school for those younger and less familiar. The teachers were conscious of the diminution of the competition typical of a peer group. They noted that the older children gained reinforcement for their own learning by their occasional function as teachers. Thus, second-year children in a group admitting new children had a changed role; and in particular, those slow or uneven in development, could avert an unnecessary and premature sense of failure. Some teachers spoke of the second year as consolidating in these children what the first year had begun. They hoped that in the third year the child would blossom. They pointed over and over again to children who had started in this easy, unpressured way and had begun to blossom in the third year, very often in the process of helping a younger child.

Mixed-age grouping, moreover, made it easier for the teacher who, faced with a few children at a time, could help these begin at their own point of readiness. The teacher's support and planning of such beginnings, adjusted to individual pace and need, were a built-in feature of family grouping. Not only was it easier for children who needed the slower start to find support for individual progress, but it was also easier for children who were ready to speed ahead to find a place with older ones.

There were many ways of organizing family grouping, in which a child usually stayed with the same teacher for the entire infant school period. Brothers and sisters were not always placed in the same group if

---

[15] Lorna Ridgway and Irene Lawton, *Family Grouping in the Infants' School.* This sums up the case for family grouping. See also L. Weber, "Study of Development of Adjustment Practices."

this was judged to be a poor idea. There might be "transitional" family grouping—combining the 5s and 6s but with single-age grouping for the 7s. More rarely, a school might have the separate reception class and then family grouping. Thus a child might have the same teacher throughout or new combinations for the second and third years. Bristol, where I was told there was 93 percent family grouping, had all styles of this.

The Plowden Report is generally favorable to this type of organization on the infant school level as is the London County Council Report:

> The balance of argument, however, appears to indicate that mixed-age grouping in infants' classes may usefully be extended under favorable circumstances and the Council hopes that the training of teachers will encourage and help more schools to organize in this way.[16]

The possibility of children doing what they were ready for, regardless of age, seemed most ingrained in the structure of the family groups. However, in the schools where the basic flexible provision was the same in all classes, this was true for children, regardless of age group. Age-grouped schools, in a sense, could have all the advantages of flexibility in progression, even a free day or undifferentiated day (see pp. 90–94), and some did. One-directional progression, on the other hand, limited the possibility of beginning learning at any point of readiness without prescribed standards of achievement; it seemed to create pressures to start skill learning even for five-year-olds.

Both kinds of arrangement—age grouping and family grouping—aimed for a school organized as a *family school*, allowing for a child's movement within the whole school so that he knew and was accepted in all parts of the school. This aim was achieved in many schools where, for example, a child from one class would come in to see what the children of another class, or what his brother was doing.

Class organization, whether based on age or on family grouping, created the sense of wholeness of infant education by maintaining a unified ungraded sequence that was consistent with the goal in the infant school: to be aware of and accept variations in the development level of children, in other words, to be prepared for an individual child's point of readiness.

USE OF BUILDING SPACE: OVERFLOW AND IN-AND-OUTNESS

No matter what the original intent in the architectural plan of the infant school, the present aim was the use of *the totality of school space.*

[16] London County Council, *Evidence*, pp. 36–37.

Corridors

A common sight was that of easels, workbenches, water tables, and block buildings—all in the corridors. The impact on an American observer of seeing such corridors was unforgettable. In the United States school corridors are empty except when used for passage, for moving in orderly lines, quietly and quickly from one place to another. They are not part of the living of a school. In England, it became clear, the use of the corridors was one of the factors that made it possible, even with large classes, for the children to make use in their learning of every aspect of the school environment. The use of the corridors—and even more so, that of the big hall—was also a way of easing the tight pressures of the classroom. It was easy for a child to spread his work into the corridors, for a small group to work there together. Thus the use of the corridors facilitated the change from the traditional classroom organization to free use of the whole school by individuals.

The Big Hall

If the big hall was central, it was most easily used. It fed movement back and forth from the classroom and allowed easy access for the teacher to the activities in the hall and back into the classroom. The easy flow of work and movement in the center hall brought teachers and children into maximal contact with the headmistress. In the midst of center hall activities she could most easily and frequently stimulate, assist, demonstrate. Children and teachers from one classroom could more readily be sparked off from contact with the work of others.

Acting platforms situated in the big hall were constantly in use, indicating the value placed on improvisation, on drama, on acting, on *role playing*. This role playing was an integrative process for a child in which he put together elements from many sources in acting pieces of his own experience. In doing this or in reenacting a story, read or heard, he was ordering his thinking, recalling, selecting, deciding on sequence, hypothesizing on the possibilities of the future and the reality of the present, absorbing into himself the feeling of past—his own or storied. His acting was *with* other children: spatial relationships had to be worked out—"you be there" and "you there." His language was extended and clarified as he worked out the "how" with others, as he projected "what you say" if you are this or that one. In this way, the discrepancies in a child's hypothesis of "how it might be" were revealed and new syntheses tried. And, of course, acting might lead to writing of the play itself or of invitations, as when a group of children (often at the suggestion of the headmistress) asked the teacher to "see" the play.

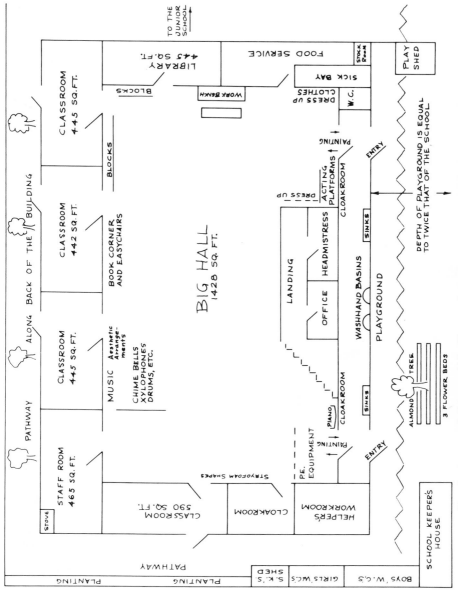

Sketch of a center hall in an old building, with measurements supplied by the headmistress.

The big hall was often the place for *mathematical exploration* with large one-foot tile squares or surveyor-link chains. It was the place for ambitious structures with styrofoam shapes. A favorite problem seemed to be measuring the height or length of the big hall, both so dramatically bigger than the classrooms.

Other observed activities were at the *workbench* and with large *blocks,* and in general, all kinds of work, from *lino-printing* to *cooking,* were going on in the big hall.

The hall was scheduled at specific times for *Morning Service,* (see pp. 97–98 for full description), for *lunch* (see pp. 98–99), and also, with modifications by some heads, for group work such as *P.E. (physical education), Music and Movement,* and the reading of *poetry* and an afternoon *story.*

Special equipment, such as the agility apparatus required for P.E., was located in the big hall, thus making it available for class or group activity. But the English talk more of an individual child's development of skill and understanding in the use of his body than of the group work in P.E. They stress *Movement* and attach much greater importance to a child's experimentation with movement than do teachers in the United States.[17] This English approach stems from their analysis that a child's development—intellectual, physical, and emotional—cannot be considered as separate pieces. Development of thought is linked to internalized movement, and English teachers discuss seriously how judgment, adaptation, and estimation develop through a child's movement of his own body in the midst of changing heights, widths, surfaces. They try to provide the experiences for the development of such judgment and of concepts of space, time, size, weight, length, and shape. They try to support the development of the "thinking body," of problem-solving skills. They think understanding of area, of spatial relationship, of direction grows through actual use of space. Movement and dance experiences reveal the variety of individual meanings children have attached to vocabulary words on movement and these can then be shared and discussed. And movement integrated, as did role playing, in emotional and intellectual terms, experiences gained in other ways—in mathematical exploration, through literature, through environmental enquiry.

A very fine *B.B.C. program* to help teachers with Music and Movement, and centering on free interpretative motion, was piped into the schools. From this series many teachers created their own form of Music and Movement, based on the interaction of teachers' and children's ideas.

Most often, *musical instruments* were available in the corridors or in the big hall. Music experiences with these instruments or with im-

---

[17] Molly Brearley, ed., *The Teaching of Young Children.*

provised ones were often a very individual pursuit by one child, or by a small group working together. Some children seemed to be experimenting with developing ways of recording the patterns they had tried with chime-bars or xylophone. Some seemed to be developing skill in reading and writing music very much as they were developing these skills with words and attempting to write their own compositions in both ways. Others were listening intently to sounds, to pitch, or with great thoughfulness and concentration working out musical patterns which were also often expressed in movement. A vivid memory: Three children, oblivious to all else, are working out a tune on the chime-bars, listening hard to make sure that the chimes match their singing. A group of five other children come up close to hear them, while one little girl, off to a side, is reading notes and tapping on a very fine kind of xylophone. Using cymbals, a boy works out a "pattern of three," and two of his barefoot friends try it out as a dance movement.

An interesting aspect of the hall function was the easy undressing by the children.[18] Children took off their shoes and socks for acting; for P.E., they shed their skirts and blouses, shirts and trousers. Barefoot and unself-conscious in panties, they used the P.E. equipment with greater safety, and were also freer in their exploration of movement. The undressing was allowed partly because the English shoes and buckle sandals are easier to get on and off and so require less teacher help than American tie shoes and partly also in recognition of a child's great need for this kind of freedom and of his enjoyment of undressing and barefootedness.

Some obvious disadvantages accompanying the use of a big hall were noise and interference from the class activities of Music and Movement, and P.E. Such interference persisted even when some teachers and heads allowed a moderate amount of the individual work going on at the side to continue, asking only that it be moved to the edges of the big hall and done more quietly. Despite the noise, children often sat in the big hall book corner while a class had Music and Movement, or they continued painting while more organized activities took over use of much of the big hall. In some of the old schools the hall had to be cleared for use as a lunchroom.

The noise, however, did not carry to all parts of the big hall. Children who were talking to each other in small groups were not competing for group attention, and so there was no shouting or yelling. As one headmistress commented: "If the children are working you don't hear any noise." Furthermore, because the free activities in the hall involved individuals or small groups, two or three children, in pursuit of these activities, were isolated from the large group in the same way that a table at a

[18] Recorded in the movie, *Infants School.*

restaurant isolates a dating couple. Children and teachers did seem to be able to concentrate and to pitch their talk so as to hear each other in their small group. No teacher said, "Say it loud," an injunction heard over and over in American classrooms and one that would seem to encourage loud voices. Clearly the noise of concurrent activity, where a pinpoint focus from all was not being sought, was less bothersome than the noise can be from a few, where total attention is demanded.

It seemed clear that in spite of such disadvantages as noise and other activities, more free activity is possible with the center hall (or center large corridor used in the same way as described for the big hall) than in any other arrangement. This arrangement seems to foster the most efficient breakthrough of classroom structure, the most mixing of classes and class to class stimulation. It seems to foster an "open" school.

With such full use of the hall, does the teacher lose sight of much that a child does and, therefore, of a whole child? Does she perhaps then miss some opportunities to help a child relate what he has done to other areas of his work? Most of the activity in a center hall or in a corridor is *near* the classroom—an *overflow* from it, a spillover outside the door, so that there is, for children and teachers, an easy in-and-out, an easy recall and collaboration with some aspects of skills. This pattern seemed essential: that the teacher know of a child's overflow activity. If she did not, she might insufficiently relate activities to skills.

Communication between teachers was certainly important; a teacher might have observed and helped with the activities of a child not actually in her class. Over coffee in the staff room, going over their "jottings," teachers shared their observations. I heard one teacher telling another that she had had Michael that day and she was puzzled about some aspect of his work. I heard the headmistress taking a few minutes with teachers to tell about what had gone on in the center hall out of their line of vision. Children were encouraged to ask their teacher to see or hear—to share what they had done with teachers and with the other children, in the same way as they were constantly drawing the heads into the orbit of their work.

> When the children have used something, the teacher wants to see what the child has made with it—if it's a material that's going to show something at the end. If it's water play, what the child has discovered from the water play. If it's junk—what the child has made from it.[19]

But the work of the children going to the various areas in the hall or corridor was often unsupervised, at least for a short period. After a time the teacher or head would come over and look at the work and talk with a child about it. Teachers did not seem to feel that they had to watch

---

[19] Cazden, *Infant School*, p. 18.

every moment of the children's work. In order to allow this, one would have to trust that a child's interest in his work would be so great that he could do it unsupervised. Trust was possible also because the "family" nature of the school encouraged older children to initiate a new child into whatever were the rules for the use of any equipment or area of work.

A tolerance for overflow situations and a trust of children not immediately "under the teacher's eye" seem to have been well established in England over a long period. In the late nineteenth and early twentieth centuries English teachers, following in the path of Froebel and then of Montessori, had encouraged individual handiwork and had introduced objects in old crowded classrooms. Since space was needed for the individual work with these objects, the teachers had to plan carefully to facilitate some movement *to* them. The free movement was introduced gradually and with care that the children understood the reasonable use of freedom. Overflow to corridor and big hall became commonplace, leading to a vital feature of informal education—in-and-outness.

The movement to and from the classroom was not entirely free, however. The teacher, with the head, regulated movement from her class, after finding out what children wanted to do and setting the limits of suitable numbers for a certain activity. A child had his classroom as base and first asked his teacher before moving into the corridor or hall. She might say that she had planned to work with him and his group on number or writing: "I'd like you and you to come with me first thing this morning. I want to go on with something we were doing yesterday." [20] Or she might suggest that he check with the head in the hall as to whether it was all right. Nor did all the children work individually, and this gregariousness also regulated movement. As one teacher described it: "The children will get into little groups. There's always a leader of a group and the children work together. So your group is naturally formed for you." [21]

Children did not move about all day doing everything. On the contrary, this informal schedule, by not interrupting or cutting across an interest and not going by the clock, allowed a child to finish, to extend and develop his interests. He was encouraged to stay with his work, though inability or unreadiness for this kind of commitment was understood and accepted. What cut down on a child's flitting from one area to another was the awareness of availability and free access and the assurance that the richness of materials and equipment would not disappear.

Nevertheless, the center hall was not the predominant physical plan of my sample, and even if present it was not always used to produce a whole and free use of the environment.[22] It would appear that in-and-

[20] *Ibid.*, p. 15.
[21] *Ibid.*, pp. 11, 13.
[22] Of the 30 schools visited, 13 had center halls; 17 had side halls. Of these, 6 had no procedures of in-and-outness. In a few others, in-and-outness was restricted to bays and corridors and did not include halls.

outness operated almost regardless of physical plant, only if it was consciously viewed as desirable. Thus, in a few cases, the center hall was used only for scheduled mass activities.

THE SIDE HALL. Not all schools had center halls. Some had side halls and in the newer schools of the New Towns, corridors tended to be eliminated and replaced by side halls. The side hall, because it did not afford easy back-and-forth access for the teacher, seemed less in use than the center hall. Still, depending on the effort of the headmistress, the side hall certainly could be well used. For example, in a remodeled school in London the side hall was the place for large block building, music, acting, measuring, and for work with large shapes. In that school, workbench, water play, and painting—activities requiring closer help—went on in the corridor opening out of classes.

Indoor and Outdoor In-and-Outness

For the most part in the old infant schools, overflow from the classroom to the free use of the school remained an indoor phenomenon.

In the good weather of the summer term (Easter through July), however, teachers and children dragged out half the equipment so that workbench, block building, clay, painting, reading, and sewing could go on outdoors—so much did the teachers believe that use of the equipment in this in-and-out way was good, and so much were they willing to trust the children to go unsupervised to equipment. Some old schools had *window-doors* opening out to the yard and garden to facilitate this free access to equipment, this flow of in-and-out activity. New schools had *inner court-yards* as well as outdoor paved bays, with overhangs for protection from bad weather, opening from each classroom. Paved bays allowed for overflow from the classroom but did not encourage mixing of classes.

The importance to informal education of in-and-outness, both indoor and outdoor, and of the overflow to corridors and big hall, is recognized by the Plowden Committee:

> The informal arrangements possible in small schools have probably done more to make teaching flexible between classes as well as inside a class than the organised time-tabled arrangements. . . . An infant school classroom is too small and too confined for all the things the children need to do. They overflow into the open air where there are no walls to shut off one class from another; they stray into corridors which are not marked out into pens like sheep folds. The classroom is the children's home, their teacher's base; but outside it any teacher may be drawn into any child's concern. The school becomes a unity.[23]

---

[23] Plowden, p. 276.

PLAN OF THE DAY—THE TIMETABLE

The plan of the day—the timetable—was a key factor in implementing the concept of informal education that stresses the free flow and wholeness of school living. An infant school timetable could consist of *simultaneous use* with *fixed points* moving toward what has been variously called the *free day*, the *undifferentiated* or *integrated day*; or it could consist of an *activity period* with simultaneous use and a *skills period* with simultaneous varied grouping. The order of activity period and skills period could be reversed and this too had consequences.

Simultaneous Use

Simultaneous use refers to the use of various aspects of the environment—one aspect by one or a few children, another aspect by others, singly or in a group, at the same time.

Activity Period

Simultaneous use was at the least a phenomenon of the activity period, a period of free choice for the children from all the areas of the environment—plastic (sand, water, clay, paint, woodwork), housekeeping, music, acting, sewing, measurement and weighing, books, games, etc. Even when it characterized solely the activity period, simultaneous use meant availability of books and number as well as of other materials. Even in such a division of the day aspects of the environment available during the period of free choice were used for the focused "skills" work, as when sand was used for weighing and water for measuring.

Skills Period

In all schools, the existing situation was of simultaneous varied grouping, no matter what the timetable arrangement. No skills work was taught *entirely* in a block classroom way, with *one* lesson for all. Even where skills were unrelated to "activities"—interpreted narrowly as painting, games, sandbox, house-play, acting—there was *always* a breakdown into several different groupings of children doing different things appropriate to their own point of progression, though all were linked in general subject. Usually in such a skills period unrelated to activities, one group might be doing reading, another writing, another number work or measuring, or perhaps individual children were engaged in these activities. Thus, the children were not all doing the same thing at the same time.

Usually, even if the whole group was doing number, children were doing three or four different activities, on different levels, handling different things. The most structured situation, for example, might be one group weighing, another measuring, another counting with number trays, another "smashing" a number such as eight and turning it into its relevant groupings.

Nevertheless, if the timetable called for the skills period to *precede* the activity period, the result was very little interpenetration of focus and interest and very little sense of the wholeness implied in informal education. This sequence of timetabling resulted in most completely isolating the free activity from the rest of the scheduled day, the least degree of free flow, the least use of the environment. Few schools timetabled in this way.

Activity and Skills Period Interrelated

More likely, some aspect of the activity period interpenetrated the skills and vice versa, and what was done was thus entirely individual. The important thing was the constant use of the concrete in the environment to give meanings to all learning. There was a constant search for what would involve children in what interests them and the intensified learning that stems from this. Therefore, activity stemming from the children's firsthand experiences took precedence over verbalisms, over "take-in" from the teacher. Plowden recommendations as well as publications of the Nuffield research teams support further development of this simultaneous multiple use of the concrete environment. Gardner's view is that activity "in isolation from the rest of the time-table . . . loses some of its potential value as providing a motive and purpose for other work." [24]

The Free (or Undifferentiated or Integrated) Day

In planning for the free day there is no separation of activities or skills and no separate scheduling of any one activity other than the fixed points (Morning Service, P.E., Music and Movement, and lunch) designed for all children in the school. As a result, one might see all aspects of the environment—reading, writing, number, painting, acting, music—in use at all times. A group getting the teacher's special help or stimulus could be found at any time.

At some time of the day a child did number, reading, and writing, adjusted to his stage of progress and depending on his interest and his need of the moment. Gardner, describing this day, says:

[24] D. E. M. Gardner and Joan Cass, *Role of the Teacher in Infant and Nursery School*, p. 7.

Good teachers have done so much to foster the interests of the children and open up fresh possibilities to them that in some schools there is no need to safeguard particular "subjects" such as reading, writing and arithmetic by reserving special times for them, since the children can be relied upon to choose them sufficiently and sometimes for longer periods than would have been allocated by a time-table.[25]

Sometimes the schedule was thought out over a period longer than a day and it was not felt necessary that every child do every thing every day. In such a school a child who was engrossed in something could continue exploring the bounds of his work without regard for schedule, at least for a while.

In Bristol, after some period of use of this undifferentiated day plan, it was clear that *play time* as a release into movement from an immobile learning situation was no longer necessary—the children had freedom and movement all through the day. Of course, some teachers have criticized this because the discard of play time means a loss of these free moments for the teacher, who remains responsible *all* day. While there is a loss of *group* free time, teachers continue to take a break for coffee sometime during the morning.

It should be emphasized that the undifferentiated day was not conceived simply in terms of simultaneity of all different aspects of the environment, nor in terms of a child's use of any one aspect as a separate use at a single moment in time. The English viewed a child's use of the environment as cutting across subject areas in pursuit of his interests. This kind of scheduling not only supported a child's integration of experience but also sustained his involvement.

Not only my observations but the literature also seemed to indicate a trend towards *more* simultaneous varied grouping and towards the undifferentiated or integrated day. In fact, most of the schools visited had for the greater part of the day a combination of the activity period related to skills and simultaneous varied grouping. Schools with activity periods unrelated to skills were in the minority. For the most part, the schools that were family-grouped had an undifferentiated day.

Some steps toward a looser timetabling had been made by all the schools of my sample, but the variety of their arrangements indicates that the undifferentiated day is the end point of a continuum. The work of the Froebel Institute focuses on a child's free choice of activity rather than on the free day, and recognizes that some teachers

might still think it indispensable to set their children (at any rate from 7–8 onward) some definite broad theme. They might perhaps also want to start from a prepared talk, and to introduce further such talks, or in

[25] *Ibid.*, p. 7.

fact lessons, at intervals. This might then become an arguable question of degree. . . . It might well be felt by a good many thoughtful teachers that some such carefully limited degree of direction would lead to more positive and valuable results, anyway from 7 to 8 or 9 onward, than any quite unplanned freedom of choice. But so far the trend of our evidence rather points the other way. In that connection it seems particularly worth noting that some teachers began along partly pre-planned lines but themselves became more and more critical of these as they went along. They found in fact that the less pattern they imposed, the better appeared to be the results. . . . And it seems important to register that there may well be room for a great variety of different procedures and techniques, determined, at least in part, by what comes naturally and easily to the teacher—provided only that the last word always rests with the child.[26]

The Nuffield Teacher's Guide, dealing expressly with problems of transition to informality in the junior school and recognizing the difficulties of this approach for many teachers, suggested that "it is best to begin in a fairly formal way and to introduce new ways gradually." [27] The teacher then "can meet a limited number of problems at a time instead of being faced with many all at once." [28] For teachers used to a stricter timetable, the Guide suggests small blocks of one hour of time as a starter, though it describes some teachers who seem able to make the change in one step. Earlier accounts of the development of this kind of planning in the infant schools also suggested activity periods of one hour as a starter.[29] These accounts described the necessary changes in room arrangement and the process of overflow to the whole day as activity period and skills were related. Mary Brown, writing after Plowden (and of the integrated day), speaks of the necessity for the teacher to have *evolved* to this.[30]

The undifferentiated day has attracted great attention in the United States as a major, and by implication, necessary and immediate, feature of what I have called informal education.[31] Examination of English writing however, indicates that there was a continuum of many steps in its evolution in the infant school. Furthermore, the English anticipated that such a continuum would characterize the evolution of informal education in the junior school.

The Plowden Report confirms the undifferentiated day as a desirable

[26] National Froebel Foundation, *Children Learning through Scientific Interests*, pp. 140, 141.
[27] Nuffield Foundation, *Teacher's Guide 1*, p. 184.
[28] *Ibid.*, p. 185.
[29] C. Sturmey, ed., *Activity Methods for Children Under Eight*.
[30] Mary Brown and Norman Precious, *The Integrated Day in the Primary School*, p. 16.
[31] Edward Yeomans, *Education for Initiative and Responsibility*.

goal and terms the trend towards this "widespread." It stresses that free use of the rich environment is connected to looser timetabling.

> The strongest influence making for the free day has been the conviction of some teachers and other educationalists that it is through play that young children learn. . . . The tendency is spreading in junior schools. Children may plan when to do work assigned to them and also have time in which to follow personal or group interests of their own choice.[32]

A Child's Whole Day

Within the undifferentiated or free day, a child's life had a pattern or rhythm even though the day had no specific schedule except for the fixed points listed below.

On arrival he might help with the preparation of the classroom workshop or with the care of the animals; in effect, he entered the school as a responsible participant, knowing that materials were accessible and available to him—to prepare, to use, to restore. He might get to work on something already underway, resuming his investigation almost without pause. After a period of satisfying work, he and all the other children joined in the Morning Service. He then returned with his class to his room and teacher, who perhaps suggested that he work for a short while on a specific skill task appropriate to his own needs. After this work he could return to his own pursuits elsewhere in the classroom, corridor, and hall, or even outside in the playground. He might need to consult with the teacher on a beginning of a new investigation. As the morning wore on a child might join his class for the scheduled Music and Movement or work on the P.E. apparatus. Until then, and while other groups had their scheduled periods, he might continue his own work.

The hall had to be cleared for lunch use. A child knew where he might safely put aside his work, ready to be taken up later. He replaced materials already used, doing his part with all the other children to restore the school to working order for the afternoon. Earlier he might have helped collect dinner money and also, in answer to his own question, computed the amount collected. Now he might be one of a group of children helping set the lunch tables.

After lunch he again met with his classmates and teacher before another period of his own investigation, mixing use of "free" activities and skills. His teacher might join him at his work—the measuring, the reading, the acting, the painting, the weighing—discussing it with him in the terms of his purposes but also posing new possibilities for trial the next day. Or she might suggest trial of a new area altogether.

[32] Plowden, p. 197.

Nearing the end of the day, as he and other children reached the end of their work or a reasonable point of interruption, they began to tidy their work areas knowing that materials not returned to storage centers would not be available for their use the next day. If he finished earlier than the others, he might read, play a quiet game, hold a guinea pig, talk with a friend, or help with another's tidying.

The day might end with the reading of a story or some poetry and a discussion. Thus, a child's day had a rhythm of sustained involvement in his own work, interposed with periods of coming together with his fellows in class and school.

Fixed Points

Whether timetabled for activity period and skills or for the undifferentiated day, the plan of the day also included scheduled activities—Morning Service (for detailed description, see pp. 97–98), P.E., Music and Movement, lunch, and playtime. These activities became the fixed points of the day, though their scheduling (except for lunch) often reflected some flexibility. The Morning Service, for example, the only officially required activity in an English school, was supposed to take place the first thing in the morning, but may heads found that it came more appropriately after some activity, and had quietly made their own adjustment of schedule. The Plowden Report notes this flexibility.

In an attempt to produce greater impact and intimacy, the heads of some schools arranged for a classroom kind of Morning Service a few mornings a week and an all-school service only once or twice a week, but this was not the usual procedure. In a few schools the 5s did not, either as a group or even regularly, join the Morning Service. In a very few instances a number of other departures from the pattern of all-school gathering may be noted.

Obviously the activities that brought together all the children or utilized the big hall limited some of the free-flowing use of the school. But the significance of these activities is not that they set limitations to free flow or to the free day, for more than timetable was involved. These activities were considered to be integrative for the children and for the school. They were expressions of the communal life of the school.

THE HEADMISTRESS AND THE TEACHER IN ACTION

Schools called "informal" were all trying to create a wholeness in the living within the school through their adaptations for family grouping, for in-and-outness, for use of the hall and corridor, and for a timetable that allowed simultaneous use of the rich environment. Whether these adaptations worked depended on their implementation by people who understood their purpose, people who understood what was meant by informal education. It is in this context that the work of the headmistress in promoting the fullest use of the whole school must be examined. The results of her efforts were reflected in the communal life of the school that developed around the fixed points of scheduling, the children's participation in all the life and work of the school, the free flow of movement, and the informality of interaction and communication between staff and children. Similarly, the teacher's planning and her purposes behind this planning revealed her grasp of informal education.

THE HEADMISTRESS AND COMMUNAL LIFE OF THE SCHOOL

Communal life may be defined as "wholeness" and "inner" unity in the life of the school. More than on operational unity, it depended on the head's conscious use of the whole school as a unifying force. The majority of the schools visited had a strong sense of this communal life.

Every school was a single unit of operation, its head the single responsible executive who unified the school and was a symbol of that unity. She not only made decisions on allocations to classrooms but she also related directly to each classroom. One headmistress in a New Town, for example, tried to strengthen her unifying role in the school by taking over each class for one half-hour a week. But a headmistress who encouraged communal life in the sense I have described did not merely come into classrooms as a principal might in an American school. The head moved in and out from hall to classroom, joining an activity, saying a word to the children, to the teacher. And the children and teachers could move easily to the head, whose office was often situated on a half-landing above the big hall and was very much in the center of all the life of the school. Most of the time the headmistress was in the school, *not* in her office. This open access and movement set the "style" of the teaching-learning process in the school. By demonstration and participation the headmistress helped teachers continue their development toward maximum effectiveness.

It was in the big hall that one could best see the headmistress function. She could usually be found there, and her presence was the central factor in its use and in the movement and relationship of children from any class to this use. All day long, beginning with the Morning Service, the headmistress drew the attention of the school as a whole to the work of particular individuals or groups or to new aspects of environmental provision. She fostered the overflow use of the whole school by coordinating with the teacher the flow of movement from class to hall. She made judgments on whether or not an activity could be trusted to proceed unsupervised, and on reasonable time allotments to ensure some sharing of equipment. In one school when children asked if they could be at the workbench, the headmistress might ask if they were friends, what they had in mind, and then suggest that they set a clock to time turns.

The headmistress was the terminus and the reason for errands. She listened to all the various communications, she admired what had been produced, she discussed problems of work in progress. The headmistress might raise playing to the level of a play, for she was the audience, someone who had not already seen or heard it, as the teacher had, and who therefore needed explanation of it. The headmistress was the appreciator, the extra ear, the receptor, the transmitter, and therefore, the stimulator of all sorts of communication.

The training and selection of the headmistress have been described in chapter 1. Every aspect of this training, including initial teacher college education, work and responsibility as a teacher and as a deputy head, and additional training in the Institutes of Education, had prepared her for this role in the school. It was essentially an *educational*, not an administrative, training, quite different from that of principals in the United States. As headmistress, she remained a teacher, a master teacher, who had a hand in all the teaching of the school. As one headmistress described her efforts:

> I go to a teacher and say, "Have you any children I can have for a little while who need some special help with number?" She says, "Oh, yes." And she takes out a little group—we have a good look first to see that we're not dragging them away from some other special interest. But generally I can gather a little group. If I can't get enough from her, I say to another teacher, "Have you any?" Then I take the children out— they can come out into the hall with me—and we talk.[33]

It was the headmistress who smoothed over some of the difficulties resulting from teacher mobility and teacher shortage. She was the extra teacher, and it was she who could experiment with combinations of experienced and inexperienced teachers and help make the training of the teacher a continuous one (as described earlier in this chapter, p. 71).

It was the headmistress who produced the blurring of lines between all aspects of the day, the unsegmentalized whole living of a child. The agents of the educational system external to the school itself, whether inspectors, advisors, or Institute of Education lecturers, all were in full

[33] Cazden, *Infant School*, p. 8.

agreement on the significance of the head's role as a condition for the development of informal education in the infant school. How these agents and the headmistress interacted will be discussed more fully in chapter 3.

Fixed Points and Communal Life

Fixed points—or scheduled periods—fostered the communal life of the school. At these times, either the whole school came together or the big hall was used for a common class activity. These periods could be used to enhance a child's whole living in a whole school in which all the parts and all the relationships we,re open to him. They could be used to further strengthen his sense of important interaction and exchange with school and class, his sharing of his work and thinking with a group certain to be interested.

Conscious awareness of the school as the boundary of his activities was considered a necessary precondition for a child's free use of the whole small school. Within this boundary or enclosure a child could use every-thing freely to further his own individual pattern or growth. But a child in this school was not an isolated individual atom. Rather he was an individual in a community of working individuals in which social inter-, change and discussion spurred the development of judgment in all areas— intellectual, emotional, social, and moral.

THE MORNING SERVICE. Though superficially reminiscent of the As-sembly Period in American schools, which centers around the flag rituals of salute and song, the Morning Service reflects continuing Church-State connections in England: an Act of Worship in a Morning Service is the only required school activity specified in the 1944 Education Act. The Plowden Report discusses the corporate Act of Worship in the context of the increasing diversity of English society and the increasing number of its citizens who question religious education as part of the school cur-riculum. Plowden recommends that this activity continue as a recognized part of education but that those teachers and children who have different views be reinforced in their right to withdraw from participation.

The role religious education can play within informal education is now being seriously studied. Goals and content of the Morning Service are being reformulated in the light of what is now known of children's development and their real understanding of such services. Value con-siderations formerly linked to religious education are now sometimes at-tached in broader fashion to moral education and even more broadly to the development of moral judgment. For this reason, the Morning Service often consists of discussions, stories, or poems that, it is believed, may lead a child from his limited self-focused vision to a beginning perception of another point of view, thus supporting his expanding frame of moral judgment.

No specific ritual or format had ever been imposed on the Morning Service, and consequently, an enormous variety of ways of conducting it evolved. Heads seemed to feel they could interpret and implement the requirements in their own fashion, with no limit whatsoever on their ingenuity. Most schools that are committed to informal education and the support of the individual development of each child value the integrative, unifying function of Morning Service. It often sets the tone for the day.

For example, November 5th is Guy Fawkes Day, commemorating the Catholic Gunpowder Plot to blow up Parliament in 1605. On that night bonfires are lit all over England to burn the effigies, the "Guys," made by the children. "Remember, remember / The Fifth of November / Gunpowder, Treason and Plot."

On the day before this holiday a headmistress was heard talking with the children about their fabulous Guys, the paintings and stories about the day, the wood work, the Houses of Parliament made with junk boxes, or about one child's Big Ben. The headmistress then spoke with the children seriously, saying more or less that Guy Fawkes really should not have tried to blow up Parliament, that it could have hurt a lot of people. She explained a bit why Guy Fawkes felt the way he did. Then she suggested that the children think about something they really believed to be right.

At a Morning Service observed in another London school, parents participated, along with babies and with toddlers—the noise and crowding of all being freely accepted. It was a very cold, windy day, and the service consisted of the reading by one of the teachers of a hymn by St. Francis of Assisi, "Thou rushing wind that art so strong," and a Christina Rossetti poem on the wind, a reading of a story on wind by a seven-year-old, and then a free discussion on "what was good about the wind," with the children offering suggestions that the wind dries clothes, that it blows the leaves off trees, etc.

At another school, older children (seven-year-olds) conducted the service—making decisions on program and leading discussion. At still another service, the headmistress brought in a ballet record and suggested to the children that they might listen during the morning, that they might hear music that they never had heard before, as "the Lord, when He was seven, perhaps? had heard things that He had never heard before," and that they might then think of some dance or something to do with this music, which they had never done before. Doing something for the "first time in your life," something never done before, was the theme here.

THE LUNCH PERIOD. This time of the day, graced usually with the English amenities of conversation, the blessing, and orderly service in which children helped, was another communal period creating unity. Lunch was planned to foster social life by having children in groups of eight or nine sitting together; classroom and age groupings were broken in the seating arrangements. A definite attempt was made to encourage social communication, to have some sharing beyond classroom boundaries. The general pattern was for teachers to have their lunch with the children, one teacher sitting with each group. Though this is now a voluntary rather than an expected pattern, I noticed that it was still in operation on my return visit in 1969. Even without the old pattern of a teacher at each table, a genuine effort was made to preserve the old atmosphere, the easy conversational interchange. A new threat to communal life would result from any rise in charges which would reduce the number of children taking school lunch. Children not participating of course would not benefit from the social interchange of the communal eating pattern.

THE ACTIVITY PERIOD AND COMMUNAL LIFE. This period broke through class boundaries. Children sought out activities given in one class and not in another. Thus, a teacher who might be helping with lino-printing welcomed all comers. Children sought out siblings, cousins, friends. They showed each other things. They visited other classrooms. No difficulties were put in the way of siblings being together, friends being togther—all things Americans worry about. Such freedom was considered vital to the natural flow of communication and to the healthy growth of relationships.

THE FREE DAY AND COMMUNAL LIFE. The schools that had created wholeness of the day and of the use of the school required fewer specific arrangements to create communal life, since it already was flourishing; for example, if mixing of the children occurs all day long, play time is no longer significant in this respect.

Shared Areas and Communal Life

BIG HALL. Many of the activities of the hall or corridor (workbench, animals, music, etc.) were shared by the school functioning as a whole, with individual children from one class joining individual children from another. P.E. and Music and Movement were group or class, not whole-school, activities, but use of the big hall gave these activities an added importance and supported the unity of each class with the school. One school in Bristol valued the communal life of the school so much that it tried to counteract its diminution created by the architectural structure of the side hall by planning the afternoon as workshop areas, with each classroom functioning as a different workshop area to which children from all over the school would go after making their choices.

PLAY YARD. Play time, where scheduled, facilitated the breakthrough of class boundaries and enhanced school awareness and unity. Once again, this was in part through children's coming together at a common time, but also in part through their use of a common area for common purposes.

Participation in the Work of the School

The children had work and errands to do not only for their class but for the school as a whole—setting tables for lunch, collecting dinner money, distributing milk, servicing the snack bar, participating in Morning Service, in plays for festival days (Christmas, etc.), taking and delivering the register to the head's office, carrying messages. The children knew the whole school and helped in the preparations of its common areas and of its materials for use. Thus unity was reinforced by the easy movement of the children through the hall on errands, on the work of the school.

A Family School

The intent of the school was to be a family school with movement and interaction between classes, emphasizing help to each other and particularly to the youngest. Schools with partial-hearing units (in Bristol and London) and with children who were spastics (in Bristol) included these in the communal life of the school, separating them from the others only for their very special needs.

The sense of the school as a whole was valued for the children, inspiring in them awareness of their own progress and their own contributions to the life of the school—of what they had done, what they still might do, what they started with, and where they were going.

A family school included a child's family in its communal life. In most infant schools the door was open as it had been in the nursery schools, and the parents came in with their children, sometimes to ask questions, sometimes to see something a child wanted to show. They talked with the head; they knew the teachers. In some schools they joined in the Morning Service on a regular basis; they contributed materials for the junk or box assemblage. In these schools the relationship of home and school was close. In addition, visits from the Board of Managers (whose members were drawn from the community) created bridges of communication and help between school and community. Many schools were used in after-school hours by community or parent groups. The Plowden Report suggests that an increasing openness to such use of the school by parents and community will enlarge public understanding and support of the school.

INTERACTION AND COMMUNICATION

Interaction, as reflected in both movement and responsiveness, was an inevitable outgrowth of organizational adaptations resulting in the free day and use of the whole school. Movement that had the effect of freeing the children and freeing the teachers was so typical of the infant school that exceptions stand out. Even in schools with little movement of children, there was movement of teachers and headmistress *to* the children, since in all schools both staff and children were working simultaneously at different things.

In the majority of schools, even where activity and skills were separated, free movement was characteristic of every activity period, and a good deal of movement existed during a skill period, though to a lesser degree than where timetabling had produced a freer and fuller use of the whole school. Children moved about to exchange apparatus, children talked to each other over work, or got up to get something or to look at something. They were not assigned to permanent seats which could define their area of function.

In those few infant schools where the timetable featured activity periods unrelated to skills, and generally one-directional progression, there was little movement of children except at activity periods or in the reception classes. Classrooms with little movement of the children were in schools characterized by little in-and-outness, a lesser variety of provision of environment, and little communal life.

Communication

Response to a child's own exploratory trials of the environment is a key feature of any description of informal education. Any test of teachers' implementation of informality would ask: Is the school responsive to any overtures from a child? Is there talk, spontaneous conversation going on, or is it silent?

For the most part, children in English infant schools functioned in an atmosphere where it was very easy to talk, to ask questions, to tell things about home to each other and to the headmistress and other adults in the school. Children functioned not as in a traditional "show and tell" program of limited talk, but as individuals, with individual concerns and with individual styles of talking. Even in whole-school activities, it was easy for children to offer their own comments on a point brought up by the headmistress. As already noted in the descriptions of some typical Morning Services (p. 98), the atmosphere was intimate, unintimidating, and with no obstacles to communication.

Many of the schools that were so striking in interaction, in communication and responsiveness, had a population of poor children. As in the nursery schools, there was no lack of good feeling in teacher-child relationships because of poverty. Closeness resulted from shared experiences—of war, evacuation, neighborhood problems—and this closeness was very evident.

Since the poor and the immigrant children overlap in this school population, the question arises: Is there real interaction unless background is understood? Is the teacher ready with possibilities that a child can use as starting points of his learning if she does not understand home, out-of-school life on the street, the neighborhood? This question continues to be raised by English teachers as they reexamine their rich environmental provision and as they study how communication and interaction are fostered.

Perhaps it could be said that the teacher, knowing very little of a child's background so different from her own, might proceed as though the uniqueness of it wasn't there. By missing this uniqueness, she might insufficiently mesh with a child's view; she might insufficiently build on this view. Though the atmosphere of communication in an infant school was all-pervasive, the interaction might be limited to the life of the school and thus not include *all* the life of a child.

The quality of interaction and communication with an immigrant child is particularly questioned by the Plowden Committee as part of its effort to increase educational services in the priority areas. Its Report stresses the need for the school's close, warm, and supporting relationship with parents. Such a relationship may in turn help the parents understand and support a child's educational experience. It is true that the open door exists in most infant schools and that the heads, as in nursery schools, are turned to as sources of social services. But parents who feel strange may not come through even an open door. The Plowden Report therefore urges active invitation, active encouragement of parent engagement with the school, and active school service to parents. It suggests many new ways in infant, and even in junior, schools, in which school-home relationships can be strengthened. Frequent slide recordings of children's work are being used as aids to discussion with parents. Parents take charge of Saturday games and excursions. In some schools, a parent roster helps with some of the work of the school very much as in a cooperative.

In the free and easy communication of the two years spent in the infant school, non-English-speaking immigrant children seemed to learn English. Nevertheless, there is great concern that language disability results in misplacement of an undue number of West Indian children as ESN, and there is now special focus on English as a Second Language for brief periods of the day, using the extra teachers assigned to priority areas. In many of the schools I visited, teachers, asked if the West Indian or Jamaican children could read, were surprised. "Oh, they're very keen. It's the English children that are a bit dim." At most, teachers mentioned difficulties in social adjustment, not learning. They referred to social habits and to problems that American teachers too have found in the adjustment of rural children to city life. If unaccepted by the teacher, these differences could of course limit her warm interaction with an immigrant child.

On the whole, the heads and teachers appeared to be sympathetically aware of strangeness, of disorientation, of loneliness, and of isolation due to difference. They tried to bridge the barriers with efforts ranging from a few words of greeting in the language of a child, to the use of interpreters (both children and parents), to invoking the helping atmosphere of the infant school to encourage children to help each other. Maps and globes, stories and pictures, were used to help children tell about themselves and learn about each other. The usefulness of these various efforts was being constantly assessed. At one school, I saw a genuine relating to a child's background, and there I also saw enormous self-pride in the children and much sharing with others of their background. The Morning Service at this school was occasionally led by a representative from a child's own religious group. Children in this school asked me, "Where do you come from?" and, dragging me over to the globe, offered to point out to me their place of origin. All over the walls words from one language were matched with words from another. Children offered to learn a word in one child's language in exchange for a word in theirs. They praised the head's pronunciation of her greeting to them in their language and reciprocated proudly with an English reply. The very nature of informal education—its openness, its responsiveness, its allowing individuals to move at their own pace and to get involved in activities at many levels and many points of individual interest—made it possible to put forth these efforts, thus giving a child who found the setting strange *time* to reestablish his orientation.

Visitors in the classroom and in the school were encouraged to feel at ease in approaching the children. No interruption of class work was involved because no "class" work was going on. Visitors could talk to children, and children to visitors. In my case, the children approached me and asked for a word, or if they could read to me, or for help with buttoning, and so on. In a New Town school, I recall that they asked about America, about my trip, and about the differences in time between their country and mine. I remember a child at one Bristol school telling me breathlessly that he knew something about America. When I asked what, he said, "Sports." And what sport did he know about America? "Gambling," he said with great intensity. There followed a discussion about how gambling was fairly common in England as well, at which point he recovered himself and cited other sports, such as tennis.

In another school, where I was the only adult at the lunch table, a discussion started because a five-year-old boy in this family-grouped school said, "Can't you even eat your custard right?" A seven-year-old, explaining my use of one implement, added, "She can't help it, she's American. It's very awkward."

Where schools lacked a responsive atmosphere there was an attitude of waiting for direction and a greater degree of functioning as a class, rather than as individuals. In such schools, there was a noticeably less fluid and alive atmosphere. No schools, however, enforced silence as a condition for work. Though it was a matter of degree, in none was there more than a few moments of the teacher talking *at* the children, requesting their quiet.

TEACHER PLANNING

The planning of the teacher is as necessary a component of informal education as it is of formal education. Teacher planning in informal education, however, may be very different: "coverage" of any specific subject matter is not its purpose, nor is "effective" lesson planning. Though plans for informal learning may also be prepared outside the classroom, a child is so central to this kind of planning that he can almost be said to participate in it.

Planning for informal education follows from the way a child approaches the environment—cutting across subject areas as he pursues his own interests and searches for answers to his own questions. It is a planning based on observation of this approach and of the level of development revealed in a child's solution of problems and his use of materials. But it is important to note that a teacher cannot plan to support a child's level of comprehension without herself understanding the content of the area of his investigation. Indeed, she cannot even recognize a child's understanding without a solid base in her own. That teachers realized this crucial point was evident in their frequent use of Teachers Centres (described in chapter 3), where they could refer to a wealth of resource materials from the Nuffield Projects and the Schools Council.[34]

Accepting the necessity of the teacher's understanding as obvious, the Froebelians underline that a child's response to what the teacher has projected largely determines her next steps in planning, and they consider this response to be the touchstone of teaching effectiveness—even in a teacher's formal presentations. They accept a teacher's presentation if

(i) the main aim of the initial talk was to arouse children's interest and to stimulate them into asking questions and freely discussing; (ii) they could then choose the enquiries that interested them most (within the broad set field) and leave off when their interest gave out; and (iii) the teacher's further talks were again intended not as instructional lessons,

[34] Teachers Centres, originally sponsored by the Nuffield Project, are now run by the Schools Council, which was set up by the Department of Education and Science to initiate and evaluate experimentation in the schools. The Schools Council also carries on the Nuffield work in the schools. In 1967, the Nuffield Junior Science Project ended its sponsorship of school activities, though it continues to publish materials.

but rather as a means of pulling together what had in fact been achieved and of re-stimulating children's interest in going on.[35]

They contend that "nothing is educationally valid or satisfactory unless it evokes the right positive responses from children. The touchstone is whether it actually gets taken up by them and used to add to or enrich their growth." [36]

My overall impression was of tremendous teacher involvement in planning a setting that would reach all the children and in planning differentially for each child. The immediacy, relevancy, and glowing quality of the school setting, even in old buildings, and the easy movement of children, their independence in getting supplies for their work, the quick picking up and reorganizing, the swift construction of new workshop areas to meet the need of the moment—all required a high degree of planning on the teacher's part.

In the early morning, before the school day began, or in the late afternoon after the children had gone, teachers were observed adding things to the environmental provision, because the children were ready for those items or because this or that child would need them for the next step; consequently, the relevancy of materials revealed the actual "unprescribed" and flexible curriculum. Proper preparation could be made only on the basis of prior analysis of each child's developmental level and interests; and the continuing adjustments in preparation to stimulate further development indicated a continuing analysis and planning. The teachers obviously were *thinking* about what was needed all the time, particularly as it affected the progress of each child.

On one typical day, I noted that their planning considered such questions as: Were the children ready for a store? Would weighing be a part of it? Would cooking come into it? Would money add to the involvement? Could the children's activity be related to some holiday or outside event? Could they use a trip to spur a deepening of interests and some needed growth? In their planning, the environment was shifted around for better use, for greater stimulation, or for more concentration and privacy. Additions of words, additions to chart material, additions of books for particular activities and interests—all were part of the daily planning.

One head explained her planning as

child-discovery . . . guided by the teacher. It's a talking together. . . . But the teacher has got to be ready . . . to be aware—all the time. . . . I didn't say that she doesn't have a plan . . . she has in mind what she will do tomorrow. . . . The different ideas evolve, then the teacher can get her work prepared. You can't just leave it to chance. . . . Very often the teacher will put exciting material down which will suggest something

[35] National Froebel Foundation, *Children Learning*, p. 140.
[36] *Ibid.*, p. 141.

to the child. She might put some cardboard boxes and think, "That will give the children an idea. They might start making a train." Then she must be prepared to find that it's been turned into a robot.[37]

More direct teaching in which the teacher works with a group of four to ten children is not excluded.

> If you find that children are having difficulty with one particular aspect, and you want to make quite sure to establish that, then you gather these children together. And you work away at that until you are sure that they understand. Then you send them back again to their play with this knowledge. . . . The teacher gathers the group together, and they have a long—no, not a long [talk], about twenty minutes—but at any rate they do have her entirely to themselves while they all work out, with the scales, that the four ounces match with the quarter of a pound weight. They weigh different things. They really get that established. And then she sends them back again to make their cakes with that knowledge.[38]

Activity Cards

Activity or work cards prepared by teachers were very widely used to foster independent work by children. Such cards indicated the teacher's estimation of possibilities as well as her planning for the general level, for the variation in levels, and for the interests of children. They might open up an area of investigation or pose a possibility for a child to consider in his own investigation. Formerly, these cards were often labeled "assignment" or "task" cards and tended to list short-run tasks and to suggest practice in skill areas. Used in this way, they imposed on a child specific teacher-directed tasks, as in a lesson. But now the real challenge to the teacher is to suggest *extensions* of a child's interests. Such suggestions were not necessarily expressed in words; for example, a pattern offered by the teacher might stimulate exploration, or one child's word displayed and discussed might suggest similar or variant trials. For that matter suggestion could come from the addition of a new piece of apparatus, different in use from the old, or from material presenting an anomaly, for example, two rocks similar in size but not in weight placed near the scale. Suggestion also could spring from a picture, or a book placed in the work area.

Flexibility about ways of suggestion and ways of sustaining a child's concentration was evident in the best situations. In no case was it intended that work or activity cards take the place of the teacher's discussion with a child of his understanding of his investigation, of his questions. Thus, whether or not work or activity cards were used as the basic support for

[37] Cazden, *Infant School,* pp. 3–11.
[38] *Ibid.,* p. 8.

ongoing work, the teacher was prepared with on-the-spot suggestions of extensions that could mesh with the particular point of progression possible for a child. Both the prepared work cards and the suggestions after discussion indicated good planning based on solid thinking and a sizable amount of observation. Work cards were brought up to date frequently and adapted to particular children's needs. Sometimes children added to the accumulation of work cards by making their own.

Beginning Points of Learning

A basic aspect of teacher planning is provision for meeting the needs of each individual's stage of development. What is implied in this is that beginning learning must be possible at any time. Whenever a child begins to learn, the teacher must be ready to mesh with his point of learning, encourage him, and lead him further. The school calendar cannot be the organizer of school learning, ruling out of order any beginning that does not match the September school opening date. This in itself speaks against block classroom teaching, prescribed syllabus, and standard of progression; it speaks for the recognition of individual differences. Lochhead wrote in the late 1920s of individual work—of proceeding at one's own rate—as an accepted principle in English infant schools.[39] At that time, according to her description, it was largely Montessori kind of work, but free choice and a child as active agent of his learning were, even then, key features of English infant education.

Preparation of materials to meet the variations in children's development is assumed and expected. Students in training colleges are constantly appraised on their ability to work on many levels and on their preparation of the environment. The Hadow and Plowden Reports both emphasize acceptance of variation of level and of beginning points of learning throughout the infant school years:

> In none of this should a uniform standard to be reached by all children be expected. The infant school has no business with uniform standards of attainment. Its business is to see that children in the infant school stage grow in body and mind at their natural rate. Neither faster nor slower, and if it performs its business properly there will be as much variety of attainment as there is of intellectual ability. The only uniformity at which the infant school should aim is that every child at the end of the course should have acquired the power to attack new work and feel a zest in doing so.[40]

[39] Lochhead, *Education of Young Children.*
[40] Hadow, p. 146.

In effect, the acceptance of this principle of individual variations has steered English education away from block classroom teaching and fixed standards of progression toward arrangements that stress individual pace of growth. The same acceptance led to discarding "payment by results" (see p. 162), and is now the basis for the trend to informal junior schools. English educators consider a prescribed syllabus and a required "standard" performance a straitjacket for teaching and a denial of the facts of development in children, resulting in much failure for teachers as well as children.

Though this acceptance of variation of levels seemed almost universal in my sample,[41] such acceptance was often colored by fears of the difficulty of transition to the more standardized junior school with its different method and philosophy. Preparation for the junior school tended to interfere with opportunities for general beginning learning, though at the same time, such preparation operated to support beginning learning points in reading. This was the head's responsible reaction to the necessity for helping children meet the junior school standard and thus ease their transition.

But, commitment to continuity, in defense of the facts of child development and of the implementation of learning in this way, is pushing toward an extended infant school and toward a junior school that will be in continuity with the informal approach of the infant school. As the junior school changes, the full acceptance of variation of levels will be easier.

The possibilities for beginning learning were different with different organizations of the schools. With two exceptions, all the infant schools with nursery classes featured such possibilities throughout. In family-grouped schools where beginning learning was most usually possible, children were often pointed out who were just getting started at age 7 at "working well." Points of beginning learning could be found more readily in the groups of the 5s and 6s; "getting on" might be the feeling in the 7s, with an eye on the junior school. At all points, the teacher was definitely prepared for beginning reading.

As already noted, all informal infant school organization is in effect an unstandardized sequence with no retardation at any point, in which there is no teaching in a block classroom way according to a prescribed standard.

---

[41] Only 4 of all schools studied—and these were largely JMI schools—could be said to have an incomplete acceptance of this. In one Bristol school the reason for this seemed linked with the ambitions of professional parents; in the other schools, the reason was linked with the use of one-directional progression. The one and only infant school (in Birmingham), with incomplete acceptance of variation of level, was well equipped, but characterized by great direction and one-way progression.

Teacher Direction or Implementation

If the teacher's commitment was to informal education, what was her role? Toward what purposes did the teacher direct her activity, her planning? What was the relationship of teacher activity to the organizational arrangements and other aspects of functioning informal education?

These questions on the teacher's role are well answered by the Froebelians:

> In view of the . . . emphasis on children's own free choices and initiatives, it may perhaps be worth underlining how far this is from implying that the teacher just stands by. The hypothesis under test does *not* suggest that if only they are left alone, children will educate themselves. On the contrary, on this hypothesis the teacher actually has a more active directing part to play than on any planned instructional programme through which pupils are processed in an almost routine way. But the part to be played is of course a very different kind. It is based on not *imposing* anything on children, but on so closely co-operating with their native interests and drives that whatever they are led to do is felt as something that comes out of themselves. The teacher provides starting experiences which produce that result; invites questions and discussion; raises questions of his own; puts out suggestions; indicates possible lines of activity; introduces provocative new stimuli; makes thought-arousing comments, etc. Some of these 'take', others do not; those that do, get adopted and what then follows is the child's own response.[42]

The teacher's role in informal education could be summed up as *implementing and opening up a child's purposes.* Where she thought her role was to direct the children's learning, then informal education in the school was incompletely conceived and certainly incompletely realized. Implementation of a child's purpose could not be kept in reserve until the timetabled activity periods, with a teacher imposing *her* purposes at all other points. It was not, for instance, a conception that differentiated between her role in play and routines. The whole of a teacher's relationship to a child reflected her conception of the learning process. It was an evolving conception—both in arrangements of timetable and in what a teacher did; and, in the infant schools, no separation could be properly made between the purposes permeating the general atmosphere and the purposes of periods led by a teacher. The factor of respect for a child's own question and a child's own purpose, as serious forces in learning, was added in the infant school in a conscious and pervasive way—when it was added. An activity period could be separated from skills, but it would seem that

---

[42] National Froebel Foundation, *Children Learning*, pp. 141, 142.

no inconsistency about the *purposes* of the teacher-child relationship could exist in an infant school called "informal." Thus, in informal schools, implementation of a child's purposes permeated any teaching-learning of skills.

But even those teachers consciously seeking this goal might have difficulty in moving toward it. The difficulties of implementation are recognized, and some advice is given in the *Nuffield's Teacher's Guides* and in Froebel Institute publications. Since it is assumed that most infant teachers now accept informality easily, it is junior teachers, who for the most part are "changing over" from formal to informal, to whom the advice is directed. The new studies are still "hammering out" the meaning of implementation; thus one can expect to find a varied practice.

More than any other single factor, implementation was a function of the atmosphere of the school, and the atmosphere, as already noted, emanated from the headmistress. When implementation correlated inconsistently with arrangements that were clearly intended to further informal education, very often the reason was that such arrangements were being imitated in a superficial, outward way. Implementation implied a high degree of understanding. Heads varied in their grasp of the idea of informal education, but within the extent of their understanding, they created the climate and setting that supported a teacher's implementation of a child's purposes.

In this context, it seemed to me implementation was not attributable to the presence of genius in the teacher. A teacher, however inexperienced, working where a headmistress had created *an atmosphere of implementation*, could function and continue to grow professionally. Perhaps it is in our isolated and encapsulated classrooms that only genius can succeed. In the English informal school, teachers not especially different from their American counterparts could function successfully.

My observations of the schools added up to a continuum—formal (entirely direction and imposition), formal with informal elements, and informal with formal elements.[43]

Only in the cases where the sequencing and one-way directional pattern of progression was very strong, could the word "direction" characterize the teacher's role in the school. But even where this pattern existed, it was not consistently carried out in every particular. Some schools with great

---

[43] Fifteen schools had a preponderance of informal with formal elements; 15 seemed to be formal with informal elements; and none was completely formal. Of all the schools visited, 13 had a preponderance of implementation; 7 had a moderate amount of implementation; 10 had great direction. No school was completely directive. In any activity period, even one unrelated to skills, there was a free choice.

direction had attempted—and some had actually achieved—arrangements for informal education; still others, which had rich environment, family grouping, etc., plus great direction, were what may be termed "confused" in atmosphere. In one case a change in headmistress had resulted in taking over the outward arrangements for informal education without belief in it. These variations in the schools led me to the conclusion that where great direction is the case and where other arrangements for rich environment are very good, what emerges is an enriched, *formal*, rather than an informal, school.

Implementation seems closely linked with in-and-outness, communal life, the undifferentiated day, and family grouping, but it does not always follow from these. While a school characterized by implementation might not have family grouping, it would inevitably have an activity period related to skills, in-and-outness, and rich provision of environment. But a school could allow movement, have in-and-outness, family grouping, the undifferentiated day, and communal life, and still not be implementative of a child's purposes and interests; it could still be directive of children's choices. Such a school could even keep the children moving, in a pre-planned, carousel-like rotation.

Some degree of direction is implied in all learning. There are degrees of movement toward the concept of informal education and, in all cases, the adult has the role of correcting a child's misconceptions, of offering new possibilities, of suggesting new variants for trial, of sharing, as it fits, his own wider experience, of transmitting in this way the culture and the language. Thus, a school called informal had to have a blend of some direction and a great deal of implementation of a child's purposes. Its aim remains the greatest possible degree of implementation.

Records

The teacher's intelligent observation of a child at work is essential if she is to ascertain the level of his understanding and the process by which he arrived at this understanding, his style of work, and his interests. "Jottings," anecdotal records, notes on possible starting points and on possible difficulties, were therefore considered the most important recordings.

Records on attainment, if these were unrelated to information on style of work and interests, were considered thin. It was expected that teachers keep such records of the progression of a child's work—the work cards he had attempted and his success, his progress in reading. But it was considered more to the point to keep a separate account for each child of the progress of all the work he had undertaken in which the motive force was his own strong interest. These accounts might cut across subject areas and thus might focus on the process of a child's thinking. It was considered important to watch for and foster a child's growing ability to initiate, to sustain, to tell about, and to make judgments about his work. Children were encouraged to keep records of their own, of where they were in their work and of what they had attempted; work itself—the books they made, the paintings, the charts—provided the clearest records. Folders of dated examples of such work indicated growth and progression and could be shared with parents.

In all schools I saw teachers keeping such records of where a child was with his reading, his number understanding, his writing. The Hadow Report had stressed the necessity of records in any system of individual work. Testing for reading level, one of the duties of the head, seemed very prevalent at age 7.

Schools with strong implementation, with undifferentiated day or at least activity period related to skills, and with simultaneous use as a major characteristic of their timetable, kept complete records on each child, observations which guided the teacher's activity. The headmistress used these records and her own observations for a summary assessment of each child on completion of infant school. In Bristol and elsewhere, the complete individual records amounted to a folder containing a sample of a child's work in each area of work at a particular chosen time, as for example, within one week, or it might be a folder of all children's work at a particular time in order to show one child's work in comparison with the class. This was then put together, in accordion-pleated style, so that one could see the work of a child at a particular time, the progression for a child, and/or a class comparison.

In a number of schools I saw teachers' notebooks and plans, and heads' notebooks of anecdotal records—the jottings of brief observations of a child's reaction to a situation or to particular aspects of environment that indicated his interest and pointed to possible sparking-off points which the teacher would then use to build on.

Gardner describes variation in recordkeeping. A teacher

1. Keeps many records including (a) a weekly report of the main developments in the free choice period together with a forecast of expected developments, (b) an individual record of each child's background, personality, special interests and attainments, and (c) notes of each child's present achievements in the basic skills especially reading and number.
2. Keep records together with plan or 'forecast' of free choice periods together with records of achievements in the basic skills.

3. Keeps only individual records on each child which include background, personality, interests and attainments in reading, arithmetic, etc.[44]

All the teachers in the Gardner sample kept at least the minimal records of attainment.

Some of the Head teachers stressed the importance of such records and planning, which range from the rough "diary" kept ready to hand in the classroom in which the teacher jots down observations and developments as they occur or at the first convenient moment afterwards, to a regular review of what has happened during the past week. In both cases these records contain suggestions for a follow up of various activities and reminders of material and equipment needed to further a child's purposes. Head teachers too sometimes glance through these records and are able, as a result, to offer helpful suggestions. One Head teacher commented on the danger of teachers in their enthusiasm spending too much time on recording at great length, but another described such work as "Time well spent in trying to evaluate the experience the children are getting, if one wants to maintain a sense of direction and ensure progress in the very 'free' situation." She added that under normal conditions it should not take a teacher more than an hour a week to keep the kind of records she asked for in this connection, though the individual records passed in at the end of each term were more time absorbing. She said that the better teachers often undertook, for their own satisfaction, more than the minimum asked for. She said the accepting of a weekly record can, in different ways, help many teachers, "reassuring the nervous, encouraging the stronger and in some measure keeping the potentially casual nearer to the mark." [45]

Nuffield Junior Math and Junior Science publications discuss record-keeping at length and suggest many varieties. Visual records—slides—are now often added to other forms of recording and much thought has been given to sharing such records with parents. A child's keeping track of his own progress and his recording of his work in a variety of ways are described. It is pointed out that experience can be presented and therefore recorded in all the multiple ways available in the infant school. A child can reveal his understanding through telling about it, writing about it, graphing it, and also through his use of plastic media, movement, and acting.

Tests

There is both interest in and wariness about testing for the diagnostic purposes that would assist in achieving a more accurate mesh with an in-

[44] Gardner and Cass, *Role of Teacher*, p. 146.
[45] *Ibid.*, p. 147.

dividual child's level of development. The wariness results from a fear of overuse of and overdependence on such tests and from an awareness of their limitations. Thus, there is relatively little testing for this purpose of better match between teacher planning and individual need. There is even less use of any programmed individualization based on diagnostic testing. The hesitancy about diagnostic testing is reinforced by the English view that such testing is very often used for purposes of tracking or ability grouping. Ability grouping—or streaming, as it is called—is disappearing from the junior school as that education level establishes continuity with infant methods, and with its disappearance there may be less wariness about diagnostic testing. Testing children for achievement of a *fixed* standard is *not* the general practice in infant schools. Grade placement is *not* dependent on such tests.

Research is underway on the use of programmed learning for attaining a better match with a child's point of progression and for help with specific disabilities, but it is generally felt that children's learning is too complicated for a machine-teaching approach. Certainly a child's own purposes and his individual pattern of learning cannot be implemented by a program of individualized instruction that recognizes individual difference only in *pace* of learning and in which "each pupil is free to go more or less rapidly exactly where he is told to go." [46] Programmed sequences are recognized as a possible aid in relieving the teachers of routine tasks and in helping answer a child's specific questions or need for specific practice.

SCHOOL ENVIRONMENT AND CURRICULUM

MATERIALS

Ideally English educators considered free access to materials an essential element in the support of a child's individual pattern of learning, which is the essence of informal education. They therefore believed that materials and equipment should be placed throughout the school. The amount and variety tended to be full and rich in all schools, far more so than is customary for this age group in American schools. All English teachers aimed for this profusion of materials; they maintained that a high level of supply was needed to sustain stimulation and that having just one or two interesting items was insufficient. The following categories of materials were the minimal standard in the infant schools:

[46] Anthony Oettinger and Sema Marks, "Educational Technology: New Myths and Old Realities," *Harvard Educational Review*, Vol. 38, No. 4, Fall 1968.

Library
Book Corners
Esthetic Corners
Musical Instruments
Wendy House
Dress-up Items
Sewing Materials
Puppetry
Acting Platforms
Cooking Materials
Clay
Sand
Paint
Art Materials
Printing Materials

Workbench and Materials
Junk Materials
Blocks (Bricks)
Manipulative and Construction Toys
Math, Concrete and Structural: Number, Weighing, Measuring, Exploration of Time and Money [47]
Science: Nature and Interest Tables and Other Materials (Pendulums, Pulleys, Thermometers, etc.) [48]
Water and Equipment
Animals
P.E.: Agility Equipment, Balls, Hoops, Ropes, Tires, Sticks

The natural materials—*clay, sand,* and *water*—were to be found in every single room in many schools.

The *agility apparatus,* utilized in P.E., which resembles the climbers that are located outdoors in most nursery schools, is more complex and involves greater skills. The children used it in individual ways—finding different spatial areas to go through and trying out different kinds of balance. A great variety of other material—ropes, balls, tires, sticks, all kinds of balancing boards, and tall boxes for jumping—was also in evidence. Every school had a trolley, like a shopping cart, ready to be used outside or inside, stocked with these extra things. Individual grace and skill and balance, a commando kind of agility, was encouraged. Inventiveness seemed prized. The emphasis in P.E. was obviously individual rather than on a mass kind of conformity, even though P.E. was usually conducted with a class working together. (Movement, which takes the place of P.E., is discussed on pp. 84, 85.)

Painting supplies were often available in the big hall or corridor in addition to the usual very full provision in the classrooms. A child's organizing of his experience in representation and image was considered essential to the development of his understanding, and children were given every opportunity to do this on their own level. In painting, a child integrated his experiences and it was considered that variety and richness of experience in other areas fed the variety and richness of representation and image. Thus poetry, stories, trips, science, even math, could feed the de-

[47] Detailed lists may be found in the Nuffield Junior Math publications; in Eileen M. Churchill's *Counting and Measuring;* and in the Leicestershire materials published by Education Development Center, Newton, Mass.
[48] Detailed lists may be found in Nuffield Junior Science *Teacher's Guides 1 & 2, Apparatus,* and *Junior Science Resource Book.*

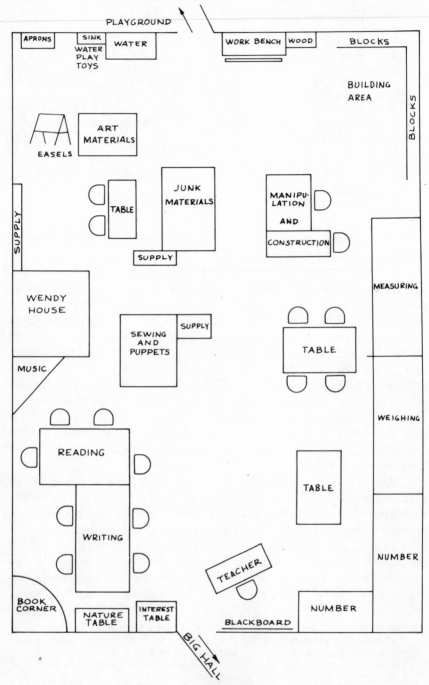

PLAN OF CLASSROOM

PLAYGROUND

| APRONS | SINK WATER PLAY TOYS | WATER | | WORK BENCH | WOOD | BLOCKS |

BUILDING AREA

BLOCKS

EASELS

ART MATERIALS

SUPPLY

TABLE

JUNK MATERIALS

MANIPU-LATION AND CONSTRUCTION

SUPPLY

MEASURING

WENDY HOUSE

SEWING AND PUPPETS

SUPPLY

TABLE

MUSIC

WEIGHING

READING

WRITING

TABLE

NUMBER

BOOK CORNER

NATURE TABLE

INTEREST TABLE

TEACHER

NUMBER

BLACKBOARD

BIG HALL

Sketch of classroom plan from a quick on-the-scene drawing.

116

velopment of image. Most of the schools offered a variety of art materials, including supplies for printing, weaving, and so forth.

The *workbench* was sometimes situated in a classroom, but the hall or corridor or outdoor bay was usually its place, thus making it accessible for several classes. A *stove* for cooking might also be located in the hall for general use.

For the school as a whole there almost always was a *special area*—perhaps a corner in the hall—with easy chairs and books, and on its walls were exhibits of some poems written large, well-mounted children's paintings, or reproductions on loan.[49] This area might also be an esthetically pleasing corner, full of a lovely display of glass, or fabric, or sculpture, or pebbles, shells, and leaves. The arrangement of this display was often worked out by a group of children and often changed. A very attractive room frequently served for a regular *library*, and if the school had more than one corridor, distinct book areas could be found in the corridors all over the school. Book areas also existed in every classroom.

Additional standard equipment included the *large semi-circular hollow blocks.* Several of these blocks put together by children could be turned into an acting platform or an acting area (described on pp. 82–84). Costumes and drapes of material suitable for role playing could be found all over and were left to children's ingenuity for use; sometimes a couple of drapes would be sewn together with a few rough stitches for a more ambitious costume.

The role playing in these acting areas was considered a very sophisticated form of communication, not displacing the role playing in the Wendy House (housekeeping corner) of the classrooms, but often adding more complexity, since children from different classes came together and bits of experience from many different areas were integrated. (See pp. 82, 84 for analysis of role playing.)

One school might offer more encouragement of musical experiences than another, but the provision of a variety of *musical instruments* for the children's use and free access to these existed in every school, in every classroom. Music of many different kinds and on many different levels was sometimes initiated by a teacher: sometimes it was a quiet individual pursuit. Some schools might have amazingly interesting and truly fine-toned instruments [50]—tuned bells, xylophones of different kinds, marimbas, drums—for the children to handle and to make music of their own. Chimebars were fairly standard; they were extremely good in tone, each note usually a hollow tube on a wooden bar, each mounted separately. Children

---

[49] The Art School Service Committee offers schools good reproductions from which children and teachers can make selections for their changing displays.

[50] Methods and instruments developed by Karl Orff are seen in many infant schools.

could work out tunes using a few at a time. Many schools had recorders available, at least for the seven-year-olds. (See pp. 84–85 for further description of musical experiences.)

The supply of *blocks*, which was sometimes very small in the nursery school, was quite large in the infant school. Thus, very often children of this age in England had far more opportunities for block building than did children of nursery age.

Certain materials were used more often in the classroom than in the hall. In a corner of the classroom there were usually some materials for sewing or for knitting—lengths of fabrics, thread, large needles, wool yarn. Every room had its *Wendy House*, a housekeeping corner that encouraged a wide range of play. Dress-up clothes were located nearby. Quite often there was a store, or the Wendy House could very easily be converted to one. The store was frequently moved to the hall so that children could solicit trade from a larger group; sometimes the sale was of good things cooked by another group. Such sales, with transactions in real money, required signs and occasionally even the printing of a flyer announcing what was for sale.

Equipment always included "junk materials," by which was meant all sorts of discards from food packaging of all shapes and sizes. These were then put together extremely inventively, and as individual "assemblages" they were highly prized for the judgment and estimation of shape, size, and material needed in covering them and for the ingenuity of the whole process.

The use of *manipulative toys* was particularly interesting. In the nursery school, so-called baby toys, such as color cones, were used with an emphasis on hand manipulation, concentration, the puzzle aspects, and general enjoyment. In the infant school the same manipulative toys were used in the concrete math corner. Thus, the old Russian toy doll (with its seemingly infinite insides), or the color cone, or the nesting boxes were utilized to illuminate the concepts of seriation, order, and larger/smaller. This idea of using materials encountered earlier in new ways, and of letting a child return to these and discover new uses for them, seemed to be an important one in the provision of material.

MATHEMATICS

My observations of the children's delight and excitement as they worked at what the English call "maths" led me to understand how informal education could work to enhance skills and how well integrated with the other activities skills teaching could be.

The junk materials, the manipulative toys, the blocks, and the many construction toys (connector rods, tinker-toys, Lego) were all considered mathematics materials. In addition, every room contained a variety of materials that were used even more specifically for investigation of mathematical concepts: number trays for the collecting, sorting, and counting of bottle caps, screws, pins, buttons, shells, conkers, nails, sticks, and more; equipment for weighing, such as a variety of scales and good weights; equipment for measuring, which included not only rulers but a yard wheel, one-foot surveyor link chains, and knotted string.

The amount of concrete materials close at hand through which number concepts could be gained was impressive. One New Town school, in addition to the supply of concrete math material in each classroom, had a special resource room saturated with such material where children could carry their explorations further. But children in every infant school explored number with an alive interest—weighing, measuring, exploring space and liquid measure—and not just memorizing equivalences. Structural aids (Cuisenaire, Unifix, Stern, Dienes, etc.) were used to clarify and emphasize what a child had already begun to understand through firsthand experience in ordinary life situations. The possibilities for mathematical exploration in a child's use of the ordinary materials of the environment were always stressed, and structural aids were employed as only one aspect of number work in English schools.

English infant schools have seriously absorbed Piaget's work on children's conception of number, with the result that overall school materials are enriched with relevance to supporting this development. Occasionally one could feel that the introduction of concrete math was simply an "extra" and that the underlying intent of covering the "four rules" remained, as though an infant syllabus did exist. Sometimes it seemed that Piaget's fundamental modification—of going as slowly as needed for a child's developing understanding—had not really occurred, but this was rare.

Basic material through which number concepts could be gained remained available all through infant school, except for some schools characterized by what I have termed "one-directional progression" (see p. 76). Grouping, ordering, patterning of the concrete objects in the number trays, making comparisons, finding equivalences were all experiences in the daily life of children in the infant school. Children counted the number of everything—of trucks, of chairs, of shoes, of children, of buttons on cloth. Everything was fodder for counting. Children marked the register and counted traffic. Using real money, they collected milk money, lunch money, ran a snack or sweet shop, and sold services for animals. Thus, number was one of the discoveries flowing naturally from the many encounters with the school environment.

Time impinges on a child in every way and so there was lots of interest in clocks and their history, in shadows and in the apparent movement of the sun, in timing for turns, in noting the time of BBC–TV programs.

All sorts of experiences might lead to discoveries on ordination and sequence: steps, house numbers for mail delivery, the sequence of before and after in enacting a story, play with a "baby" manipulative toy like the stacking Russian doll. There were signs announcing "the fifth house," "the second flower is red." A boy had painted a picture of a row of trees: under it was written his story, "The second one is very tall, the fifth one has apples on it." A sign under another picture showed: "Pat lives at No. 19— Anne lives six houses on." Young children were making simple groupings and comparisons. A little girl made a book of "lots of things." One sign read: "This house is bigger than . . ." Signs compared the number of children with sweaters with the number without.

Variety, the chance to "see" and explore and experience in many ways, characterized daily living at infant school, as for example in the activity of measuring of perimeters, areas, things made at the workbench, length of playground with:

Hands	Foot-tile Squares
Feet	Tape
Inch Cubes	Foot-link Surveyor Chains
String	Yard Wheels
One-inch Squared Paper	

If you had measured the span of your hands, you might want to measure how much string it took to go around the outside edge of your hand, even in and out of the fingers. You might then want to measure the height of the room. And so, in a different way, if you had measured a thing with one-inch unifix cubes, you might then use a string knotted at ten-inch intervals, and then remeasure with ten unifix cubes locked. You might measure a large distance, pacing it with footsteps and then using a yard wheel that clicked off yards as it went, even clear across the playground. A bed being built for the housekeeping corner involved measuring everyone to find an average and proper length. Children asked the question, "Is height the same standing up as lying down?" and then checked their observations on many willing volunteers.

Every infant class had scales and balances in much use. Scales were needed for cooking, for comparing the weight of one kind of material with another, for following the increase of one's weight and comparing it with that of other children, even for finding who wore the heaviest shoes. Rocks of various shapes were weighed and compared, and dry sand compared with wet sand. Guinea pigs were weighed before and after feeding as well as weekly. Eggs from new hens were compared in numbers and in weight with those from old hens. When, by way of saying goodbye at the school where *Infants School* was filmed, I was trying to figure out how many "Smarties" (our M&M candies) I would need to buy to give each of the children four, I was quickly told, "Why you'd weigh up an ounce, Miss," and then almost as quickly told how much to order for the 280 children.

Constant comparison fed the ability to judge, to estimate. Comparisons were then charted, so all could see: the number of girls with blue eyes against those with brown, the number of birthdays in March as against the other months, etc. The visitor to an infant school was often met with such questions as, "Miss, can I weigh your shoe?"; "Miss, will you stand up here so we can add you to our chart?"; "Miss, do you know how much string it takes to go around, and then in and out of your fingers?" Children first talked about their work, and then they painted or drew pictures, wrote, charted, or graphed. The charts, many of them pictorial representations, were on the walls in all the infant schools I visited.

Exploration of shape was part of working with the junk materials. Similar shapes were found in the living snake, shells, the inside of clocks, the mattress coil found on a junk heap. Shape was discovered in molding materials three-dimensionally—paper, clay, junk materials, block building, wood work. Children began to realize that the inherent qualities of materials set limitations on shape, and thoughtful selection was necessary if a specific shape was being sought. Shape was explored in every way—in Movement, in dance and P.E., in the shaping of space itself. It was discovered in moving acting platforms and in making patterns with styrofoam pieces, tile squares, and surveyor link chains. Spaces were noticed from different viewpoints—the inner spaces, the closed spaces of boxes and containers, the "insides" as well as the "arounds" or outer edges. These were noted not only as volumes, areas, or perimeters but as problems in estimation and comparison. There were all sorts of investigation of relationships—space, shape, size. Children figured out areas on squared paper. How many rice grains on a spoon? How many in a one-inch square? In comparison, how many kidney beans on that spoon? How "much" is 100 grains of rice? What does it look like piled high, or on squared paper? What does it weigh and how did all this compare with marbles?

Ways of printing pursued further this exploration of inner or outer space and pattern—even into repetition, symmetry, and reversed pattern. Pattern—in shell, in leaf, in bark, on fabric—was noticed. A fabric pattern, a rug pattern from a different country or from a different period, was sometimes the exhibit in the esthetic arrangement. Sewing—on checked gingham, burlap, monk's cloth, even on pegboard—called for accurate counting, spacing, and combinations of stitches. Estimation, of course, was also part of the experience of cutting out and then sewing dolls' clothes. Knitting with its rows, its knit one, purl one, and weaving for older children enhanced the analysis of mathematical patterns. Pattern was also discovered in painting, in drawing, and in writing. Children's written work often noted patterns: "I have made a pattern with curves," "with half-circles," "with Vs," "with Ws," "with acute angles," "my knitting is in 1s and then 2s."

Eileen Churchill's list of desired equipment for the development of mathematical concepts includes all the items already given as standard for infant schools but adds many interesting items not ordinarily conceived as mathematical. Thus, for painting she suggests "brushes of various thicknesses, thick and thin pencils, paper of various colours and shapes." [51] For weighing she suggests

> Bags of silver sand or grit weighing 1 oz., 2 oz., ½ lb. Boxes of different sizes filled with a variety of substances, e.g., lead shot, sand, flour, cotton, wool—made up so that the children may discover that weight is not correlated with size.[52]

Also on her list are: mirrors, lens, locks, springs, sprayers, timers, pulleys, and pendulums, in a variety of sizes, shapes, functions. That she places enormous value on rich, concrete experiences integrated with the whole of a child's living is clear from the following quotation from her chapter on the exploration of space, of places to go to, and things to look at with parents and teachers:

> *In and from the Sky:* cloud shapes, sunshine effects, rainbows, eclipses, moon shapes, star patterns, snow falling and lying, snow crystals, ice, frost and rain. How things look in foggy weather. Thunder and lightning. What the wind does to trees, clouds, weather vanes, kites, balloons, and people's hair. Aeroplanes, helicopters, jets, parachutes.[53]

Additionally, the Nuffield Junior Math Project pamphlets—*Beginnings, Mathematics Begins, I Do and I Understand, Shape and Size, Pictorial Representation,* and others—constitute a treasure house of illustrations of actual work using this approach.[54]

SCIENCE

The "science" in the environment could not be summed up or described by listing the many specific science materials. It was based on a

[51] Churchill, *Counting and Measuring*, p. 126.
[52] *Ibid.*, p. 127.
[53] *Ibid.*, p. 200.
[54] Nuffield Junior Math Project.

conception of a child asking questions of the world. These questions were presumed to be proper subjects of investigation. In this view, science as a subject did not exist separately, and the method of "teaching" was related to the *way* in which a child *asked* the questions, the process by which he gained understanding of the world. Everything a child did was based on concrete observation and led to further concrete observation. It was a child's kind of observation that was talked about, with no necessary implication of adult "note-taking."

> *Observing will mean doing every imaginable thing in a situation and then judging the response through all the appropriate senses . . . practical problem-solving is essentially a scientific way of working, so that the task in school is not one of teaching science to children, but rather of utilizing the children's own scientific way of working as a potent educational tool.*[55] (Italics in original)

The teacher, tuned to be sensitive to children, was urged to be particularly alert to what puzzles them. Only a teacher who had participated in discovery experiences herself and had thought her way through the many potential questions could be attuned helpfully to a child's own questions. Workshops giving teachers a chance to have such discovery experiences were the chief feature of the Nuffield Institutes. This method of inquiry, a scientific-process approach to *all* learning regardless of its content, was clearly seen as "a particular way of working to be employed at any time if it will lead to greater understanding." [56]

The whole school was treated as a source of inquiry and investigation, relationships as well as things. A child's sorting of materials in the school, his help with arranging and with planning, his use of the whole school and its spaces and relationships—all were considered discovery.

More obvious than the question of method was the integration of "science" with other subject areas of curriculum. Much of the investigation of number can relate to "science" observations and can properly be called science investigation in the sense of asking questions of the environment. Thus, children who were cooking had experiences of measurement and weight but also might become fascinated with the discovery of change and relate change to temperature as the final cooked product emerged different from the uncooked separate ingredients. Estimating the weight and the weighing of the ingredients might begin speculation on concepts of mass. When the children measured their playground with trundle wheel and then with string which could even become a ball of string, they dealt with number, but they also might speculate on space that was coiled and

---

[55] Nuffield Junior Science *Teacher's Guide 1*, pp. 21, 22.
[56] *Ibid.*, p. 43.

space that was stretched out. Estimation, comparison, equivalence, difference—the various ways of measuring, of weighing, of perceiving shape and size and space and pattern—were clearly all part of the thinking that was beginning to be scientific as well as mathematical.

Further, just as investigation of number was integrated with *all* aspects of curriculum, so in a "science" inquiry, language and painting, even acting and movement—which could in their own right be subjects of such inquiry—might be ways for children to share their investigation in other areas or "tell about it." The Nuffield Junior Science Project material makes very clear this integration of environmental investigation with all aspects of a child's life.[57] But integration was sometimes even more than what *tended* towards specifically mathematical or science thinking or towards *use* of all expressive media to "tell about it." Consider how change, observed in the course of an inquiry, often extended this inquiry to "changes." Some child might be interested in "how it was," of "how people used to do it," in other words, in the uses and history of the thing about which he was asking. One result of a child's question might be his search for the "history" among the many little resource or information books in the infant school library.

Just as an investigation might lead to "history," so might it include the investigation of the social surroundings and relationships along with the physical surroundings. The external world a child was trying to understand was social and cultural as well as physical. The pictorial representation of the playground, the walk to school, might lead to mapping. Interest in roads, in traffic, in building, in places where children used to live or where their relatives now live, would lead—depending on a child's question—to work we might call math or science or social studies.

Thus, in its conception of environmental investigation as truly integrative of all aspects of a child's search for understanding, the Nuffield Junior Science Project extended the more focused Piagetian awareness already described for mathematics. It expressed what I had observed: that the whole atmosphere of the infant school is one of "finding out" from the concrete world around. In contrast with the overspecific definition of science in American elementary schools, it had seemed to me that the Nuffield Project perhaps had no goals for "specific," "essential," and "sequential" science learnings.[58] The same lack of "essential" or "sequential" development characterized English social studies. But this analysis would ignore the *actual* learning, of children inquiring about things and people in the infant school's very rich environment. The prepared but "unprescribed" environment was the "hidden" curriculum built on the various

[57] Nuffield Junior Science, *Teacher's Guides, 1 & 2.*
[58] Lillian Weber, "Impressions of Infant School Science," *The Teacher*, London, January 13, 1967.

possibilities that could be expected from an analysis of children's development and interests. The learnings that concern us for children of infant school age—the family, the neighborhood, the work around us—were part of the living, the discussion, the storytelling, the books read, the painting, the acting, the movement, the role playing in Wendy House. Nevertheless, the things we call "science" for children of this age were also made available in such specific terms as exploration of the properties of all materials used, whether paint or clay or sand or wood, a nature table, animals, a weather station, water, cooking, junk materials, pendulums, balances, and the wealth of material already described for math.

The *weather station*, to cite an example observed in a Bristol school, often led to a much wider inquiry than we would consider likely for children that age, such as questions about wind, shadows, and the effects on different materials of changes in moisture and temperature. Such inquiry might include seaweed or other items a child had brought in as samples of the different reactions. Since there was no fixed amount of science material in infant schools, the nature table in a particular infant school might be less than the lovely esthetically pleasing one of the nursery school. It might be somewhat dusty, less or more a piece of the decor and not exactly a reflection of the active interest in change, sequence, and growth; it might have given way to a discovery or a find, a junk or interest table. It might feature the self-conscious "science" of an arrangement of mirrors and a question on reflection or repetition, a display of a rusted nail in water and a question on this, and an assignment card on sink and float and on magnets.

Compared with nursery schools, infant schools might not so often be stocked with animals. On the other hand, a greater variety in nature experience was sometimes available in infant schools, particularly in those where all sorts of animals—guinea pigs, tortoises, and stick insects—lived all about the school. In a number of schools children were busy in aviaries bright with bird variety, in hen roost, dove cote, or rabbit hutch. The care of animals might involve handling a thermometer and charting temperatures. It might lead to comparison of groups of hens for number and weight of eggs produced. It might lead to sale of eggs and experiences with money. It meant experiences in feeding animals, in loving them, in observations of their bodily processes and their breeding. It meant also experiences in practical management—cleaning cages, clipping nails of guinea pigs—and in writing and reading about animals.

While far fewer infant schools than nursery schools had gardens, in some there was even a fairly large area available for what children identified as "farming." In a Bristol school, for example, growing tomatoes was, in addition to a science activity, a math experience to find the amount of water needed, and an observation of growth or change.

Water was not merely available for washing, for use with clay or paints, or with boats and the usual sink and float collection. In a more specific "science" way, water was part of the daily environment: children could find out about liquid measure using good equipment; a standard water trolley as big as a sand table could be used by several children at once. Water was used in ways *very rare* in American schools. Discoveries came through *any* handling, but pouring and repouring into vessels of different sizes and shapes raised all the Piagetian questions, and using siphons, or pumps, or making a fountain, raised more. Children could find out about the properties of water and the properties of things in water; they could discover the displacement of water with things in water, and the fact that water has no shape without the container that holds it; and they could learn that water frozen *becomes* the shape of its container, or in turning to steam, it "disappears." Water was used for cooking and for further exploration of its properties as it was heated.

Cooking in itself was a constant source of exploration. Children could be seen reading recipes posted over a stove, carefully measuring and weighing. There were observations on heat and temperature, change, and perhaps there were money experiences as well, since the cooked items were sold at the snack bar. Children also wrote about their cooking experiments.

"Science" in the infant school was intended to encourage a questioning attitude. An ingenious headmistress indicated how far a school committed to inquiry might go to stimulate questions. She suggested that mirrors built into a school might be

> placed to show repeated images, to function as periscopes or to see 'round a corner, prisms angled to throw spectrum colors from the sun, mobiles suspended in a current of air.[59]

In the infant school a child was encouraged in his observation, in alternate solutions, in his own solution, and thinking, judgment, estimation were thereby fostered. The infant school was *ready* to help a child ask the questions of the world that he needed to further develop his frame of understanding, and to provide the environment so that he could do this. This, more than specifics, was its science.

READING

The infant school was full of books—books were read to children, children read books, children made books. A child's firsthand experiences created a need and a desire for information that was in the books. English

[59] Brown and Precious, *The Integrated Day*, p. 16.

educators believed that only the reading that grew out of this context would result in its further development and use: As a child met difficulties with reading he used in this way, the teacher worked on particular skills with him. *But the teachers considered that discrete skills taught outside the context of interest and need could result in early attrition of the desire to read and therefore in little use of reading skills.* Thus reading rooted in interest and need was what most infant teachers attempted.

There has never been, apparently, objection to early reading or number work if it happens to arise naturally from a child's interests and if it is not forced. I saw evidence in my visits of offering a word, a sign for block building, or writing a child's story about his experience at his dictation, and this might start a child reading. I looked for evidence of excess offering that might push a child to read before his own response made that the inevitable next step. While the teachers may have started early on some writing and reading with a small group they considered ready, they acknowledged that this was not really reading, and they easily accepted the fact of some children not joining this small group.

This attitude of having a reading atmosphere "around" may be distorted by particular teachers into a too positive encouragement that could deprive a child of the development of his play, as was briefly discussed under Class Organization (p. 79). However, I saw very little scanting of play; most of the "reading" work with 5s was on a reading-readiness level. Most teachers were quite ready to be patient, not to "flog" it, to think it would "come along." A head described this process:

We teach the sounds, too, the phonetics. . . . You must know whether your child knows the sounds or not. He suddenly discovers, by looking at a book, that the first letter of his name is exactly the same as the first letter of somebody else's name. He says, "Oh, look! You've got that and so have I!" And then if you are there, you say: "Ah, yes, that says 'buh' for Bobby. And that says 'buh' for Betsy. What else can we think of that starts with 'buh'?" . . . The teacher says, "What have you painted?" And the child will begin to say what the picture is about. The teacher will supply words and, again, build up the vocabulary. She might say to that child, "Would you like to write what you've painted?" The child might, perhaps, have painted a picture of a lady—"That's Mummy." "Would you like me to write 'Mummy'?" The child might say, "Yes" or he might say, "No." If the child says, "Yes," the teacher writes "Mummy" beside the picture. And the child can then go over on top of the writing or copy it out underneath, according to his skill. The next time that child might paint another picture of "Mummy," or there might be a picture of "Me with Mummy." The teacher says, "Would you like me to write what you've painted: 'Mummy–Me'?" Then, you see, the steps go on, farther and farther. The next time it is, "This is my Mummy. This is me." Or "This is Mummy and me going shopping." We do not correct any grammatical error. We write it just as the child says it. . . . because the child

is only going to read what he said. If he says, "Me is going to do this"—
I don't often hear that—"Me is going shopping," you would write "Me
is going shopping." Because the next time the child reads it, he would
read, "Me is going shopping," even if you write "I am going shopping."
So don't waste your time and his. Write what he says.

Then the next step, after the child has been doing that for some time, we
get quite a lot of, "This is a house." Children love to paint houses, so
you'll get that over and over again. "This is a house." "This is a boat."
"This is Mummy." "This is my toy." "This is—" And it keeps coming
and coming. You might put one up on the wall. You could also collect the
children's work together and make up a "This is" book. When the
children have done that for a certain time, you say to the child who you
know would be able to do it, "Could you write 'This is' for me, and I'll
put the rest of it?" The child has drawn perhaps a picture of his birthday
cake, and he goes and writes "This is" on the side. "Can you find the
word 'my' anywhere in the classroom?" Yes, because you've got the pictures all around, and you've been talking about them. You've been reading all the words that other children have asked for, and the child might
be able to find "my." If he can't, you write it on his paper. And then you
supply "birthday cake." That is just showing how very simply and
gradually it builds up.[60]

The pattern everywhere was discussion with a child of his painting
or drawing. A child of five drew his picture; under it the teacher wrote
what he told her about it and his name. He might trace over what she had
written at his dictation; he might copy it. Soon, the teacher wrote what
he said on a separate paper; "soon" could mean after a number of months
filled with many, many experiences, all bearing on reading readiness. She
might write what he told her as separate words, if a child was now at the
point where he could pick out the words he wanted. Soon she gave him
just a word, letting him find the rest from written signs around the room.
At that stage children asked other children for separate words. On my
visits to schools, they asked me for words. Word lists were common for all
the children after the beginning reading period, and as they collected their
word lists, they began to be able to sort words for beginning sounds.

Writing went on all the time, parallel with reading. Some of the
children seemed to learn reading by writing, and the writing was valued
by the children as *uniquely their production*. It was writing that said
what *they* wanted to say. In one New Town school with an amazing amount
of "free" or "creative" writing going on, the writing a child did about
the painting was not even recopied in good hand. The feeling was that the
child who wrote it could read it. In most schools it might be copied in
good hand before being put under the painting. Productions were in this
way part of reading. Children became familiar with a number of words

[60] Cazden, *Infant School*, pp. 11, 3, 20, 21.

and matched these. Their own books of their experiences grew—all this before and going along with later books. Writing might start as patterns, but it went on from there, even while patternmaking continued.

I was so startled by the amount of writing so early that it first struck me as a pressure. Were the teachers worried by the transition to junior school and therefore overeager to start reading and writing? But the fact of the *amount*—not timed or forced—seemed to be a tribute to a child's *desire* to communicate. In this system, experience is communicated either through discussion or writing and, eventually, through both. The desire to communicate flourished because in this free atmosphere every child was doing something interesting; every child was doing something different. The encouragement to communication as a product of the diverse activities cannot be too greatly stressed. In such an atmosphere, communication is *necessary*. How else could anyone know what you've done? And it is made very clear that the headmistress and teacher are tremendously eager to hear, to read, to support the communication. English reports recommended that writing not be *demanded*. The English are aware that the too automatic request for recording can be a damper to discovery work. The *Nuffield Teacher's Guide* is one of many publications that discuss the many ways of communication—talking, painting, charting, etc.[61]

At one school, where talking was considered the most important pre-reading activity, the headmistress stated, "We use no set introductory book. We make our own from the vocabulary used by that child. The first books, therefore, are made by the teacher."

The use of everything a child had done for beginning reading was strikingly demonstrated at the first infant school I saw: A teacher took a small group that had been weighing flour and making dough, and talked with them. "Tell us, the rest of us, what you used." An experience story was quickly constructed. The aim was to talk, to find words. A lot of the vocabulary was around the room. They could match words from a group experience story to their own. One child brought over his label and read it to me, "I made a boat and it is red and black." He could not yet read but he could remember what he had said. This incident illustrated Nora Goddard's statement: "Children recognize sentences, phrases and words by their general pattern or shape before they have been taught letters or sounds." [62]

Children were sparked off to read and write through the *needs* of life at school. The printing of circulars for the animal clinic, for example, created needs to write and read. In schools with an undifferentiated day, where some reading was going on at all times, it was often reported to me that, just as at a certain point of discovery the combinations of the 100s

---

[61] Nuffield Junior Science, *Teacher's Guide 1*.
[62] Nora L. Goddard, *Reading in the Modern Infants' School*, p. 9.

board can be overwhelmingly interesting and absorb a child all day for a week or a month, so, at a certain point, the new skill of reading may be overwhelmingly absorbing. There was a willingness to go along with the rhythms of interest in a child. The role of the school was seen to be that of finding a motivating point and helping to keep it going by using whatever was needed.

Nora Goddard sums up how a child was led to reading through his serious pursuit of his firsthand experience.

> In approaching reading through interest the natural sequence is: first, that the child has something he wants to say, second, that we write it down for him, and last, that he reads it, and *wants* to read it because it tells of something that is of real interest to him.[63]

> . . . we try to base our reading material upon the child's natural speaking vocabulary.[64]

> It is this talking about what he is doing that is so necessary as a preparation for learning to read. The child will not be successful in learning to read words that describe things that are outside his experience. For this reason we seek to extend and supplement the experience of the child from the less fortunate home.[65]

> We need to be sensitive so that we follow his real interests, and not what we imagine these interests should be. . . . We know, for instance, that most children are interested in events in their own lives, in their homes and families, in things that they themselves make, in living and growing things, in listening to stories, and in new experiences that come to them within the secure environment of the home or classroom. . . . His tasks will be self-chosen.[66]

The Department of Education and Science continues to support a reading approach which stresses "the width and depth of the experiences about which language is employed." [67] It is particularly concerned about reading schemes that impose language on a child. Therefore, the Schools Council Programme, *Breakthrough to Literacy* (developed over a six-year period and published in 1970) aims to promote initial literacy through a child's *own* listening and speaking vocabulary and within his total experience of language.

In addition to the stimulus to his reading from firsthand experience, a

[63] *Ibid.*, p. 12.
[64] *Ibid.*, p. 15.
[65] *Ibid.*, p. 20.
[66] *Ibid.*, p. 30.
[67] Department of Education and Science, "Learning To Read" from *Reports on Education*, No. 64.

child was led to reading through his interest in the stories that were read to him. He discovered that he could find out about some things only in books. Stories and poetry were part of his experience every single day in the infant school. Stories could bring a child the indirect experiences of situations and feelings which stretched his understanding past his own frame of reference to a beginning empathy with the experience of another. Shared in a group, or even in Morning Service, the meaning attached to these experiences by other children could be used by an individual child in his own integration of meaning. The concern evidenced in all the other areas for carefully planned extension of a child's level of understanding—emotionally, morally, and intellectually—was also reflected in the careful selection of stories and poems, literature of quality and depth.

A wealth of "little" books could be found in the infant school, books that could be read at a single sitting, books that could be read so quickly that a child felt a quick satisfaction and an immediate comprehension of a complete story. Many of these books were made by the child or other children, many were two or three page books to which he could turn to find out what he needed to know or wanted to know—about an animal, some water activity, or any other interest. At the water table the child might find a four-page book (as, for example, one of the series entitled *The Young Investigator*) that he could read himself, with only one new difficult word—perhaps, in this case, "porous." He grew in power as he read *many* books and as he read these quickly.

Phonics

A child learned some phonics in connection with the reading he did to find out about things and in connection with the writing he did to tell about the things he had done. A few minutes might be spent on the sound of a word a child had requested. Phonics usually was absorbed incidentally —beginnings, endings, word-building, blends—in the creation of word lists. In the course of some reading with the teacher, a few minutes might be given to analysis of a word family and the finding of additional examples.

As the child neared 7, a more direct tackling of phonics was undertaken, but it never dominated the teaching of reading. A certain amount of phonics could be found along with all other methods, perhaps in all schools. But not until the seven-year-old period was it taught, and even then, it was never taught as a separate thing. (In 10 percent of the schools, ITA (Initial Teaching Alphabet) is used.) [68]

Series readers could be found in *almost* all schools though only a few schools used one series. More often a great variety of books on a par-

[68] John Blackie, *Inside the Primary School*, p. 61.

ticular level was available. Where there were several series, a child could pick what he was interested in and be helped with this.

This account does not mean that the teacher in many infant schools is not "hearing" the reading of one child at a time or of three or four children in a group, or doing some direct special teaching of it. Direct teaching, always with individuals or small groups, was part of teaching of reading in many infant schools. Tansley describes such direct teaching— using phonics with slow learners—*within* the context of English infant education.[69] He stresses teaching to the *individual*, simultaneous multiple activities, and rich experiential reinforcement; he warns against teaching phonics as an isolated skill. The direct and systematic teaching of reading, according to Moyle, "is not out of place nor yet need it spoil the informal atmosphere of a classroom for it is usually best done individually." [70] Both spokesmen for more direct teaching than is now the case in many infant schools are thus within the framework of individualized infant education.

But direct teaching was only one aspect of the total reading and writing atmosphere; the multiple activities related to interests that drew on reading, writing, and speaking. In addition to any specific teaching of skills, the use and pursuit of the skills were entwined with a child's serious and sustained exploration of the total environment. *Incidental* teaching, teaching right at the moment of a child's need in following up his interest, is integral to any description of informal education, and resulted in far more reading than ever happens when reliance is mainly on formal teaching of reading.

SUMMARY AND ESTIMATES

THE FRAMEWORK OF CONDITIONS

Everything in the infant school was directed toward maintaining a child as the unique individual he was. When he came to the infant school he came with his own pattern of learning, with his own five-year-old frame of reference already synthesized as a result of the workings of his curiosity, his interests, the active forces for learning within him. The experiences he had had, the quality of the human beings with whom he had been in interaction, and the focus of his attention and interests all helped determine the patterns he brought to school. It was essential, in the minds of those committed to informal education, that the planning and activity of the school not interrupt the development of these patterns, but meet,

---

[69] A. E. Tansley, *Reading and Remedial Reading.*
[70] Donald Moyle, *The Teaching of Reading*, p. 101.

extend, and carry them further. Recognition of individual differences and of a child's own firsthand experiences was focal in this commitment, which guided all attempts to actualize informal education in the infant school.

I have described and analyzed the conditions I observed in the schools, concentrating on those factors which I consider to be the supports for the framework of informal relationships. No single condition separately could support what was meant by informal education; even in the presence of *all* the conditions, without the conscious intent on the part of heads and teachers to weave a purposeful web of support, the informal structure remained weak.

Thus a center hall, with in-and-outness from classrooms, made possible simultaneous use of environment, movement, and communal life of the school, but again, only if the intent to produce this kind of school living had allowed this in-and-outness. A lack of in-and-outness limited the communal life of the school. Some of the new schools had encapsulated classrooms, even when they were family-grouped, if schoolwide in-and-outness had disappeared with the corridors. The headmistress, relating to the in-and-outness, was the real producer of the communal life of the school.

Movement was necessary for use of the environment in a simultaneous way and for a real communal life in the school. Limitation on movement certainly limited use of the environment and contradicted other informal characteristics.

Family grouping seemed to make all other features of informal education most possible but these features—in-and-outness, communal life of the school, rich environment and simultaneous use, interaction and movement, an activity period related to skills, teacher planning, acceptance of variation of level, easy transition, even an undifferentiated day and implementation—could coexist with age grouping in a family school. Only one-directional progression contradicted the purposes of informal education.

Relating the work in the activity period to the skills was basic to the concept of informal education, and this implied simultaneous varied grouping. In many schools, full simultaneous use and full relating of activities to skills seemed to be leading to the undifferentiated day. Only where a skills period preceded an activity period could one find the relatedness, continuity, and meaningful use of the learning situation by a child severely limited. Such a situation constituted a partial contradiction of all that is implied in informal education, though certainly an activity period, even at the end of the day, was better than nothing.

Teacher implementation, which encompassed teacher planning for individual children and acceptance of variation of level and beginning learning, was a vital aspect of any school preponderantly informal. Its aim was to give children the chance to achieve the fullest involvement that comes through pursuit of their own purposes and questions and choices. That aim certainly could only be realized with implementation rather than direction. Implementation was a result of—but not an inevitable accompaniment to—the many arrangements for informal education. But when the aim was missing, these arrangements remained as the outward structure only. Thus, teacher direction sometimes existed even with all the arrangements that seemed to be aspects of informal method.

Infant schools of my sample can be described as existing in a continuum of development. In all the schools I observed, there existed a certain core of activity period, of movement, of provision of rich environment, of simultaneous use, of acceptance of variation of level, of acceptance of beginning learning at a child's point of readiness. The essence of these features is the acceptance of individual differences, of a child as an individual in this learning. Naturally then, the fullest extension of the concept was in family grouping and in plans allowing for use of the whole school with in-and-outness and the undifferentiated day. The fullest extension of concept combined the communal life of the school with implementation of a child's individual purposes.

IMPRESSIONS OF CHILDREN'S BEHAVIOR AND ATTITUDES

The children's responsive and active participation in the life of the infant school and in their own learning was the goal of informal education. In order to judge its achievement, therefore, we would have to look at the children. What was apparent in the emotional bearing of the children? How did they seem to respond to this way of education? The following impressions, which are culled from my notes and are not in any way the heads' estimates, are based on watching the children at their work and in their interaction with the headmistress, the teacher, each other, and myself.

The schools where the children showed great friendliness, initiative, curiosity, and intellectual excitement were family grouped and had an undifferentiated day, a general modality of implementation, and a strong communal life. At *no* school were the children apathetic. The gradients of description range from cheerful, waiting for teacher direction, and not being particularly involved, to great initiative, spontaneity, creativity, curiosity, caring for each other, and intellectual excitement. Using these gradients the estimates on all infant schools were positive; less positive estimates (cheery, waiting for teacher direction, not particularly involved) applied in only four schools (2 infant with nursery classes and 2 JMI schools). Even such an estimate was not related to apathy but to the fact that these schools had not developed a strong, purposeful involvement on the part of all the children. In the one school (infant school with nursery classes) where the children seemed inarticulate, there was no tie-in of activity with skills. In this school I also noted more obvious discipline, more structure, more noise level.

The infant schools where my impressions of the children were most positive were informal. None had one-directional progression; all had family grouping, in-and-outness, activity periods related to skills, and going on to undifferentiated day. Of the JMI schools, the two schools where the children displayed the greatest initiative were informal and family-grouped.

Some of the schools producing the most positive impression had children of predominantly poor economic backgrounds; in such schools I made special note of the intellectually stimulating atmosphere. One school with an 84 percent immigrant population was memorable for its strong emphasis on creative writing. Another school (further described on p. 103), also with a heavily immigrant population diverse in origin, was noteworthy for its intellectually excited children who were genuinely pleased with themselves.

All the informal schools had a special glow of intellectual stimulation, as reflected in the children's writing of poetry and stories (often stories continued over a period of time), in the large amount of mathematical exploration, and in the quality and depth of children's activities in movement, music, plastic media, and acting.

Children who are willing, responsible participants in school life seem to expect that requests from the adults will be sensible and necessary, as illustrated in this episode recorded at one infant school: The children listened to a Morning Service, as would ours in Assembly. They then dispersed in the English infant school way, talking, arms about each other. The headmistress, suddenly remembering something, called out in a voice only slightly raised, "Oh, children, I've forgotten to tell you, would you please tell your mothers. . . ?" Instantly, the children stopped talking and listened. Hard as it was for me to imagine a parallel American situation, in which a teacher so easily regained children's attention when they were midstream from one activity to another, I realized that in the free English schools it was easy to get the children's attention. The teachers consistently used a natural tone of voice; they talked to *individuals* and very rarely did they talk *at* the children. I heard no yelling. Teachers expected to be listened to but asked this of children infrequently and only when its necessity was self-evident. Far more often they listened *to* children.

I have already described the nursery school teacher's style of speaking which is based on the use of suggestion. This manner is found, it seemed to me, on all levels of English society and in all situations. In their way of saying, "It will do, won't it?" "You do think, don't you?" the English teachers create a setting of agreement that very possibly may account for a low degree of resistance in the classroom. Furthermore, teachers did not seem to fear what would happen if the children were moving around or were unsupervised for a time. No one assumed that a child going somewhere in the school outside his classroom was doing something wrong. Children were moving around all the time. They were *trusted.* They were expected to have identified the school as theirs and to be using it responsibly. They were expected to help each other and to turn to each other—even for words and skills. I was continually impressed by the unclouded mental functioning of the children in this kind of situation. When they were asked a question they didn't seem to have to hesitate, to put it into a frame of the rules, to ask themselves, "What is expected of me?", "What does she want me to say?" They could answer right off. Since what they were doing was their own choice and their own construct, they understood it clearly and could tell you about it. They were also freely curious. If something about me puzzled them, they asked questions: about my bifocal glasses, my accent, my food habits, my table manners; did I know their Aunty in America; did I sleep on the boat coming over to England, etc.

American parents and teachers have asked me many times, "but aren't these children really different? Isn't that why they pose so few discipline problems?" Part of the answer is that with the children working in ones and twos on different things instead of as a unit, the impact of aggression is diluted. It is not that there are no discipline problems but that these become less disruptive to everyone else's work. Certainly, all heads pointed to a number of children needing special help. The National Study states that 5 percent of the children have serious adjustment problems and another 10 percent show stress symptoms of various kinds.[71] But other observers also report the striking fact of few discipline problems:

> When the class seldom meets as a unit, when the children work independently discipline is less of a problem. It does not disappear as a problem but it becomes less paramount.[72]

Some American teachers who have seen the spectacle of children in British classes working diligently on their own have raised another question: they have wondered whether British children are fundamentally different from American children. Certainly British grown-ups are different from Americans, and there may well be important differences in national character. Yet middle-aged English visitors to the informal schools often react with the same disbelief as Americans: they find it hard to credit British children

[71] M. L. K. Pringle, N. L. Butler, R. Davie, *11,000 Seven-Year-Olds.* First Report of the National Child Development Study (London: Longmans Green & Co., Ltd., 1965), p. 155.
[72] Joseph Featherstone, "Schools for Children," *The New Republic,* August 19, 1967, p. 20.

with so much initiative and so much responsibility. Also, formal schools in Britain suffer from discipline problems, so it is hard to know how to speculate intelligently on the question.[73]

English teachers all recalled the time of formal classes, when classes functioned as single units, as a time when a large percentage of their efforts had to be directed to maintaining discipline. Control of a group functioning as a unit demands attention and quiet focus from all the children as a unit. Regardless of differences between English and American children, English children present fewer discipline problems in these schools organized for informal education. Just as it was not a question of *different* teachers but a context that supported this kind of function, so it was not, it seemed to me, a question of *different* children, but a context that supported the children's involvement in learning. This context is what I have described as informal education.

TRANSITION TO THE JUNIOR SCHOOL

The impact of the infant school experience on a child cannot be discussed in isolation from his transition to the next level. At the time of my study, children from infant schools moved on to largely unchanged junior schools in which traditional whole-class, subject-oriented teaching dominated. Many junior schools have changed, but observations and heads' estimates of transition problems dating from that period will continue to have validity for some situations because change comes slowly.

Difficulties in the process of transition arose from the fact that a child's free movement and his free interaction with adults and children were interrupted, and—a more serious discontinuity—unchanged junior schools did not accept him at the level of his understanding without fixing standards for achievement. The unchanged junior schools, for the most part, were not expected to help a child with beginning reading, nor did they accept this responsibility. Thus, an important component of a child's easy transition to the junior school was his ability to read. My information on reading achievement is based largely on the estimates made by the heads. In every school but one, the head's report was of few non-readers (2 percent was the usual figure, representing the children who had made no start at all in "catching on" to reading). My observation, from visiting schools and having groups of 7s or individual children who were 7 read to me, was that most children could read.

Reading was certainly a point of concentration with all groups, but

[73] Joseph Featherstone, "Teaching Children to Think," *The New Republic,* September 9, 1967, p. 15.

especially with the 7s. Heads interested themselves in the reading—regularly hearing the reading of children who were going on to junior school, taking small groups of nonreaders, or arranging for them and for poor readers to have special help with a .5 remedial teacher or a library teacher, etc. Though these procedures did not in themselves produce easy transition, they were part of the all-out effort. Though of course many infant heads resisted the pressure coming from the junior school, fear of difficult transition often had the effect of tightening the learning atmosphere for the 7s groups in the infant school, since these children went on to junior schools after a long holiday in which their new found skills might slip a certain amount. Furthermore, for the many children who were at the beginning of reading, the change produced confusion.

The English are aware that concern about seven-year-olds may be unrealistic, viewed at the 11-year-old level. For instance, John Blackie, former Chief Inspector for Primary Education, has stated that the percentage of nonreaders at the end of primary school, age 11, is small but that 15 percent at that age are poor readers.[74] Nevertheless, English educators have been anxious to examine all factors that affect the reading in infant schools.

The National Child Development Study, in findings that were the basis for recommendations by the Plowden Committee, summarizes:

> Nevertheless, a considerable number of children in this sample of 7-year-olds were described by their teachers as being either non-readers (about 3 percent) or poor readers (about 24 percent). An even larger proportion (almost half the sample) had not achieved a sufficient mastery of this subject near the end of their infant schooling to use it as an efficient tool for further learning; rather, reading must continue to be specifically taught, because full mastery of the skill has not yet been attained. Thus, on the evidence of the children's present reading abilities about a quarter will need a continuation of 'infant methods' if they are to progress with this basic subject . . .[75]

> About 45 per cent of children appear not to reach full mastery of reading skills by the time they are due to leave infant schools. This means that the teaching of reading needs to be continued at the junior level; also there should be some continuity in teaching methods and reading schemes.[76]

Therefore, to ease transition, the Plowden Committee recommended prolongation of the infant school experience itself and continuity of informal methods in the junior school. The National Study stated: "If the length of schooling is one of these factors [in reading success], then it may

[74] Blackie, *Inside the Primary School*, p. 59.
[75] Pringle, Butler, Davie, *11,000 Seven-Year-Olds*, p. 154.
[76] *Ibid.*, p. 156.

be possible to take practical steps." [77] In line with this thinking, the Plowden Committee concluded

> that children should have three years in the infant schools and that they should not transfer until the age of eight. A three-year course will allow teachers and children to work steadily without anxiety. It will give infant school teachers the satisfaction of seeing more results to their labours and of knowing that children have reached, before leaving them, a stage at which they can tolerate a change of school. . . . We recommend that transfer to junior schools should take place in the September following a child's eighth birthday.[78]

Long ago, Susan Isaacs wrote: ". . . lack of continuity between the methods of the Infants' School and those of the Primary School accounts for quite a large number of cases of backwardness in reading." [79]

The Plowden Report emphasizes the need for continuity: "It will still be necessary to ensure that there is no sharp break between 'infant' and 'junior' methods. . . ." [80] Its recommendation for transfer at age 8 derived from similar recommendations made by heads and from research indicating that reading was consolidated between the seventh and eighth year for most children:

> At this age many children are at a turning point in their mastery of reading.[81]

> Evidence from research has confirmed that transfer at seven can have disastrous results on children's achievement in reading.[82]

> For all children and more particularly for the average and slow developing child, three years is desirable. The third year is a period of consolidation during which rapid progress may be made.[83]

Plowden suggested that the newly reorganized infant schools be called First Schools, recognizing them as the first step in compulsory education, and that the reorganized junior schools be called Middle Schools. Some experimental situations observed at the time of my study had already incorporated this organization for age of transfer; for example, the Eveline

[77] *Ibid.*, p. 130.
[78] Plowden, pp. 140, 141.
[79] Susan Isaacs, *The Children We Teach*, p. 59.
[80] Plowden, p. 164.
[81] *Ibid.*, p. 212.
[82] *Ibid.*, p. 213.
[83] Goddard, *Reading in the Modern Infants' School*, p. 94.

Lowe school, described in an HMSO pamphlet, is organized according to new ages for transfer as well as for experiment with several combinations of age grouping and group size.[84]

In the period since the appearance of the Plowden Report, many LEAs have submitted plans for new units or for reorganization based on a new age of transfer. Eight is now becoming more customary as transfer age to junior or middle school.

Plowden further recommended, as ways of easing transition, what many good heads already practiced. Heads had tried to mitigate the difficulties by arranging visits of the junior school head to see the work of the children, by encouraging friendships of infant teachers with junior school teachers, by sending along with him the book a child was up to when he went to the junior school. In addition to reports of his progress, a child could take a folder with samples of his work. In turn the junior school sometimes tried to have an infant teacher or a teacher conversant with infant methods take seven- and eight-year-olds. These arrangements had produced a much easier transition (in the opinion of the heads).

At the time of my sample in 1966, any ease in transition was very largely the result of such work of the infant heads. At that time, inclusion of the infant school in an unchanged junior school under a single head did not ease the pressure of transition or the pressure to produce few non-readers. One exception was a JMI school in Bristol that was completely geared for implementation and informal education, with beginning points all through the school. This school reported 40 percent nonreaders at the beginning junior school level, a result of a consciously slackened pressure on reading with the thought that all children would be reading on the 11-year-old level; and indeed, according to the head's report *all* children were reading *well* at the end of junior school. I was told that there were 15 such informal junior schools in Bristol, family-grouped in a two-year system; approximately 15 percent of junior schools elsewhere were in the process of change in the direction of greater continuity with infant school methods, convinced that fuller implementation of a child's own pace and development depended on the junior schools' being in tune with this way of working.

The trend seemed to be toward increasing continuity and blurring of the lines of division. Nora Goddard,[85] Infant Inspector, ILEA, spoke of this as a blurring between class and class, between stages (nursery, infant, and junior), in subject matter divisions, and between home and school. Before planning the new experimental Eveline Lowe School, the architects, "watching the fluent improvisation . . . in an old building," noted:

---

[84] *Eveline Lowe Primary School, London.*
[85] In her address to the Nursery School Association, September 21, 1966.

. . . the distinction between teaching and non-teaching areas was disappearing. The whole school and its surroundings—corridors, cloakrooms, porches, entrances, medical rooms and even stairways—were being called into use . . . there was a fruitful blurring of some of the subdivisions traditionally found in primary schools. Sometimes children of different ages formed "family" groups and there was much coming and going between neighbouring classes. Few "subject" barriers appeared to remain, for knowledge and skill were now seen as a whole. A session was not necessarily broken up into set periods, and in some schools "playtime" had disappeared. A school day consisted largely of a planned sequence of varying activities, with "breaks" suitably interposed. "Work" and "play" were harder to distinguish, for every pursuit had a purpose which was clearly understood and valued by the children engaged in it.[86]

Open use of the school, the overflow from class to school, is extending even to some junior schools.

A similar situation is becoming more usual also in the junior school. Room for individual work is found in corridors and foyer. . . . In an increasing number of schools, classroom doors are, metaphorically at least, open. Teachers know what is going on all over the school. Children are encouraged to visit classes other than their own, to use equipment kept there, or to consult a teacher who has the particular knowledge that they need.[87]

This open use is being further extended for parent and community. The Eveline Lowe School, for example, was planned as just such an "open" school.

On my return to England in 1969, I looked for evidence of further developments in arrangements. Junior heads told me of their use of the work folders sent up from the infant school: Incoming children found samples of their work—writing or number or painting—on the walls of their new rooms, welcoming them.

I saw junior schools in Yorkshire that were certainly informal in all the ways I have described. Children in these schools, even in the last weeks of the summer term, seemed to be working with purpose on their different kinds of work. I saw an easy directness of discussion with each other and with the teachers who moved from one intent group to another. Of course, the rich environment was adapted to the more sustained interests of older children. In one junior school, the oldest children were taking infant children, who would be entering that school the following term, to see the things around their school. An 11-year-old girl was moving through the school showing four infant children some handiwork and explaining the technique of the production. "You won't be able to do it *right* away,

---

[86] *Eveline Lowe Primary School*, p. 9.
[87] Plowden, pp. 276–77.

but after a while you might like to." Or this, "Here's something you could try, mightn't you?" "I didn't do this one but I think this is how it works. I did this one." An 11-year-old boy demonstrated some air experiments and then showed his little group some math equipment. "We have that," a little one spoke up. "You do, do you?" the 11-year-old looked at him a moment with interest. "Well, you can always try new things with it, can't you?" Later, the infant children were treated to a "tea" prepared and hosted by the older children. The attitude of the older ones was solicitous, tender, and confident that school had good things in store for these new-comers. I spoke with some of the 11-year-olds at the end of the day. In response to my compliments on how the day had gone, a girl explained, "I remember *my* first day. I'd want them to like this school."

A wind of change was, in fact, blowing through the junior schools. In newspapers, on TV, in workshops, since the publication of the Plowden Report, the climate of discussion is producing a "change of heart" in many junior headmasters. The old junior school image of desks in rows is reported to be rare now. Local study groups are at work analyzing the meaning of Plowden recommendations for continuity. The work of the Nuffield Projects and their publications are a major influence, implementing the change. A new interest has arisen in better communication between infant and junior schools, as evidenced by increased intervisitation. The situation is so fluid that the percentage of changed schools is significantly different even within a very short period. The 15 percent reported to be changed in 1966 had increased to an estimated 25 percent in 1969. These changes occurred within the context of others, such as the elimination of *the 11+ examinations* that determined placement in one type or another of secondary school, and the plans for comprehensive secondary education. Though some authorities have produced alternate selection plans which may be no better, the discard of the 11+ through much of the country has facilitated change in the junior schools, just as the discard of the "payment by results" policy in 1897 (see p. 163) had made possible the changes in the infant school. The majority of LEAs now have plans to go over to comprehensive education, though the actual changeover so far has been slower than had been hoped for. But change is not stopped. The attack on selection procedures under any guise continues, and a new sophistication and flexibility seem to permeate discussion of what educational encounter can be—on all levels—with much of the discussion stressing active engagement, informality, continuity.

ESTIMATES

Finally, how successful is informal education? Gardner answered the question in her book, *Experiment and Tradition in Primary Schools.* Her testing of many items comparing children ages 7 and 10 (carefully matched), in informal (experimental) schools and formal (traditional) schools, showed the success of informal schools in all areas except mechanical arithmetic.

> Some of these results confirmed expectations which were based on my previous work. I had grounds for expecting that the experimental school children would do better in free drawing and in English language and also that they might do well in a social situation. Nor was I surprised at their superiority in the test for ingenuity, indeed I expected an even higher result in this test. . . .

> The greater opportunities in experimental schools for children to exchange ideas and participate in discussion appear to have had a very favourable effect on their power over language, which, by the age of ten, is showing in their written English.[88]

Gardner estimated in 1966 that well over 50 percent of the infant schools were weighted towards informal methods, that almost all had at least some core of activity period, individual and small group teaching, and thus had made a breakthrough from the teacher-controlled, block, whole-class method.[89] She felt that the battle of the infant school had to continue, to extend even further the ways of this kind of teaching and the number of schools successful in this way. But she estimated that the battle of the next period was already on in the junior school.

How does the Plowden Committee report on this continuum? From an HMI survey of all the primary schools in England, the Report lists the percentage of schools for each of nine gradients of evaluation. The survey assessment included junior along with infant schools, and so its finding that 33 percent can be classed as "good" is even more startling.

1. Outstanding
2. Good with Outstanding Features
3. Good without Special Distinction
4. Signs of Life and Seeds of Growth
5. Weak but Especially Good Personal Relationships
6. Decent, Run of the Mill
7. Good and Bad Aspects
8. Out of Touch
9. Bad

1.	2.	3.	4.	5.	6.	7.	8.	9.
1%	9%	23%	16%	6%	28%	9%	5%	0.1%

33% Good   50% Relatively Good

We were at pains to discover. . . . What was done about them [the 9th gradient] when they were identified. Each of the 28 schools [the

---

[88] Gardner, *Experiment and Tradition in Primary Schools*, pp. 200, 201.
[89] ————, Lectures at the Institute of Education, University of London, 1966.

"bad" 0.1 percent] was followed up by the local authorities and by
H.M. Inspectors, and action taken. . . . We doubt whether any school
in this category would be suffered to stay there long.[90]

The Plowden Report confirms Gardner's estimate and the conclusions
from my sample; it confirms the trend towards changes in the junior
school. Above all, the Report pronounces an overwhelmingly favorable
judgment on the infant schools: "Learning is going on all the time. . . ." [91]
And again:

> Many infant schools are outstanding for the quality of the relationships
> between teachers and children. They excel in the opportunities they pro-
> vide for play and the talk that accompanies it, the stress they put on in-
> dividual learning and the skill with which teachers select from the various
> methods of teaching reading those that suit themselves and the individual
> children.[92]

Therefore, the Plowden Committee recommends continuity and development of methods from such models as are described in its Report and
in this chapter, as well as in chapter 1. These are the models for English
primary education.

[90] Plowden, pp. 101, 102. The survey included 20,664 primary schools in England
apart from 676 which were considered "too new to be assessed or, for some other
reason, could not be classified. The whole body of H. M. Inspectors responsible
for the inspection of primary schools took part." Category I contained 109 schools,
about 29,000 children; Category II contained 1,538 schools; Category III contained 4,155 schools. It is these 3 categories that add up to the 33% considered
quite clearly good.
[91] *Ibid.*, p. 103.
[92] *Ibid.*, p. 140.

part two

INFORMAL EDUCATION
The Entity
and the Theory

chapter 3

THE INFANT SCHOOL ENTITY
Dissemination
and History

Diverse as infant schools might be there were more similarities than differences between them even within their many original and special approaches. The composite that emerged was an entity that could be described as follows: An infant school was of a certain small size and architectural shape meant to create some communal living; either it already offered this prospect or its architectural shape was bent to do it. It had a headmistress whose role as communications facilitator, master teacher, and master agent creating the entity was in some sense understood by all. It had an agreed-on range of environment and an agreed-on aim to use this environment freely. In every way—in timetable, in group structure (age or family), in mode of relationship of teacher and child—it tried to foster the use of this environment to create a whole, full, rich setting in which each child could live and learn in his own individually different way.

DISSEMINATION THROUGH THE HEADMISTRESS

What I have described as informal education was more than the mechanical adding up of conditions and arrangements. These conditions and arrangements had to be consciously adapted by the headmistress into the entity that implemented informal education. It was she who through such adaptation made the idea actuality. Her awareness and understanding of the shared concept of entity and of informal education not only directed her adaptations, but accounted for the differences between schools with similar arrangements. The differences in the understanding of concept— from one headmistress to another—were of degree, not of kind.

This common idea of informal education, moreover, existed without specific prescription from public authority. Heads I had met in the United States and England regarded, almost with horror, the idea of a "fixed" or "prescribed" syllabus, the idea of all schools functioning in the same way. The headmistress felt free of control and free even to interpret aims in her own way. It was not only the *feeling* of freedom that she had experienced but also the fact of freedom, acknowledged in government reports. As the Plowden Report stated it:

> "The only uniformity of practice that the Board of Education desire to see in the teaching of public elementary schools is that each teacher shall think for himself, and work out for himself such methods of teaching as may use his powers to the best advantage and be best suited to the particular needs and conditions of the school. Uniformity in detail of practice (except in the mere routine of school management) is not desirable, even if it were attainable. But freedom implies a corresponding responsibility in its use." [1918 Code] This passage was reprinted in the preface to the 1937 edition of the Handbook. In 1944 the Code, which had become increasingly permissive, finally disappeared, and in the 1944 Education Act the only statutory requirement that remained was that children should be educated according to "their age, ability and aptitude." [1]

The freedom, as commented on by Plowden, coupled with an existing concept of desired result and a standard of evaluation, made it possible for heads to experiment and develop their own patterns, which later could become the models for the future long before they had won general acceptance. Both concept and standard were, of course, still evolving, but at least they were already somewhat formulated in the common history that heads had inherited and shaped. In fact, the culture of the educational world in which the headmistress lived and was educated was rooted in this history. Through her relationship to this history—which is basic to the development and operation of all the other factors—the infant school entity was disseminated.

The mechanisms that influenced her were the teachers' colleges, the Institutes of Education, the inspectorates, local and HMI, and the in-

[1] Plowden, p. 189.

service training. All of these operated in a reciprocal relationship with the head. And all, in their turn, gained reinforcement from the history of the development as embodied in the literature and in the reports produced by the Department of Education and the Institutes.

The Teachers' Colleges and Institutes of Education

The head's first experiences as a student learning to be a teacher in a teachers' college would appear to be a major mechanism of the spread of a common idea. Certainly the colleges of education *maintain* the wide spread. But while teachers gained some of their ability to function informally from their experiences at teachers' colleges, good practice sometimes even preceded the development of supportive programs in the colleges. Examples of good practice, in fact, were sought out by the colleges. And even now good practice in the schools is ahead of some of the training in the teachers' colleges, while the very goals set by the colleges for the education of teachers, and the criteria used for evaluating their qualifications, have come from the analysis of examples of good practice.

In qualifying teachers, the Department of Education and Science accepts these criteria rather than imposing its own standards. In any case, the criteria for good practice and the implications for education and qualification of teachers are developing rather than static criteria. They are examined and reexamined, and as little as possible is defined externally by the Department of Education and Science, while as much as possible continues to develop within the schools, the professional organizations, the colleges of education and the Institutes of Education. Inevitably then, the process of influence on the development of criteria is a reciprocal one.

The Education of the Teacher

For the English, teacher education (see also chapter 1) is broken down into three major areas: the study of children, practice and curriculum, and a self-chosen individual exploration in some field of study. Emphasizing the continuity of a child's development, the program is multilevel, including experience on the level preceding the chosen area of concentration and on the level following. Inherent in this training is the acceptance of variation in children's development, an individual approach, and the assumption of responsibility for preparing the environment and for providing varied and multileveled material.

Child study is at the core of the integrated three-year course, which is offered as a unit, not as separate credit courses, and in which theory and practice are interwoven. In each of the three years the student has a block of practice. The Hadow Report had pointed out that child study was the basis of good teacher education, that the best teacher would be one who had made a careful study of the physical and mental development of children. So much importance is given to child study that the student is encouraged to work with babies in private homes, in institutional settings, etc., either prior to entrance into college or at some point along the way.

The area of concentration stresses the students' individual exploration and personal development, and this emphasis becomes a significant part of their own experiences as students, highlighting as it must the lecturer's relation to them and expectation from them. The students are treated as individuals, develop individual projects, and learn in their own way how to appreciate individual work and the depth to which this can develop. It is hoped that they apply this understanding to their teaching of children.

In her final teaching practice (approximately five weeks), a student takes over an infant school class and is expected to function independently with responsibility for all aspects of the class, including the preparation of varied material that can be used on many levels. The student can even change things about—physical arrangement, content, method. The class teacher accepts this independent role but permits the student teacher to call on her for help if needed. (For continuity the class teacher also maintains daily contact with her children.) The headmistress, as always, plays a strong supportive role, and college supervision of the student teacher is close—twice a week, and often more—since the student can be supervised by subject tutors as well as education tutors.

This close supervision may be diluted, at least temporarily, by the current expansion of teachers' colleges. But various ways of keeping this supervision a real and vital part of the training are being explored, such as the Plowden recommendations for increased use of the cooperating teacher and headmistress. Expanded use of the practice school's teaching force to train teachers is logical. After all, it was the pioneer experiments in the infant schools that were turned to originally by those in the training colleges who were convinced that this kind of education best maintained a child's drive to learn. And even though methods, theories, and aims of informal education can be studied in teacher colleges, it is still recognized that the young teacher is lucky to work under a head in whose school "informal" has real meaning, in an atmosphere of a successful model. If the young teacher does not get this experience in her practice, it is hoped that she will be lucky enough to get it in her first year of teaching.

The first year of teaching is one of probation, in which the young teacher works under careful supervision, and is assessed very seriously at least twice by the LEAs. The latter also receive reports from the school heads, which have been shared with and signed by the probationer. While there exists a strong obligation to make that year successful, and sometimes an extended probation in a more sympathetic situation is recommended, not all young teachers pass their probation to receive final qualification.

The Institutes

The twenty Institutes of Education attached to the universities act as "area organizations" coordinating facilities. This responsibility is delegated by the Department of Education and Science. The Institutes are responsible with the colleges for the system of external assessment and examination—an evaluation of candidate teachers by those outside the college—which insures interpenetration of viewpoint and aims. The Department of Education and Science now qualifies teachers for their first teaching post only after recommendation by the Institutes. The Department also confers final qualification at the end of the probationary year.

Some colleges were early pioneers, exploring the implications of the ideas of informal education for teacher education, but the idea is no longer limited to any one college.[2] Naturally there are variations in colleges and, more seriously, in supervisors, but the programs of each college are discussed in consultation with its Institute. The views of the Department of Education and Science are taken into account and have influence on the college programs. But each Institute, working with a college in its area, has the last word on how that college program develops. Thus, the differences in emphasis and even in nuance and philosophy in the Institutes and in the colleges are maintained, if for nothing else, as encouragement to variation and experimentation. These variations and the variations in school practice met by student teachers in their assignments to schools are a constant inducement to reexamination.

At the Institutes of Education, prospective teacher trainers and prospective heads take advanced courses. Such courses are not meant to constitute steps in a continuous, uninterrupted sequence proceeding from the initial education of the teacher; they are taken by teachers after they have taught awhile. It is usually after at least five years that mature teachers (or heads) can be released by their LEAs and given grants, after admission, for courses leading to advanced diplomas in child development, etc. Those who will educate teachers are themselves inducted into deeper understanding of their field (child development) but they also concern themselves with the question of how "informal" teaching can be conveyed. In fact, the difficulties involved in conveying informal education were under

---

[2] Gardner in *Education Under Eight* mentions the Froebel Institute, the Rachel McMillan College, the Mather Training College in Manchester, and the Moray House College in Edinburgh as early leaders in training for informal education.

continuous discussion in all teacher education circles while I was in England. It was felt that the "formality" of secondary education and its effects on the minds of the entrants to teachers' colleges were a major source of these difficulties. As Susan Isaacs had observed, commenting on these entrants, "Nor have they any ability to think or observe independently. Their life has so far been dominated by a narrow series of examinations." [3] At the Institutes, the question was asked: Can informal, or activity, or individual methods be conveyed to students who, coming out of the formal education of the grammar school, are immersed in the passive formality of a lecture room? The laboratory approach of the main course, in which individual exploration and an individual response were expected from the student, was part of the attempt to answer this question.

Grappling with the problem in an earlier period, Gardner described experiences in a play center that, in addition to providing teaching practice, could help student teachers gain a better understanding of informal education. These experiences with mixed-age and large groups were experiences in "bending" environmental circumstance. Gardner considered these a very necessary part of teacher training.

> The experience of ages given in school practice is necessarily very limited, and it is in Play Centre that a Senior teacher can get first-hand experience of the behaviour of little children (which is so necessary for a real understanding of older ones), and a Junior teacher can realize clearly the later stages to which her children are developing. . . .
>
> The students' attitude to discipline is often greatly helped by Play Centre experience. They become leaders rather than authorities, and we often find that after a period of leadership in a Play Centre gang, or of organizing a Play Centre department, the student has developed tremendously in her power of inspiring children in their classroom activities. She has learnt not to be afraid of having children moving about, employed on various constructive activities, instead of sitting quietly, all occupied in in one way. . . .
>
> We have found very often such instances of development in the power to handle large numbers of children. . . .
>
> Another quality which seems to be developed is that of tackling difficulties with enterprise, instead of acquiescing in bad conditions. Students who have painted and distempered play rooms and furniture, and extracted from the changing conditions through which Play Centre has passed all possible opportunities for the children's advantage, do not submit willingly to school conditions which tell them it is impossible to carry out creative work.[4]

[3] Susan Isaacs, in her introduction to D. E. M. Gardner's *The Children's Play Centre*, p. xii.
[4] Gardner, *The Children's Play Centre*, pp. 127, 128, 129.

Inservice Courses

In the general revision of all primary education towards "informality," much of the needed education and reeducation of teachers has been and continues to be conducted outside the colleges. Heads who were ready to experiment wanted far more reeducation than could be serviced by the colleges. They came to depend for their professional growth on the many inservice courses offered, some of them organized directly by the inspectors. Certainly the HMIs and local inspectorate conducted inservice training all the time, just by their advice and by sharing the good programs they had seen. But regular inservice courses were given by the LEAs, by the Department of Education, by the Nursery Association, by the Froebel Institute, by the Institutes of Education and teachers' colleges, and more recently, by the Nuffield Foundation. These courses were always oversubscribed even though no increment was given for attendance. Even educational magazines and unions (National Union of Teachers) ran courses.

Whenever the Department of Education or any of the other educational agencies felt methods had changed, courses were given to assist in retraining, and schools in trouble were aided financially in order to get teachers or even the headmistress released to participate. Every newspaper carried accounts of courses offered by the LEAs. Moreover, the education authorities supported the spread of particular ideas by publishing accounts of these ideas, by offering courses and releasing teachers and heads to attend the courses, by setting up or helping to set up trial situations. Thus a great many Nuffield Math and Science experimental groups were set up in the schools, even though the Nuffield Foundation existed outside the official structure. In almost every school, the headmistress spoke of conferences, special weekend courses, special leaves granted to teachers to take advanced courses at the Institutes of Education. She frequently referred to a teacher out for a special course, a teacher on leave for special training, or an extra, mature teacher working in the school as part of a retraining course. Some LEAs owned old mansions set very pleasantly in the country where they kept weekend or longer courses in constant session. All of this had official sanction. In addition, the Nuffield Foundation ran week-long or weekend residential courses at Teachers Centres or residence halls of colleges all over the country, demonstrating and giving teachers experience in their approach to science and math by involving teachers in working with the materials as would children. The Teachers Centres served to bring together learning materials, publications, and reports of current research. They were often laboratories, giving teachers a chance to become directly acquainted with learning materials, immersing them, workshop fashion, in direct trials of new methods.

The Bristol Teachers Centre, for example, staffed with personnel from the Nuffield Junior Science and Mathematics Project, consisted of several rooms fitted out as environmental workshops for exploration of almost anything.[5] Teachers came in groups on certain afternoons, with 20 sessions planned for each teacher. The plan was to eventually include *all* the teachers in the Bristol primary schools.

The Plowden Report has much to say about inservice courses, but even more interesting is the effect of the Report itself in stimulating study prior to and since publication. Working groups assigned to study the Report have been set up by many LEAs as well as by teachers' colleges. Studies initiated for the Report and recommended by it to continue have been continued. Other studies recommended by the Report are underway.

Thus, variety—experiment, model situations, trial situations—seemed to be built into the process. The 1964 London County Council Report to the Central Advisory Committee on Education described two trial model schools built for the study and evaluation of many new ideas in education. An HMSO publication describes one of these, the Eveline Lowe School, spreading further the study of the new organization.[6]

Any new ideas gained by the head through attendance at institutes or courses were very easily spread to the teachers in her school. The spread followed from the very nature of her function in the school. She was herself always sharing, and teaching teachers by the example of her own teaching. And the open school, where teachers could be influenced by contact both with other teachers and the head, and could see what took place beyond their own classroom, fostered this sharing and this dissemination through example. The Plowden Report, describing the prevalence of such training, strongly recommended that heads continue to teach: "The fact that the head continues to teach raises the whole status of teaching." [7]

The Inspectorate

The participation of the inspectorate in the careful processing of applicants for headships has already been described (p. 45). The inspectorate also functioned as one of the institutionalized safeguards around the practice of freedom. But perhaps more important than either role, the inspectorate helped maintain, *after* employment of the head, the *quality* of the initial selection. This relationship accounts for at least some of

---

[5] When I left England in 1966, 45 such Centres had been set up by the Nuffield Foundation specifically to support the Nuffield work. Teachers Centres have proliferated since the Plowden Report. A recent report estimated that there are now some 280 (Antonia Trauttmansdorff, *The Times Educational Supplement,* London, July 4, 1969).

[6] *Eveline Lowe Primary School,* London, HMSO, 1967.

[7] Plowden, p. 332.

the heads' astonishing performance and for the widespread acceptance of the *idea* behind this performance.

In this role, inspectors helped the continuing growth of concept. They made sure that communication remained open so that information and ideas could circulate. They aimed their efforts at maintaining a receptive atmosphere. They made suggestions by releasing teachers for courses, visits, and conferences, and teachers were persuaded. By sharing all the good examples they saw, they stimulated a constant process of new implementations of the common idea. In short, they were very much part of the mechanism for spreading the idea of informal education and a significant force creating similarities within the freedom of practice.

The inspectorate had the same professional background as the heads and the college teacher trainers, but they had the additional perspective of their varied work experiences. Prior to appointment, they may have been heads and then lecturers at colleges.[8] Whatever the case there was movement back-and-forth in these assignments. Their influence seemed incomparable. They encouraged the work of the headmistress, supporting experiments to further clarify and implement the basic idea. They fostered the trying-out of interesting variations of the idea, carrying news of all this work in their reports and in conversations with heads. The experiments themselves served as models which inspectors then suggested to others for visits and observation.

In this setting, which allowed heads freedom of action and developed an encouraging but noninterfering relationship, experiments had time to achieve depth. Isolated experiments of heads, developed within this freedom, became models for the spread of a concept that molded all infant education. Moreover, news transmitted by the inspectors in their unstructured manner could be accepted as suggestion, not prescription, and tried out with new variations and further experimentation. The Plowden Committee described this process:

> Advances in education or practice are often surprisingly local and often owe much to local inspectors and advisers. They can be made widely known by H.M. Inspectors.[9]

As an institutional safeguard within freedom, the inspectorial function more and more restricted itself to a suggesting, advising, persuading role, even when inspectors had doubts (as certainly was sometimes the case in the early pioneering days). If the provision for good living clearly existed and the life of the school was rich, inspection served not to

---

[8] D. E. M. Gardner, once a local inspector or Supervisor of Schools, is an example of this shared background. E. R. Wastnedge, after heading the Nuffield Junior Science Project, went on to become an HMI.
[9] Plowden, p. 335.

produce a narrower, restricted, defined usage, but to encourage ingenuity and variation towards maximal development.

Public discussion by teachers associations and by HMIs more than ever favors interpretation of the inspectorial role as adviser, suggestor, disseminator. The principle of inspection (derived in the 19th century from the need to supervise the expenditure of public money) has not, however, been discarded. Thus, the Plowden Report says:

> Assessment of a school is a necessary preamble to giving relevant advice. . . . Very occasionally children and the public still need to be protected. . . . Yet we welcome the growing stress on the role of adviser rather than of inspector. . . . The more informal the schools become in their organisation and relationships, the more informal ought to be the routines of inspection.[10]

Reports and Literature

A series of remarkable government reports at the turn of the century helped set the direction for the development of English infant schools. The reports had a style and a method that are, perhaps, the very essence of the spread of a common entity within freedom. They became the pivotal points of the infant school's evolving unity of concept. Used at the time of their issuance to buttress experimental action, they are still studied in the teachers' colleges. They are studied not as prescriptions but as suggestive *illustrations* derived *from* the schools, and they reflect the interaction of stimulation between the practice and such reports of practice. They have been the texts, not to be separated from the major educational literature, for the study of educational practice. Their unique role goes far beyond legislative acts or administrative rulings. All succeeding literature from the Ministry (now the Department of Education and Science) reflected this evolving unity of concept and served, in turn, as the instrument of further unity.

Thus, case studies were published describing experiments of practice in particular schools without trying to generalize or to pronounce absolutes. Each case was allowed to stand on its own and the generalizing and application were made independently. New reports arose from these independent and various applications.

I had thought of my observations in the schools as discoveries, and that I as an outsider had noticed things taken for granted or overlooked by the English, only to find, when I started delving into the literature, *all* my discoveries in the Hadow Report and in other reports and government publications (though *not* with the same emphasis I had given them). The

10 *Ibid.,* p. 335.

reports reflected very specific and concrete knowledge of the schools. They summarized the current situations and described the best of what they had seen. For example, by reporting the best, the Hadow Report influenced the spread of the best into other schools. It urged the acceptance of variation of level. It suggested that the limitations imposed by buildings could be broken down. Speaking for individual work, it pointed out that whole-class teaching organization was no longer appropriate.

> The primary school should not . . . be regarded merely as a preparatory department for the subsequent stage, and the courses should be planned and conditioned, not mainly by the supposed requirements of the secondary stage, nor by the exigencies of an examination at the age of eleven, but by the needs of the child at that particular phase in his physical and mental development.[11]

Along with summaries from Hadow, this handbook reports:

> In many schools, the hall, the corridors and other spaces outside the class-room are used almost as fully as the rooms or playground and garden, and almost everywhere in the building children may be seen hard at work at their different employments.[12]

The same handbook suggests that materials should be available throughout the day. It reports family grouping in some schools. The head as teacher and leader is discussed in just the way I had understood from my observation. Such handbooks had been published from 1905 on and represented a distillation of the inspectorate's experience in the schools.

The Ministry published illustrative examples supporting ideas that came from schools not in expectation of their being copied in detail but— as elsewhere—in the hopes that they would stimulate specific concrete solutions and thinking. The pamphlets it published describing new ideas from the schools were, in effect, a distillation from the many, many good ways observed, and each pamphlet was prefaced by an account of a child's way of learning.[13] A permissive atmosphere was created for experiments that would further break through the old classroom structure. Similarly, the Nuffield Junior Science Project *Teacher's Guide 2* continued the tradition of publishing, without generalizing, case histories and specific examples from the teacher's work in the classroom.

On the adult level, this approach, stressing experiment, was consistent with the methods of English infant education. Just as a child is allowed to ask his own questions, so an adult, presented with a case history

---

[11] Hadow, as quoted in *Primary Education*, p. 6.
[12] *Primary Education*, p. 45.
[13] *Science in the Primary Schools, Mathematics in Primary Schools, Slow Learners at School.*

of another teacher's work, can ask *his* own questions, select what is pertinent, and decide whether or not to apply it.

Underlying all inspectorate reports, drawing from them and then adding to them in new statements, are the Parliamentary Committee reports. These reports collect examples of current practice as a base for their conclusions and spread descriptions of the best of these as widely as possible. Thirty years or more may come between reports of a Parliamentary Committee (as the Hadow Report, 1933, is the report on primary education directly prior to the Plowden Report of 1967), but the committee, when it has reported, has really drawn on the experience of the whole current scene, from schools, training colleges, the university Institutes of Education, HMIs and LEAs to doctors, psychologists, teachers, heads, and parents. An examination of the list of those giving testimony to the Plowden Committee reveals this widespread involvement. A Parliamentary Committee report thus embodies the most serious thought and aims of each period and serves as a guide for their dissemination. The descriptions of practice in the report are, in effect, its recommendations, and they influence, guide, and stimulate change for a long time to come. When the changes themselves, as well as societal change and the new knowledge, suggest new accommodations, or when the logic of implementation has resulted in new forms that no longer need the accommodation, it is the time very often for a new report.

In England, there has been only minimal legislative prescription of practice. As a consequence, the reports have a dimension and a significance for English education that cannot be weighed in terms of enacted legislation or administrative ruling. Their influence is as synthesizer and collector of the best existing practice in the schools, and such reporting constitutes recommendation, creating the permissive frame for further extension of exploration. In addition, as mentioned, the preparation for the report is itself a stimulating process, helpful in perfecting the method, and not merely a process of passive collection.

Thus even during its preparation the Plowden Report informed heads about more successful ways of doing what they wanted to do, which they then tried out. Based on three years of study, on research reports especially prepared for it, the Plowden Report stimulated new syntheses by stimulating study, stimulating research, and stimulating new experiments among groups and individuals preparing statements of testimony for the Committee.[14] Moreover, just as the Hadow Report is still studied and restudied in teachers' colleges, the Plowden Report has come under examination, eliciting arguments and defense, with a new Education Act the

14 Michael Young and Patrick McGeeney, *Learning Begins at Home*. This study, sponsored by the Institute of Community Studies, is illustration of this.

likely result. The Report will be text and source and touchstone for years. Even without legislative implementation it is the inspiration for further surveys and studies suggested in the Report, which are meant to prepare for the implementation of the recommendations. Some of these—on home and school, on the NNEB, on teacher education—are completed or in preparation. The Report has stimulated the Schools Council to prepare curriculum bulletins that can serve as suggestion for further experimentation. LEAs are preparing reorganization plans for changed entry ages. Since the Report's publication the decision on age of transfer has largely been left to LEAs, and age of transfer is no longer the same in every area.

Furthermore, the Report has already had an effect because so much of it requires neither legislation nor funding. Within the freedom for experimentation in English schools, much can be done if the head is convinced, and the Plowden Report convinced many heads to move towards greater inclusion of parents and towards a change of method in junior schools. Such changes need support, and the Plowden Committee addressed itself to this point by involving the parents and the public, not merely the profession. Thus, programs that followed on radio, ITV (Independent Television), and BBC (British Broadcasting Corporation), and the discussion in newspapers and magazines, have drawn *all* of English society, parents as well as professionals, into a vast discussion on the Plowden recommendations, on the Plowden description of how children learn. The BBC's followup on the Plowden Report is most illustrative. It prepared short filmed case histories of good practice, of new methods, and of how children learn. At the time of this writing, the BBC had completed ten on "Discovery and Experience," six on "The Mother Tongue," and six (for parents) on child development, entitled "The Springs of Learning"; another ten programs on the primary schools were being prepared and LEAs and colleges of education had ordered 250 prints.[15]

It was not only in official reports that experiences were collected. Studies sponsored by the Institutes also gathered and synthesized and evaluated the experiences of the schools and described the ideas on which these experiences were based. Gardner, for instance, from her position as head of the Child Development Department, Institute of Education, University of London, distilled the good practices observed by her and described to her, synthesized the common analysis on child development, presenting comparative evidence on results of practice, and wrote books that were both theoretical and practical, sharing all her experiences, as well as the work and experience of the many heads she knew. Her research on results bulwarked the defense of experimentation and gave needed encouragement to further experimentation.

[15] Information from Eileen Molony, producer, October 1968.

The heads also told their own story as shapers and inheritors of their history. Freedom had resulted in experiments, and the teachers and heads wrote of them, contributing to the collection of experiences from which others were free to select. *Play in the Infant School* by E. R. Boyce was one such early and influential sharing of a very fully developed experiment. (This description of East End London children, in fact, brings to mind many analogies with American ghetto children. In the free atmosphere of the school, children were encouraged in their spontaneous talk about everyday life at home and on the street, and much of the book is about communication.) The descriptions of good practice accumulated because many heads, actively participating in the process of dissemination, shared their experiments.[16] The process was two-way. The heads acted and were acted on. Experience collected from schools and heads was given back in the reports and in the literature disseminated to the heads. Reported experiences were tried, extended, reworked into new variations, and then tested again. It is no wonder that the similarities of practice are so great, even without prescription.

In America, as the English pointed out, research was brought to the teacher from the university. In England, so the analysis went, teachers who wanted to make things better did so, and then the researchers evaluated the effort. It was not quite like that, but close enough. It was rather, as I've described, a reciprocal influence, and teachers were much influenced by their reading and by the research reported in their reading. A Plowden statement of how the heads influence and are influenced, of how the mechanics of dissemination work, makes a similar point:

> A deliberate change in the curriculum has been brought about not by the issue of programmes by states or universities as is often done in the U.S.A., but by pioneer work by teachers, clarified and focused by advisory services to teachers, and diffused on a national scale by in-service training in which self help has played a major and essential part.[17]

And at another point, the Report again gives the credit for change to the teacher: "The willingness of teachers to experiment, to innovate and to change has been one of the mainsprings of progress in the primary schools." [18]

THE HISTORY

The reciprocal relationship between heads, the history of the idea, and the organizational and functional entity more than anything gave the in-

[16] E.g., Mellor, Marshall, Gordon, Sturmey, Ridgway, Daniel, and more recently and post-Plowden, Brown, Precious.
[17] Plowden, p. 236.
[18] *Ibid.*, p. 423.

fant school development its peculiar continuity. One did not act on the other without being acted on in turn. The history was both inherited and shaped by the heads; it was cumulative rather than a response to the urgency of the moment. The history, in fact, dates back to the founding of the first infant school by Robert Owen [19] in the early part of the 19th century, and to Margaret McMillan's work, particularly her advocacy of open-air-type schools and compulsory medical inspection, and her work with young children in the slums of Deptford and Bradford that culminated in her successful campaign, waged in 1917, for permissive legislation and state grants for nursery education.

Thus, even though nursery schools were not actually a part of state education until the Education Act of 1918, their influence on the infant school had a long history and, again, the history was reciprocal. In this history, moreover, the development of both the nursery school and the infant school is inextricably linked, even up to the present time in the Plowden Report. Thus the Hadow Report suggested that the nursery school provide a center in which problems connected with the general development and nurture of children could be investigated. It suggested that the nursery school be supported as a model for possible applications in the infant school.

> We hope that the valuable ideas in the nursery school will be increasingly realised within the existing infant school system. Meanwhile it seems highly desirable that the nursery school should be developed separately and be left free to perfect its methods and to fulfill its special purpose. The infant school has admittedly suffered in the past from bookish and academic traditions; the nursery school is one means of counteracting these influences by extending upwards its own special tradition of health, of reasonable freedom and of joyous spontaneous pursuits. It is true that this new spirit which is found in the best nursery schools is also to be found in its genuine form in the very many infant schools. Nevertheless at the present stage in the development of infant education the nursery school has a value of its own as an educational instrument.[20]

Gardner, in her succinct presentation of the history of the nursery and infant schools, notes that Owen, setting up the first infant school in 1816, wanted children out of doors as much as possible, that he wanted learning to come as a response to curiosity, that he wanted dancing and singing. Even though his school was called "Infant School," it anticipated the present nursery school movement by 100 years. Moreover, both Owen and Margaret McMillan held in common the concept of a child developing in a natural way in a garden. Faced with the child labor of the early Industrial Revolution, Owen, one of the all-around men of that period—

---

[19] See Harold Silver (ed.), *Robert Owen on Education* (Cambridge, England: Cambridge University Press, 1969).
[20] Hadow, p. 108.

industrialist, philanthropist, economist, and socialist—wanted to preserve childhood for the children, at least until age 8.

In any case, 19th century educators and reformers were always concerned with two-, three-, four-, and five-year-old children. Children of that age *were* in school, for one thing, and their presence in the infant school population produced an inevitable interlocking of educational ideas from the nursery and infant school level. In 1870, the date of English statutory compulsory education, the age for schooling was set at 5, but poor children of 2 to 7, who *were* already in the infant schools, were allowed to remain if the schools could accommodate them. As life at home and in the streets made school an increasingly practical necessity—for children as well as their working mothers—it was seen that such accommodation could not be left to chance. By 1888, government reports were urging that ample accommodation be encouraged for infants under 5. Between 1870 and 1900, 45 percent of the under-5 population was in school, and attention began to focus on what was really happening in the schools. It was a time that bred reformers and, because concern for conditions in the schools was part of the general social concern for a better society, some of these reformers worked in the schools.[21]

During this time, too, the followers of Froebel,[22] active in England since approximately 1854, began to experiment with free kindergartens— the first founded in Manchester by the philanthropist, Sir William Mather, in 1873.[23] In 1874, the London School Board invited the Froebelians to lecture to infant school teachers. They set themselves up as an examining board in 1876, and in 1888 were accepted as examiners by the Board, creating for the first time a body of people who could give serious and knowledgeable attention to the problems of educating young children.

The infant schools, in the meantime, were no longer the Robert Owen schools. They had become full and bursting, responding to their charges with a "minding" kind of care and with a class organization much more reminiscent of the monitorial system of Joseph Lancaster and Andrew Bell than of Robert Owen.[24] "Payment by results"—the allocation of funds according to success with a specific prescribed attainment set for entry at

---

[21] Albert Fried and Richard Elman (eds.), *Charles Booth's London* (New York: Pantheon Books, 1968).

[22] See Friedrich Froebel, *A Selection from His Writings* by Irene M. Lilley (Cambridge, England: Cambridge University Press, 1967), and Evelyn Lawrence, *Froebel and English Education*.

[23] Gardner, *Education Under Eight*, p. 7.

[24] Such organizations were adaptations within the schools of the Industrial Revolution's extension of the division of labor. Educational trends in England towards nonconformism and towards utilitarianism were also reflected in these developments. See Barnard, H. C., *A History of English Education* (London: University of London Press, 1961), p. 54, and also D. Salmon (ed.), *Lancaster's Improvements and Bell's Experiment* (1932).

the six-year-old level—made this situation even worse (1862). This commercial arrangement did not extend downward below the six-year-olds but nevertheless, while it lasted, it held the infant schools in a straitjacket by its demands. The history of this period, in fact, describes an examination-oriented, prescribed, and narrow curriculum, though modifications were made as early as the 1870s.[25] The system was abandoned in 1897, but the aura of it remained for a long time. Legal release was a necessary prior condition for change, but *actual* change was slower. Abandonment of "payment by results" did not, of course, mean abandonment of accountability. Accountability remained through the funneling of questions to a board of managers and in turn to and through the inspectorate. Changes in philosophy, in concept of standard, in desired result, gave new meaning both to responsibility and to the role of the inspectorate. Responsibility remained but it was responsibility to a new standard, a new evaluation of result. Released from "payment by results," the infant school was freed to develop.

A series of government reports, referred to earlier in this chapter, began to guide infant schools towards new developments. The code of 1902, repeating what had been urged in an 1893 circular from the HMI, included a statement on children's needs for spontaneous activity.[26] The school's goal was stated as support for the harmonious and complete development of the whole of a child's growth.

In 1905, a report of the Committee of Inspectors had the effect of stemming the direct public interest in the under-5s in infant school even while it defined the necessities of life for under-5s as later organized in the nursery school. It urged that under-5s be excluded from infant school because routine activity was mind dulling and restriction of movement was prejudicial to health.

If a *better* school situation could have immediately been put in place of the damaging one, the critique would have accomplished its purpose. If, immediately, nursery schools could have been set up to provide for all the three- to five-year-olds in a better way, if immediately, infant schools had been revised, the worthy motives of the Committee in protection of the children would have been served. In fact, however, the number of three-to-five-year-olds for whom the state assumed responsibility declined. From the 45 percent of the three- to five-year-old population in the schools in 1900, by 1910 the population of three- to five-year-olds in the schools went down to 22+ percent and in 1930 to 13+ percent. The Hadow Report lists 13 percent in 1932.

A reconsideration of this state of affairs in 1907—when the medical inspectors found so many physical defects in the five-year-olds—helped

---

[25] Barnard, *History of English Education*, p. 171.
[26] Gardner, *Education Under Eight*, p. 8.

define the needs of the under-5s (no rigid timetable, stimulating experiences, no formal instruction).[27]

None of these developments stemmed the tide of under-5s leaving the infant school, however. The needs of only a small number of them began to be met *outside* the infant schools by the nursery schools, and when the 1907 and 1908 reports recommended nursery schools, the way was paved for acceptance of the 1914 McMillan experiments.

Through Margaret McMillan's efforts the "umbrella of the State" was again spread. The Education Act of 1918 included permissive legislation covering education for under-5s, and the financial support, though limited, made possible the establishment of the excellent model nursery schools described and supported by the Hadow Report. These did provide in a better way for three-to-five-year-olds—a few of them—but the economic difficulties of the post-World War I period limited their spread. The next advance had to wait until 1933. The Hadow Report, realizing that just getting children out of infant school was not a sufficient answer, urged the LEAs, even though they were not so obliged, to consider supporting nursery provision if it seemed needed.

The nursery schools had been set up first with the idea of serving about 40 children in each school and then with the idea that they could properly be increased to from 150 to 200 children. The Hadow Report thought that 60 to 80 children would be ideal, and nursery school was discussed in the same terms as it had been in the Report of 1893 as "the recognition of the child's spontaneous activity" and "the harmonious and complete development of the whole of the child's faculties." [28]

In the period of great economic stress that directly preceded World War II, the building of new nursery schools was again greatly reduced. Nevertheless, Gardner described beautiful prewar nursery schools for children from 2 to 7 in Bradford and other places in England and in Wales that were triumphs of the nursery idea rather than of the stodgy infant schools of the 1905 Inspectorate's Report.[29] Thus, in addition to defining the conditions of under-5 education, the critique of 1905 had led to a revision of the infant school which gave it continuity with the kind of education that had been defined as needed for under-5s.

Heads of infant schools observed children in the freer situations and drew conclusions about necessary change.[30] When they were convinced about the truth of a new practice, they bent circumstance to fit convictions. Inspectors, reporting pioneer experiments, might be startled, but they confirmed the heads in their freedom as defined by the 1918 Code.

[27] *Ibid.*, p. 8.
[28] *Ibid.*, p. 8.
[29] *Ibid.*, p. 12.
[30] Jesse Mackinder, *Individual Work in Infant Schools.*

Heads *acted*, influenced by their observations, their concern, the reports, and, of course, by all the current intellectual ideas that they could use to bolster their convictions.

In this way and even in the post-World War I period of economic stress, the private and free Froebelian kindergartens, the nursery schools, the 2–7 schools described by Gardner, and the influence of the examples and discussions summarized in committee and inspectorate reports, had resulted and were resulting in experimentation by more and more heads in revision of the infant school.

Revisions of many sorts—all necessarily adaptations to the physical circumstance of size of class—were motivated by observations of the patterns of learning, and by observation of the importance of concrete material for a child's learning. It is in this context that "overflow" into all the spaces of the school was an early revision.

Even before Susan Isaacs had given a fuller rationale for the heads' revisions, Montessori [31] ideas had affected these and had led heads to acceptance of the principle of individual pace and the responsibility for organizing the environment to allow this individual pace. Individual and group methods were applied at *least* to reading, writing, and number— even within the still formal structures in which a child's purposes were largely unrecognized. Project methods deriving from Dewey led to still wider revisions beyond the individualizing of skills; they led to integration of subject areas through activity. But in Isaacs's analysis the realities of ordinary life were preferred to the "culture epoch" approach to content. Observation had led to a recognition that learning was at a peak when a child pursued it to further his own purposes. Many pioneers, especially after Susan Isaacs, were sure that "the highest peaks of the child's thought and learning were found in the situation of spontaneous and purposeful play." [32] Project method, using the interests of the learner but unifying a whole group, was modified so that it offered many "starting points," with a stress first on a child's "choosing" and finally on his "own question." Individual work arising from individual interests remained the English focus.

Gardner summarizes the critique of the project method and its modifications:

> Good teachers . . . were quick to realise that one main interest or purpose will not satisfy all the children . . . they themselves were aware that they were playing too dominant a role in order to keep all the children working with the same end in view, and that the real interests of certain

[31] See Maria Montessori, *The Absorbent Mind* and *Spontaneous Activity in Education.* In the U.S., Montessori ideas were reintroduced by Nancy Rambusch, *Learning How to Learn.*
[32] Gardner and Cass, *Role of the Teacher,* p. 6.

children were either different from the beginning or became so after a much shorter period than the teacher was trying to maintain . . . what the children really wanted to do was generally equally rich in educational possibility if fostered and encouraged intelligently.[33]

Susan Isaacs's work [34] as chairman (1933–43) of the first Research Department of Child Development at the Institute of Education, University of London, deserves special mention in this history. The Hadow Report and her famous books (*Intellectual Growth in Young Children, Social Development in Young Children, The Children We Teach*) were almost simultaneous in publication and exerted enormous influence. A whole generation of advanced and mature students—future heads—studied with her the meshed emotional, social, and intellectual development of a child. She was, of course, in the English tradition of concern for betterment. In her youth a member of the University Socialist Federation, a lecturer to the London Workers' Education Association, she was as a teacher a unique combination of scholarship and practicality, expressing both a drive for the deepest possible understanding and a concern to help make things better.

Finally, wartime evacuation, involving teachers in caring for children in a very total way, made vivid for them the significance of "home" to a child. Teachers could understand with more sympathy both the parents' burdens and impatience, and how within any or all of their impatience they gave tremendous and necessary support to their children. Almost every head I met had, as a young teacher, or as a young girl prior to training, lived with children in evacuation conditions. Their understanding of this evacuation experience was deepened by descriptions and analysis in the writings of Anna Freud and Dorothy Burlingham.[35] Susan Isaacs's memorandum on experiential deprivations in institutions contrasted the latter with the complex richness of a child's experience in his home and street and neighborhood.[36] The teachers' sympathetic understanding of the parents' role and of home life was broadened so that they were more willing to include parents closely in the working of the school and to incorporate into school life aspects of home experience. Thus, their conception of what school life could and should be, and of the inextricable wholeness of a child's life and his responses, was extended, as was their conception of their own role.

It is this history, which preceded the 1944 Act on which today's English informal education rests, that is still the base for all the campaigning, including the Plowden recommendations, to extend the nursery school

---

[33] *Ibid.*, p. 5.
[34] See D. E. M. Gardner, *Susan Isaacs: The First Biography.*
[35] See Bibliography.
[36] Susan Isaacs, "Children in Institutions," in *Childhood and After*, p. 232.

provision, and that will serve as base for the new Education Act now under preparation. In other words, this development—in the *state* schools— toward what I've described as the infant school entity, can be traced in a *continuous* line. At times the line's progression was slow and uneven. According to Gardner, for a period after the pioneers, teachers accepted change by imitating in a surface "fashion" way. Certainly some teachers had a conception limited to provision of environment, with little conception of a *changed* teacher's role implicit in the process of changing the learning environment. This, of course, is still sometimes true, that a structure is set, the outer shell provided, without the infusion of meaning and life that can only come from understanding. Nevertheless, it seems to have been rather clear in the work of the pioneers that the role of the teacher was not *just* providing but was "providing for, following up and stimulating, the interests and purposes of young children." [37] The teacher had to have "the art of organising and planning an environment suited to children and a deep understanding of the needs of the children as individuals." [38]

English educational history reveals adaptations, development—not breaks. The continuity of development in teaching method is described by Gardner.

> Every fresh development in Infant School education seems to require additions to the equipment of a good teacher, but never the discarding of the qualities that made a really good teacher of the older methods.[39]

Current practices are clearly a refinement, a development in a continuous line. Thus Gardner is able to say: "We have never reverted to purely class teaching again in the Infant Schools." [40] And she is able to confirm that the unity of concept underlying the wide dissemination of an entity such as I've described did not come about through a sudden revolution in 1944 and since, but rather through affirmation in 1944 of an idea already widely held:

> The progressive movement in Infant Schools was well on its way in London, for example, in 1930 when I first went into many schools through becoming an Infant Education lecturer. Indeed when I was at college— 1918–1921—pioneer schools using play under Froebel influence were in existence. Froebel-trained lecturers spread the gospel to the State Schools. People like J. P. Slight, local Inspector for Leeds, for example, exercised influence and when I went there in 1936 progressive Infant Schools were so many that I could put all my 64 first year students into one for a first

[37] Gardner and Cass, *Role of the Teacher*, p. 18.
[38] *Ibid.*, p. 2.
[39] *Ibid.*, p. 2.
[40] *Ibid.*, p. 3.

school practice. The reason Susan Isaacs' *Intellectual Growth* (1931) had so much influence was that it gave the 'Why's' to the progressive movement and led others to feel confidence in joining the pioneers who were well at work before this book appeared and so ready to see its tremendous significance for their work. The War (1939) caused a temporary setback, owing to children and teachers being moved about so much and even after the war it was some years before schools were rebuilt and populations stable and rehoused. . . . Progress was not uniform all over the country.[41]

In describing the process of disseminating the infant school idea then, one describes an active process, an evolving process. Its history, from the national vantage of inspectors' reports and Parliamentary Committees, is the dissemination of case histories culled from actual practice in state schools. It is a history, furthermore, of *early* release from prescribed curriculum and fixed standard, of early *official* support for experimentation. It is a history of rootedness in the common social concern with the conditions of the mass of people, of shared analysis of the development and learning of children. It is only in the context of this history that one can provide a proper answer to the question often asked, "Why England, not America?"

[41] Gardner, in a letter to the author, May 14, 1968, quoted with permission.

chapter 4

THE IDEA

Rationale
for Informal Education

The literature that synthesizes a description of the infant school entity, including the multiplicity of illustrations and case studies, the Hadow Report, the Plowden Report, and the Nuffield case histories, had as its touchstone a view of how children grow and learn. Each report put itself into the context of a common voice by presenting this view in its initial section—as rationale for practice. It was an analysis common to all and accounted for the infant school entity: the similarity within a nonprescriptive system. It underlay the *idea* of informal education.

The idea was indeed one of the conditions of informal education—even the key condition. As I came to comprehend this, the idea could no longer be dismissed as the "background of common premises" presupposed at the outset of this study. My observations had added facets that did not entirely fit my previous premises, and so the idea had to be found by dissection. Such dissection started with my observations, continued with gleanings from conversations with heads, and concluded with analysis of the literature that confirmed and sharpened my recall.

Central to the conversations was always a child: What does he need? What is he *interested* in? What is he *ready* for? What are his *purposes*? How does *he* follow them? What are *his questions*? What is he *playing*? These questions about children *seemed* to be uppermost in developing plans for the classroom, for plans were made not from the vantage point of a syllabus of demands which a child had to meet, but with relevance to children in the most immediate way. A plan fitted itself *to* a child. It was developed in response to the pace and internal pattern of his own growth and in support of his own purposes. It was developed through watching a child, studying him at his moments of deepest involvement in play.

Play was important to headmistresses. They often talked of curiosity. They seemed to trust curiosity as a motive force. They seemed to trust that the forces of a child's development had a forward propulsion—"how else would he adapt at all?" Their job was to keep this momentum going, to maintain it. But it was a *child* who learned and so he had to be *allowed* to do so. A free situation, activity, movement, a rich environment were just the implements, the ways of unimpeding a child's own propulsion. The prototype of a teacher as controller, or "giver-out," and a child as "taker-in" inevitably gave way to a different concept, still developing in England. With such an analysis as base, *teaching* gives way to *helping* learning. It is a difficult concept and its implications are still being explored and reached for in the real test of actual practice. The first part of the idea, however—the centrality of a child's development and school as a support for continuation of this development—is certainly accepted.

The idea had long roots, its present unique integration and character being an offshoot strand, woven from many such strands, of the main root of the history of education—from Montaigne, Rousseau, Owen, Pestalozzi, Froebel, Montessori, McMillan, Dewey. Rereading the English formulations of educational ideas and practice that were familiar to me in another way in the United States, I understood for the first time the controversies, the intellectual probing, the relationship of each part to the whole. Respect for play and spontaneous activity as a child's natural way of learning, respect for natural development, came from these early roots. From Montessori came the technique of individual work, of a child's own pace and progression, and the introduction into the classroom of more concrete materials to add to the already existent influence of the Froebelian "gifts." From Dewey came the emphasis on the experiencing of social relationships and community, on learning generated from a child's activities and his experiences. The English continued to stress individual work stemming from individual interests, but the sharing of communal functions and responsibilities in school was added to the accumulating implications of an educational method supportive of natural development.

SUSAN AND NATHAN ISAACS

Out of this background of eclecticism, too, grew the ideas of Susan Isaacs. Examining and questioning the research and researchers of her time—from Freud to Piaget—she searched for clarity. Her context of English educational history and thought and the realities of the developing English educational organization modified all ideas and practices, American or otherwise, as she absorbed them. With the way paved by a climate of opinion supporting education as implementing the natural development of children, her work found a receptive audience. She joined this conscious continuity of English development without resting her ideas solely and separately on her psychoanalytic insights, using the combined insights of past and current thinking, her self-awareness as teacher and human being and, most of all, her careful observation and study of children. From this study, Susan Isaacs produced solid evidence to bolster what had been largely a philosophic belief, and English ideas on education were thereby deepened. She gave an objective base, in the context of genetic psychology, to previous generalities on natural development, on the deep connections linking inner and outer reality, emotional and intellectual life.[1]

The connections between Susan Isaacs's developmental descriptions of children and actual school practice were still further spelled out in the writings of Nathan Isaacs. Isaacs developed the implications in his wife's work on intellectual development and reconciled these with Piaget's analyses of the development of the mental structures in a child. The slight differences between Susan Isaacs's and Piaget's analysis, probed in a mutually respectful exchange of letters, were made compatible. Nathan Isaacs accepted as corrective to previous estimates of developmental time Piaget's descriptions of the long process of constant accommodation and reaccommodation before the formation of logical relations. Susan Isaacs had considered Piaget's description an *inflexible* doctrine of stages in this time process. This she called a "pseudo-biological sequence, totally independent of experience."[2] Her own view was that stages were *broadly* descriptive of levels of development and sequence. It was not hard for Nathan Isaacs to reconcile these positions. And with this reconciliation, Nathan Isaacs demonstrated to English teachers the reinforcement to their own beliefs that could come from an understanding of Piaget.[3] His contribution is considered monumental.

[1] The arguments that linked inner and outer development were further strengthened by Ruth Griffiths's analysis of painting and intellectual development, *Imagination in Early Childhood.*

[2] Susan Isaacs, *Intellectual Growth in Young Children,* p. 67.

[3] The English emphasized the prime importance of Piaget's analysis of early assimilation and accommodation as well as his analysis of the development of a child's ideas of number, space, etc.

From the Froebel Institute, from the Nuffield Foundation, from other analyzers of informal education, have come writings which accept the formulations of the two Isaacs as core for the continuing development and extension of the definition and application of informal education. These formulations confirmed the conclusions of their own systematic observation of children, and made clear the continuity in the thinking of English informal educators on how children learn, as well as the consensus on the informal organization of the infant school.

The Plowden Report, absorbing all of this past, reaffirmed this common context of idea basic to English infant education.[4] A child, the Report affirmed, is active agent in his own learning, and the internal processes of mental structuring and restructuring contain their own self-perpetuating propulsion. The Plowden Report defined the school role in terms that follow this analysis: provision of environment to support a child's individual and unsegmentalized development; inclusion of the play life that is vital to a child's reconciliation of inner and outer reality and that is vital to his development of judgment and discrimination; allowance to each child for the time necessary for his own individual mental synthesizing.

The Plowden summary is only a summary. Presented in more full-bodied detail filtered through all these roots and the more recent contributions, the English idea based itself on the knowledge of the child's development gained from study, much of it a kind of "watching," a systematic observation of a child acting spontaneously in a natural situation. The attempt is to understand the meaning of each piece of a child's development in a total context. While all research was used, Susan Isaacs's critique of research methods was certainly accepted.

> Without such a background of the total responses of children to whole situations, partial studies of this or that response to limited experimental problems may be no more than sterile and misleading artifacts.[5]

> One could take point after point of those appearing on the various rating scales or developmental schedules, and show how far they are from being single trends which can be measured in themselves apart from specified total situations.[6]

Most important, about children under five years she noted, *"what a child does for one person under certain conditions is not a reliable index of what he may do for another person in another situation."* [7] (Italics in original) Elsewhere she continued:

[4] Plowden, pp. 187, 193–95.
[5] Susan Isaacs, *Social Development in Young Children*, p. 4.
[6] *Ibid.*, p. 8.
[7] *Ibid.*, p. 9.

For our own convenience in study, we may pick out now one, now another of the aspects of growth, but they are never separate in fact. Nor can we ever say that one dominates the rest. It is always the whole child who plays and laughs, who quarrels and loves, who thinks and asks questions, through all the hours of his day and all the years of his childhood.[8]

It is in this frame that the Plowden Report criticizes behaviorist learning theory and any analysis based on the theories of segmentalized learning.[9]

A *Child: Active, Unique, Whole*

The students of child development in England see each child as unique and active in all aspects of his individual development. No one of these aspects can be separated, they reason, because development rests within the whole that is a child. These three characterizations of a child— as active, individual, and whole—are focal to English analyses. It is only for purposes of definition that the characterizations, always intertwined in English discussion, are separated.

Recognition of a child's *active* thrust, described also as curiosity, is in the English view unavoidable, for "without some native drive towards active growth normality would not have been achieved at all." [10] It is this active growth, a child's active construction and reconstruction of his own development, that is described in Nathan Isaacs's explication of Piaget:

> Piaget's work as a whole has made plain all the vital education that goes on in the child quite independently of the set educational processes, and above all in his first few years, before those processes have even begun. Indeed, by far the most important portion of his intellectual growth is achieved by himself, through the direct working of the interchange cycle by which he actively learns to take in all the main features and the general make-up of the physical and social world around him.[11]

> This process of absorbing and organizing experiences round the activities that produce them Piaget calls *"assimilation."* He regards it as our most fundamental process of learning and growth, which indeed goes on for the rest of our lives. However, assimilation is always being modified by an accompanying process of *accommodation.* Many situations or objects resist the activity patterns the child tries on them, and in so doing impose some changes on these patterns themselves. Still others yield *new* results which go to enrich the range or scope of the patterns.[12]

This active thrust, this assimilative, accommodative process is always individual. A child is born a unique individual, and development is *in* this

8 Susan Isaacs, *The Children We Teach*, p. 80.
9 Plowden, p. 192.
10 Nathan Isaacs, *Piaget: Some Answers to Teachers' Questions*, p. 15.
11 Nathan Isaacs, *New Light on Children's Ideas of Number*, p. 35.
12 Nathan Isaacs, *The Growth of Understanding in the Young Child*, p. 9.

individual. His world of inner needs and meanings is personal, lived out in the human relationships into which he is born and with people whose world has been equally individually determined. He has particular, specific bits of experiences and particular, specific expectations, and it is these that he brings to his relationships—meeting people with differing experiences and expectations. His development is individual and uneven in pattern and pace and made even more individual by the personal route of his interests. Having made these observations, the English do not *strive for* or seek to *produce* individuality. They *recognize* it, and the individuality of learning—in process and in product—underlies all discussion of theory and practice in English education.

The active and individual process of assimilation-accommodation-reaccommodation occurs within a *child* who is a whole—uncompartmentalized, unsegmentalized—with his social, emotional, and intellectual development inextricably linked. The links are forged from the very nature of a child's existence in the world with others. The English description of these links gives additional meaning to the accommodative and reaccomodative process, to the restructuring and correction of the first learning. All familiar education components are reexamined in this context.

The wholeness, the inextricable links, long predate school. There can be no separation of inner needs and outer adaptations. A child is born into the human relationship and thereby immediately into adaptation with another who is separate.

> It is the child's first experience of instinctual frustration, or unsatisfied longing for food and love in the intervals between satisfaction, which provides the first stimulus to his appreciation of the external world. When he wants the breast and it is not there, he cries out for it and eventually it comes to him. When he wants warmth and comfort and sheltering arms, he can obtain these by his cries directed to those who will bring him what he wants. But some gap between desire and satisfaction there must inevitably be, and since it is persons who bring the child relief, he apprehends his dissatisfactions in personal terms.[13]

But while his world is personal, it is never separate.

> . . . his external world, as soon as knowledge of it begins to awaken, is understood very largely in terms of that with which he is already familiar —himself and his own feelings.[14]

His inner needs are the *force* for his outer adaptations, but they are *necessarily* exercised in a context that makes for adaptation and development. From the very beginning his unique development, both emotional and in-

[13] Susan Isaacs, *Social Development*, p. 288.
[14] *Ibid.*, p. 286.

tellectual, is affected by the reality of his environment and the reality of his relationships with the people in that environment.

> As with all mammalian young, the child's first relations are with his kind rather than directly with the physical world. . . . But whilst recognising this . . . one cannot shut one's eyes to the influence of direct contact with the physical world. The child makes a partial discovery of the limits which the physical world sets to his activities surely almost as early as he comes to know other human beings as persons.[15]

Reaccommodation: Fantasy and Play

The discrepancies between what children expect of the world and of people and what they actually meet in interaction with these are an impetus for the reaccommodation that is *also* one of expectancies. Susan Isaacs discusses the corrective to fantasy that children derive from real experience:

> . . . phantasy itself more and more takes up reality into its own tissue . . . there is a progressive penetration of feeling and phantasy by experience. . . .[16]

> What imaginative play does . . . is to create practical *situations*. . . .[17]

> Whilst it is certainly true that the *first* value which the physical world has for the child is as a canvas upon which to project his personal wishes and anxieties, and that his first form of interest in it is one of dramatic representation, yet, as I have already urged, this does not prevent him from getting direct actual experience of physical processes. Physical events become, in fact, the test and measure of reality. There is no wheedling or cajoling or bullying or deceiving *them*. Their answer is *yes* or *no*, and remains the same to-day as yesterday. It is surely they that wean the child from personal schemas, and give content to "objectivity." [18]

Ruth Griffiths similarly speaks of fantasy and its necessary role in intellectual development:

> Imagination is, in fact, the child's method not so much of avoiding the problems presented by environment, but of overcoming those difficulties in a piecemeal and indirect fashion, returning again and again in imagination to the problem, and gradually developing a socialized attitude which finally finds expression at the level of overt action and adapted behaviour.[19]

15 Susan Isaacs, *Intellectual Growth*, p. 79.
16 *Ibid.*, p. 107.
17 *Ibid.*, p. 99.
18 *Ibid.*, p. 80.
19 Griffiths, *Imagination in Early Childhood*, pp. 353, 354.

The importance of the external environment, of play, of a free situation in which a child *can use* the environment *and* play, all are implied in these analyses of reaccommodation, these analyses of how expectancies are corrected.

At no point was play conceived by these thinkers as an "extra," without bearing on intellectual development. Even in its important function of pleasure and release it was always related to learning. As Susan Isaacs stated:

> Play is the child's means of living, and of understanding life.[20]

> . . . it helps him to achieve inner balance and harmony through the active expression of his inner world of feelings and impulses, and of the people that dwell in his inner world.[21]

Play was related to reworkings:

> The child *re-creates* selectively those elements in past situations which can embody his emotional or intellectual need of the present. . . .[22]

Thus, though the first impetus to re-creation was the inner pressure of feeling and fantasy, the re-creation was made in an external world, with children using external things, being forced to adapt, and thus led to correcting themselves by the encounter. And sometimes the re-creation, which implied a remembering of past feeling, implied also an ability to see what cohered, what went with what, what future was implied in the past.

Peel sums this up, restating it in Piagetian terms:

> Play also has an important rôle in the intellectual growth of the child, being at once the cause and expression of changes from egocentric to objective judgments and of growth of language and of reversible action and judgment.[23]

Reaccommodation: Social Interchange and the Adult

It is not only a child's play but his relations to other people, even as he plays, that lead to corrections, reaccommodations, better adaptation to reality, and finally, learning. The intense egocentricity of a child, intellectually and emotionally, is corrected through companionship with children

---

[20] Susan Isaacs, *Childhood and After*, p. 66.
[21] *Ibid.*, p. 69.
[22] Susan Isaacs, *Intellectual Growth*, p. 104.
[23] E. A. Peel, *The Pupil's Thinking* (London: Oldbourne Book Co. Ltd., 1960), p. 61.

and interaction with their different purposes and points of view. From his companionship with other children he gains perspective about adults in his life, and can find allies against their pressures. Since social interchange, discussion, and differing points of view are essentials for this operation of the challenge of discrepancies, a *free* social situation is necessary. This free social interchange is "fed" best in a challenging atmosphere, rich in possible activities that can provide the "stuff" of discussion. The need for the free social interchange is expressed by Susan Isaacs:

> . . . if we deprive him of free speech with his fellows, we take away from him one of the most valuable means of intellectual and social growth.[24]

> It is not the mere presence of other children but active participation with them, doing real things together, an active interchange of feeling and experience, which educates the child.[25]

The correctives to discrepancies that result from the *actual* relationships help define the adult role. That role was spelled out in the basic biological relationship of care and the basic obligation to allow a child's growing away from his need for adult care. It was spelled out, too, in the adult's obligation to provide and to extend the environment as necessary for each child's learning, and in the adult's obligation to offer the correctives of reality and discussions of additional and alternate possibilities that might encourage and support a child's own restructurings of his first reference frames. Much of Susan Isaacs' *Intellectual Growth in Young Children* is an account of such discussions and the resulting corrections and self-corrections.

> . . . we tried to use our parental powers in such a way as to reduce the children's need for them.[26]

> To shirk or evade the responsibility for satisfying his emotional and social requirements is for society's representatives to act as bad parents themselves.[27]

> . . . the educator cannot teach the child, nor can he learn for him. All that he can do is to create such situations as will give the child opportunities to learn for himself. In this regard he has to control the social environment of the child as well as the physical, in order to make it possible for the child to learn. The child can, however, learn only by his

[24] Susan Isaacs, *The Children We Teach*, p. 171.
[25] Susan Isaacs, *Childhood and After*, p. 226.
[26] Susan Isaacs, *Intellectual Growth*, p. 33.
[27] Susan Isaacs, *Childhood and After*, p. 224.

own real experience, whether social or physical, and the educator must not stand between the child and his experience.[28]

Because the *actual* reality in which a child lives is the corrective impelling him to new accommodations, the adult's role should be mild, sane, but strong enough to support a child growth, strong enough to help him to further reaccommodations.

> Words, verbal commandments, abstract principles, have no significance except in so far as they are embodied in the actions and the personalities of the people upon whom he is dependent. What parents and teachers are, and his real experience of them, is infinitely more important than what they profess or claim to be, or tell him he ought to be.[29]

> If he neither finds fulfilment of his phantastic dreads in the outer world, nor is left at their mercy in his inner world by having no external support, but is slowly educated by a tempered, real control, mild and understanding, appropriate to each situation as it arises, he is led forward on the path of reality and towards all those indirect satisfactions in the real world, the sublimatory activities.[30]

All of these—real experiences in play, in social life, and in companionship with other children and adults—are the avenues of correctives to a child's inner fantasies, necessarily played out in an external world. They are the avenues of correctives to the discrepancies of a child's first structurings, and the process of learning in these many ways can be subsumed under the infant assimilative-accommodative-reaccommodative drive. This drive is the bedrock on which the English rest their belief in the active thrust of development, in curiosity. It is on this that they rest belief in play, in experience, in the wholeness of children as emotional, social, and intellectual beings, their belief in a child's active individuality.

Language and Experience

The English analysis of this prior-to-school learning also permeates their discussion of the relationships of language and experience. Susan Isaacs emphasized in all her books the importance of the mother's early talk to her child, the stimulation to language from ordinary living. The stimulation as the English see it occurs in an active relationship of interaction and experiencing, not only in a verbal relationship.

Obviously, the argument has never been about the importance of language. The English are a literate people.

[28] Susan Isaacs, *Social Devlopment*, p. 453.
[29] Susan Isaacs, *Childhood and After*, p. 219.
[30] Susan Isaacs, *Social Development*, p. 421.

It is only as [a child] learns to use words that he can effectively draw upon the experience of other people and deal with problems less immediate and concrete than those involved in actual handling of material.[31]

Equally, the argument is certainly not about the importance of adults to a child's development of language.

[A child] has little power for sustaining conversation as such, and needs the opportunity to talk with people who talk well. Grown-ups or older children who will listen to what he has to say and respond appropriately are of far more value to him than specific lessons in clear speech.[32]

But, the impulse to speech and the development of speech involve more. "It is under the stimulus of wishes and emotions that language develops most freely and fully." [33] And this stimulus, these drives, are exerted in interaction with an external world. "It is only in the most intimate contact with activity and actual experience that he begins to talk freely and to exchange ideas." [34] Thus, on verbalism as a mode of teaching a child new material, Susan Isaacs writes:

. . . words are only tokens of experience, and are either empty or confusing to the children until they have had enough immediate experience to give the words content. With young children, words are valueless unless they are backed by the true coin of things and doings. They have their own place as aids to experience, and to clear thought about experience.[35]

The evidence . . . shows . . . that one of the main stimuli to the expression of reasoning in words comes to young children from their practical interests in play, and from the discussions and arguments which these play interests give rise to. When occasion calls for it, they break into theoretical statement, although they cannot yet *sustain* verbal thinking.[36]

Verbal reasoning and the clear formulation of judgments are no more than wave-crests upon the flow of young children's thought. . . . Verbal thinking can hardly yet be *sustained in its own right*, in the earlier years. It draws its vitality from the actual problems of concrete understanding and of manipulation in which it takes its rise, and the solution of which it furthers.[37]

[31] Susan Isaacs, *Childhood and After*, p. 61.
[32] *Ibid.*, p. 60.
[33] *Ibid.*, pp. 60, 61.
[34] *Ibid.*, p. 60.
[35] Susan Isaacs, *Intellectual Growth*, p. 40.
[36] Susan Isaacs, *The Children We Teach*, p. 168.
[37] Susan Isaacs, *Intellectual Growth*, pp. 84, 85.

Verbal Reasoning and Preverbal Logic

The earliest learning, the prior-to-school learning, could not be taken for granted in order to concentrate on what came later. Study of coherent thinking, for one thing, could not *begin* with verbal reasoning; the earliest learning was, in effect, a preview of the later verbal reasoning, which would be inexplicable on its own. A child's manipulations and actions had a coherence, a sense not matched by his unstable, feeble verbal reasoning. This coherence revealed the whole network of his earlier learnings, his adaptations. The preverbal working logic of a child—the frame of the first accommodations he made from his engagement with outer reality—was the base for the later development of his ability to *formulate* logically, to think in language about experience.

> Right from the start we build up in our minds a kind of working model of the world around us; in other words, a model of a world of persisting and moving objects and recurring happenings set in a framework of space and time and showing a regular order.[38]

> . . . though he starts from practically nothing but the familiar "blooming, buzzing confusion" of his first few weeks, there is formed in his mind, by the age of 5–6 years, a far-reaching *functional working model* of his surrounding world.[39]

> His verbal thinking, however, lags far behind his practical logic. He can deal with the problems of right and left, of degree and order, and of social relations, *in practice*, long before he can handle the same issues in words, and in thought divorced from action.[40]

The discussion of verbal thinking in the context of its prehistory had its parallel for all forms of learning. Susan Isaacs stressed that *all* complicated ways of functioning had beginnings in prior growth, psychologically and physically. They were not independent, separate, newly-appeared qualities, but had a history of implication and of possibility. The mental process as it unfolded was propelled by its own prehistory. The beginnings may have been momentary and unstable, unmaintained in the balance of forces and meanings in which they appeared. But their appearance at all, the conditions under which they appeared and what happened to them as they appeared, was part of the history of their new function in a new stage of development. New "stages" were descriptive of a major balance of

[38] Nathan Isaacs, *The Growth of Understanding*, p. 11.
[39] Nathan Isaacs, *New Light on Children's Ideas*, p. 35.
[40] Susan Isaacs, *The Children We Teach*, p. 155.

drives and major functions. In between the stages the lines were blurred and unstable. Susan Isaacs described the unevenness of the pattern of learning in the individual, or the "many disparate types of behaviour coexisting in the same children":

> Thus any final theory of development must allow for the fact that these different levels of functioning may occur alongside each other, and that the presence of one type of behaviour under certain conditions does not justify us in assuming that no other would be found at the same age, in different circumstances. Intellectual growth certainly shows a psychological coherence; but this coherence has the elasticity and vital movement of a living process, not the rigid formality of a logical system. It is most fully expressed in the *continuity* of development in noetic synthesis, and in the way in which the later and more highly integrated forms draw their life from the simpler and earlier.[41]

The Case for Continuity

Unevenness and individuality of patterning in the learning process make even stronger the case for continuity. Nathan Isaacs quite explicitly urged the educator to intervene only in ways "continuous with the real structure that is already there." [42] He stated that the educator *must* be aware of this real structure because the learning that predates school, that is, the prehistory of school learning, is the *base* for school learning.

> Certainly outward teaching which is not related to inward growth, and to the stage which this has already reached, becomes peculiarly futile and meaningless—as meaningless as progressive educationists have long contended it to be. By the same token any approach which is not based on *clear and full understanding* of that growth must inevitably fail, even if the utmost will to educate from within is there.[43]

It was inherent in the obligations of the adult role and therefore of the school that the individual, unsegmentalized character of the assimilative-accommodative process should be understood, its continuity fostered.

The adult has the obligation not only to provide continuity, but also to provide extension. A child's prehistory of development propels him and readies him for further experience. The adult and the school provide experiences that a child can use to extend and correct his previous conclusions, whereupon new possibilities are posed. But a child's use of all new

[41] Susan Isaacs, *Intellectual Growth*, p. 97.
[42] Nathan Isaacs, *New Light on Children's Ideas*, p. 36.
[43] *Ibid.*, p. 35.

material is dependent on his own ability to make connections from new to old.

The same was felt to be true of the adult's and the school's obligation to allow *time.* Piaget's research indicated that a child needed time for all his very gradual adaptation to reality, a prolonged time of active engagement with the many concrete situations in the environment. The school's obligation was to allow *more* time than had previously been thought necessary, to allow whatever time was needed by an individual child.

The School Environment

Following from such an analysis of the primary process of interaction, the provision of rich environment is not just as supplemental enrichment or as "aids to teaching," but as the material of action, the material on which accommodation, and therefore further reordering and rebuilding and stretching of the frame of reference, happens.[44] It is the rich environment experienced in differing ways that is the "stuff" or material of discussion. As expressed by Nathan Isaacs in an analysis derived from Piaget, because human mental growth "springs essentially out of the interaction between the child and the world he finds around him, . . . [and] the character of that world must be constantly affecting his growth," the quality of the environment becomes important.[45] Growth will, to some extent, turn on the "helping or hindering features of the world." [46] Fitting Piaget's view to his own linking of inner and outer growth and the importance of the environment, Nathan Isaacs says:

> Piaget's basic view of the very process of inward growth is . . . pivoted on the continual cycle of interchanges between the child and the outward world: his action on that world and its reaction on him. It is this cycle that is the very motor of the child's mental advance, which proceeds by a constant rhythm of in turn assimilating outward reality and accommodating to it. . . . Thus outward reality is as all-important for inward growth as the inward impetus in the child himself.[47]

In this analysis, people, the social world, are included in the term "outward reality." The educator, meanwhile, is responsible for ensuring the quality of the environment and he takes the primary process of interaction as guide. He prepares the environment after familiarizing himself, as best he can, with the world that surrounds a child.

[44] Nathan Isaacs, *Piaget: Some Answers,* p. 17.
[45] *Ibid.,* p. 18.
[46] *Ibid.,* p. 19.
[47] Nathan Isaacs, *New Light on Children's Ideas,* p. 35.

Curiosity and A Child's Own Question

If a setting is prepared that allows engagement with the world to continue, then curiosity—the active thrust of a child as agent of his own development—can be trusted to extend his engagement. "A really rich and stimulating school environment engenders interests which in turn engender the energy to pursue them." [48]

And so the implications of believing and trusting in the description of a child's active thrust of development, the active and independent nature of the assimilative-accommodative process, become clear. The school must *allow* a child to *be* the active agent. It must be aware of and use a *child's* question, a *child's* purpose. A child's own question arising through *his own* experience is what will forward the next step in learning. The Nuffield *Teacher's Guide*, in fact, insists on the necessity for a child's own question:

> . . . however little we know of children's questions, we may be sure that, although they will often accept problems other people put to them, their own mean more to them. When they are allowed to exchange other people's problems for their own, it is striking how much more en- thusiastic and ready to apply themselves they are. *Their own questions seem to be the most significant and to result most often in careful in- vestigations.*[49]

It is however not only the active thrust that is stressed in this discussion, it is the *individual* patterning of a child's integration of his learning. A child helps determine the direction of his development by the experiences he chooses to pursue and the questions he asks of these.

Susan Isaacs applies this analysis in another context when she dis- cusses how we can help fatherless children.

> Moreover, the child has to find his *own* way out. Just as children show their difficulties in different ways, so they will find different ways of overcoming them, whatever sort of help we give. We cannot determine the ultimate effect of his experience upon the child's character and social attitudes. We cannot say that his development shall take this line rather than that, nor decide what sort of person he shall become in the end.[50]

A child can be the active agent only in the free situation. The free situation allows the expectancies of a child to interact with reality. He finds discrepancies and makes corrections. A child must find a solution for

[48] M. Brearley and E. Hitchfield, *Teacher's Guide to Reading Piaget*, p. 165.
[49] Nuffield Junior Science, *Teacher's Guide 1*, p. 28.
[50] Susan Isaacs, *Childhood and After*, p. 193.

the problem *he* was searching to understand, a solution that makes sense of the observations *he* has made. Discussion may help a child locate his problem more clearly but the adult cannot decide in advance on the suitable solution or even the path to a solution.

> And if the next most relevant piece of understanding is the bit which dovetails into the pattern already existing in the child's mind, it is almost impossible for a teacher to predict what it will be. It will certainly be different for every child in the group, and only the individual child is able to ask the question which will be most significant for himself.[51]
> (Italics in original)

This formulation—a child's "own questions," his "own purpose"— is a combining of activity and individual interest, but in a more sophisticated way. Nathan Isaacs speaks of this as an in-depth application of Dewey's concepts of democracy to a child's psychological development.

> The integrity of a human person is one and indivisible, and if we mean to respect it, the time to begin is when he first begins. And that holds all the more because for so long his integrity depends utterly on those in natural authority over him. They claim, indeed, not only the right but the duty to rule and mould him, and up to a point this is quite incontrovertible; but the real question is whether it shall be deliberately restricted to the unavoidable minimum. . . . For those who fully accept the principle of respect for each person's integrity the answer is not in doubt. For them the future individuality of every child is a trust, to be honoured to the utmost attainable extent from his earliest years.[52]

> It follows . . . that he must do his own growing. . . . We must understand . . . how dependent it is on the child's own positive assimilative and integrative activity; and how much it needs to be continuous and of one piece.[53]

A child can even correct his very poor image of himself as weak or helpless by finding out all he can *do* in being active. A necessity for a child's future growth, in fact, is that he be allowed decision and responsibility so that he *conceive* of himself as active agent in his own learning and growth, experiencing the outcome and integrating the fruits and consequences of his choices.

> If he has the chance to develop manipulative and creative skills, to share in the social and practical life of his home, to be *active* in learning at school, he gradually comes to believe that he can contribute to others

[51] Nuffield Junior Science, *Teacher's Guide 1*, p. 28.
[52] Nathan Isaacs, *What is Required of the Nursery-Infant Teacher in This Country Today?*, p. 4.
[53] *Ibid.*, p. 5.

as well as take from them, can make a real return for what has been done for him when he was weak and helpless. Only *active* learning, however, and active social participation and interchange with those who love him and give him responsibility can build up in him a confidence in his own future.[54]

These are the ideas basic to English infant education—summarized for the most part from formulations of Susan Isaacs and from Nathan Isaacs's use of Piagetian formulations. They are ideas of the wholeness, the continuity, the cumulative nature of development, of the need for time. They are ideas of individual and actively independent development, a development propelled further by its own prehistory and by the active thrust of curiosity and individual purpose. In this analysis, development results from each child's constant unique interactions—his integrations and reintegrations and the constructions and reconstructions of his understanding—within the human relationship into which he is born, in an outer reality that is social as well as physical.

Nathan Isaacs applied these formulations to the defense of English "activity" methods, to infant school practice.

> It can, I think, be fairly said that Piaget's fundamental psychology of mental growth not merely supports such methods, but decisively demands them. A radical "activity" approach over virtually the whole front of education is in fact now shown to be the only one that *makes psychological sense. . . .*[55]

This was a real stiffening of the past formulations of the English informal tradition which had interpreted the school's role as one of nurturance and the simple implementation of a child's development. It demanded further extension of "activity" methods over "the whole front of education," not only experiments or even only infant school.

The Formal School

The old way, the formal way, was analyzed and discarded as inconsistent with the facts of development. Peel says:

> Up to this stage [of formal schooling] their intellectual development has marched in line with a "natural" environment from which they take just what is required for their particular stage of thought-growth. But now the environment is no longer "natural," instructions are given, skills are developed and verbal and numerical habits formed that may outstrip the level of thinking reached.[56]

[54] Susan Isaacs, *Childhood and After*, p. 234.
[55] Nathan Isaacs, *Piaget: Some Answers*, pp. 7, 8.
[56] Peel, *The Pupil's Thinking*, p. 64.

But what, in fact, is this formal school, this usual concept of "teaching"? Nathan Isaacs sums this up unforgettably, in words whose aptness go far beyond the English scene.

> . . . the teaching situation so conceived involves lifting the child right out of the context of his living learning—with its own motive-springs and starting-points, its active stretching-out and all its rewarding own achievements—and setting him down in a sort of "looking-glass" world where things virtually go by opposites. Here he must acquire a new way of life (oddly known as "learning"), which is essentially behaving to order, under continuous verbal direction. Nowadays, of course, this no long starts abruptly and in full force; most children are allowed quite a long period of transition. But in the end they must fall in with the *real* aims and rules for which they are being sent to school.
>
> For [children] are in effect put there to be taught; which means expressly clearing out of their minds all that ordinarily fills these and handing them over to the teacher with, as it were, "vacant possession." Their task is to co-operate faithfully with his attempt to furnish their minds, compartment by compartment, as they ought to be furnished. They must make every effort to *take in* what he offers, as he offers it; they must listen as directed, look where directed, act when directed. Of these various demands on them, listening is the most crucial, because it is both so difficult to keep up, and so essential. For language can alone provide the necessary connecting links, give the teaching continuity and cohesion, and build up organisation. Therefore, children must above all follow the spoken word, lesson by lesson—and thus allow themselves to be slowly led, according to some master plan of which they know nothing, to various labelled but otherwise unknown destinations. These they must patiently wait to learn more about when they begin to get there.[57]

It is a shattering formulation but one's experience underlines its undeniable truth.

> Naturally most children will obediently try, as far as in them lies, to comply with what is expected of them. In their varying degrees they will endeavour to "learn" at least some part of what they are taught. A number of them will indeed get fired with real interest in this or that "subject" and put active energy into mastering it. But even then it will often remain a "school" interest, and a transitory one. Whilst in far too many cases no spark will pass at all. Something will be "learnt," but it will not begin to *mean* anything to the child, and most of his own dutiful efforts as well as those of the teacher will in the long run just go to waste. In other words, the foregoing account of the way the teaching situation operates is not the travesty it might look, but a description of the way it actually works out, psychologically, for quite a large proportion of children.[58]

[57] Nathan Isaacs, *Piaget: Some Answers*, p. 14.
[58] *Ibid.*, p. 14.

Where the education is half-successful, Isaacs attributes the success to the out-of-school learning which has fused with some of the school learning.

> Of course in a number of cases . . . true mental growth will continue outside school, strong interests will get formed, and . . . these self-educative processes may eventually pick up, and fuse with the more congenial parts of school education.[59]

In 1932, in *The Children We Teach,* Susan Isaacs offered specific applications of this theory of how children learn in order to encourage change in the schools. Moreover, the aims of her Malting House School and her description of its activities were not so far from the aims and activities of today's infant schools. Thus, it was never *only* theory. Susan Isaacs identified herself with teachers, she worked for the British Nursery Association, she taught a whole generation of advanced students at the Institute of Education, University of London. She linked herself to application in the schools. She said:

> I was a trained teacher of young children and a student of Dewey's educational theories long before I knew anything about Freud. . . .[60]

> . . . I do not hold that any entirely new or innovatory educational principle emerges from this deeper understanding of the child's relation with his parents or fellows. Such is hardly to be expected, since wise mothers and gifted teachers have long known how to treat little children satisfactorily.[61]

She wrote out of a commitment to make schools better, and out of concern. She and all the forementioned English educators felt the responsibility to *apply* all the results of their study to the service of all children.

And how long should a child be helped with this kind of learning? And how continuous should it be? The Nuffield group, speaking for the junior education that now in some cases goes up to age 13, contends that the answer is indeterminate.

> The time this process takes and the extent of the experience required will vary from child to child. How long it will take is unpredictable, but it will certainly be much longer than most people imagine. *The evidence suggests that it is not possible to hasten the forming of concepts, but that schools can make it easier by providing suitable materials and situations.*[62]

[59] Nathan Isaacs, "Memorandum for the Plowden Committee," *Froebel Journal,* June 1965, p. 20.
[60] Susan Isaacs, *Social Development,* p. 18.
[61] *Ibid.,* p. 416.
[62] Nuffield Junior Science, *Teacher's Guide 1,* p. 16.

Nathan Isaacs also answers broadly.

> Direct learning—always through exploration, experimentation and the
> striving for fresh achievement—must in fact be steadily re-stimulated
> and aided to advance further and further, until the help of planned
> teaching becomes its own next need and active demand.[63]

This active learning, if continued, "at least over the whole vital period
of the foundation-building primary years," will provide the broadest framework for the phase of systematic teaching to come.[64]

Granted their analysis of the ways of development, the English
answers and the choices of the ways of education were not niceties or
kindnesses. They seemed necessities that were consonant with the evidence
and, presented as such, provided the rationale for the infant school entity.

[63] Nathan Isaacs, "Memorandum for the Plowden Committee," *Froebel Journal*,
June 1965, p. 21.
[64] Nathan Isaacs, *Piaget: Some Answers*, p. 17.

chapter 5

OTHER IDEAS

Convergence
and Divergence

That the coherence of ideas giving theoretical backing to infant school practice is not static, deriving from a single source or fixed in formulation, is a fact so crucial to understanding these ideas that it bears repeating. A wide-ranging eclecticism has always been their characteristic. Without question the greatest external force for reexamination and reformulation for new coherence has continued to be the writings of Jean Piaget.[1] Additional developmental studies—whether from the United States or elsewhere—were, and continue to be, used almost interchangeably with native English studies to add observational weight and confirm Eng-

---

[1] American analyses of Piaget, even though some of these paused over his description of the slow accommodative-reaccommodative process in the development of mental structures, have been added to these accepted formulations. Thus, McVicker Hunt is much quoted on the importance of opportunity for variety of experience; Millie Almy's view that spontaneous play, discussion, and activity in a rich environment of people and objects are necessary ingredients of a child's mental development is certainly welcomed; also quoted is R. W. White's reassertion of active drive (included in Almy, *Early Childhood Play*). See also, Elkind and Flavell in Bibliography.

lish conclusions on child development. The slightly different emphases drawn from the different contexts of practice and application have been reciprocally stimulating. The study of these differences, and the redefinitions that from time to time reestablished congruence, maintained the web of reconfirmation and restimulation.

The eclectic English informal educators took as a matter of course that they could also use research findings originating outside the field of developmental studies, even where the premises and process of such research were clearly rooted in a different conceptual framework. They applied some of these findings even without reexamining their ideological implications. In this way they had used the IQ test to stimulate a more exact perception of one aspect of individual differences. Similarly they have been spurred by developments in programmed learning to use educational technology within their own context of informal education as a tool for sharpening the match with an individual child's differences in learning. Still other studies—on critical period, on sensory deprivation, on social and class factors in language formation, on language deficit—have been applied, after translating their language into the terms of the English informal education world, in critical reexamination of implementations of the informal idea. These studies have served to sharpen insight into particular aspects of development and individual difference. Thus, the newer studies on IQ (discussed in chapter 6) were brought to bear on the discussions of the Plowden recommendations for organizational change. Far more difficult for the English informal educators than absorbing research findings as simple additions to the context of informal education was the reexamination of informal ideas forced on them by the literature of *ideas* that accompanied the new findings—a literature analyzing the research in ways that often diverged from developmental formulations.

Ideas outside its own informal tradition—from many research sources in and around the educational world and from sources all over the world —had always been a force pushing for reexamination. Indeed the vitality of the formulations of informal education depended on constant examination of its own performance, of new ideas, and of reexamination of its own coherence. The strengthened reformulations resulting from reexamination often included *aspects* of the new ideas. Even ideas that were rejected served the useful purpose of stimulating redefinitions or at least spelling out the differences. For the English informal educators the yardstick of examination was, of course, an idea's possible contribution to and compatibility with a developmental view of a child. On this depended the absorption or rejection of an idea, and it is in these terms that an idea can be considered convergent with or divergent from the main tradition of English informal education.

From the mountain of writing demanding examination I have selected two scholars, both outside the main development of ideas on informal education, whose work most sharply made clear the need for reexamination. Each was considered spokesman for a major trend; each was influential far beyond his own field of investigation. *Jerome Bruner* investigated curriculum, teaching, and cognition.[2] *Basil Bernstein* wrote on social and class factors in language formation, and his work was then used by others writing on the disadvantaged and on language deficit. In the United States, Bruner's work was often used by those more concerned with what should be known than with the process of knowing. Quotations from Bernstein's work selected by writers in the United States came back to England as an attack on informal education. Yet the English informal educators, reading both Bruner and Bernstein in original context, considered the ideas of both writers convergent with their own. It is also useful to examine, however briefly, the writings of those in the United States who used Bernstein's work to support purposes directly contradictory to informal education. These writings are subsidiary to the direct line of Bernstein's influence but they are important in their own right because of the consequent reexamination. In the case of both Bruner and Bernstein, their ideas are used by the British educators and absorbed in selective fashion. They do not supplant, and are not in exact congruence with, the ideas of informal education already formulated.

JEROME BRUNER [3]

Bruner seems to have been particularly easy to absorb because so much of what he had to say was similar to what the English were saying. He accepted the major developmental premises; his work acknowledges inspiration from Piaget. Starting with a child, Bruner affirms, as did Piaget and Susan and Nathan Isaacs, intrinsic intellectual curiosity as the motive force in learning. Bruner, however, equated the drive to master skills with the drive for curiosity, and held that interest comes *after* the skill: "We get interested in what we get good at." [4] The active force in learning thus

[2] I consider here Bruner's work through 1966 because it is the influence of this work that still operates. Bruner's concentration now is on the processes of intellectual development in the very young child, and his present-day formulations may have a different focus.

[3] Sources for my analysis:

Process of Education, Cambridge, Mass.: Harvard University Press, 1960.

Towards a Theory of Instruction, Cambridge, Mass.: The Belknap Press of Harvard University Press, 1966.

A Study of Thinking, New York: John Wiley & Sons, Inc., 1966.

Studies in Cognitive Growth, New York: John Wiley & Sons, Inc., 1966.

[4] Jerome S. Bruner, *Towards a Theory of Instruction,* p. 118.

becomes the intrinsic reward from increased competence. This is a narrower view of the motive force in learning than is described in Isaacs or Piaget.

Nevertheless, his stress on rich environment and on much concrete experience follows logically from *any* acceptance of curiosity as motive force. Certainly Bruner affirms that experience is of primary importance. He notes the danger of going too fast into symbolism. You do so, he says, "with the risk that the learner may not possess the imagery to fall back on when his symbolic transformations fail. . . ." [5]

He notes that a child needs "multiple embodiments of the same general idea . . . a store of concrete images . . . to exemplify the abstractions." [6]

Bruner values play in a way similar to Susan Isaacs—as the corrective to inner fantasies. A child needs not only play but the conditions required for playfulness in order to develop. A child needs *"stimulation, play, identification,* and some degree of *freedom from drive and anxiety."* [7]

But it is a limited view of play: as a factor in "denaturing" a child, moving him from an emotional, or affective, context to a thinking state; and as precursor to "games" and the cognitive process.

Thus, dissimilarities with the English formulation outweigh the similarities in Bruner's discussion of play. The affective context is seen as negating cognition. Bruner separates himself from what he interprets as the "emotional adjustment" goals of the American nursery school world. But his emphasis is also different from the English view in which a child's development of his mental structures cannot be *separated* from his uncompartmentalized functioning, from the inextricable link of his social, emotional, and intellectual life. For Bruner the function of the imagination or fantasy in thinking could be discarded as belonging to an earlier period of a child's development. Having mentioned play, his focus shifts from the process of learning through play to a child's need for identification. He then enlarges this to a need for an adequate competence model and *teaching* becomes necessary.

It seems clear that Bruner's interest (at that time) was not, as in the English writings, on a child's prior-to-school learning. Bruner tends to treat very, very lightly, though he doesn't completely ignore, the working logic and the frame of reference a child has long before he has logical verbalization.

It is as though after acknowledging and explicating the early development within children, the interaction of the elements in that early learning process almost disappears in his discussion. It is even more than

[5] *Ibid.,* p. 49.
[6] *Ibid.,* p. 65.
[7] *Ibid.,* p. 134.

that, since Bruner puts learning blocks, apathy, and learning deficit firmly outside his consideration, as belonging to *other* fields. For his discussion Bruner starts with the will to learn and *assumes* the necessary curiosity. Thus his concentration, on the whole, is not on the process of learning but on intellectual powers; conceiving that they can be separately considered. He searches for a theory of instruction and for better curriculum.

> . . . there is an appropriate version of any skill or knowledge that may be imparted at whatever age one wishes to begin teaching—however preparatory the version may be.[8]

The rich environment and "discovery" learning he has described is to be planned and controlled for the discovery of "essentials," for the discovery of the inner structure and basic concepts of the disciplines.

Bruner searched for the continuity of intellectual development, and instruction and curriculum were analyzed to support this search. He sought for the continuity of the spiraling levels of a child's *insight* into the essentials of the disciplines. In Bruner's view this spiraling intellectual development leans heavily *"upon a systematic and contingent interaction between a tutor and a learner."* [9] (Italics in original) In a Socratic dialogue, through discussion with an adult instructor serving as a competence model, a child's insights are reinforced and can develop unimpeded. His spiraling is a process of knowing, and the nature of the knower and the process of knowing are premises. But the emphasis is on the *content* of the knowing.

Bruner's spiraling is different from the genetic process focused on all aspects of the developing described by Susan and Nathan Isaacs. As they saw it, the first spiraling, a child's earlier intellectual feelers toward abstract understanding, are unstable, unsustained "wave crests" that must be understood in the context of the balance of meanings in which they appear. They must be understood in the context of the unevenness of a child's developing mental patterns, in the context of the coexistence in him of differing levels of function. In this kind of spiraling, a child's mind, engaging with the outer world and with the different viewpoints of the social world, driven by curiosity, guided by his own interests and questions, and supported and stimulated by adults, works towards his constantly extended and reframed understanding of reality. A child's grasp of the logical structure of the disciplines is a later development, which he acquires, usually, after a long history of this kind of spiraling.

The Isaacses too are interested in a child entering into the inheritance of essential ideas. But for them, the better teaching that can support this entrance follows inevitably from understanding the nature of the knowing

[8] *Ibid.,* p. 35.
[9] *Ibid.,* p. 6.

or the learning. Their understanding of the developmental or genetic process of how this entrance into the inheritance is best accomplished, how it is in fact, accomplished at all, results in a different answer to the problem of better teaching.

Support for the *continuity* of a child's spiraling insights would focus on the mesh that must be made with the points that have meaning for a child, the questions discrepant for each child's grasp—*his own questions* that he asks in his own developmental groping for understanding of reality. A child extends his understanding through pursuing *these* questions; he is helped to further extension, if the teacher goes along *his* path, posing new possibilities only in ways the child can absorb as a living part of his already existent frame. His path to the inheritance of ideas is individual and personal.

Clearly, the emphasis is different and the dissimilarities are plain, between the Isaacses' and Bruner's approaches. In Bruner's theory, the familiar word "continuity" is used, but it has different emphasis. Bruner's way of producing a continuity of spiraling through systematic interaction—tutor and learner—emphasizes response only to what touches on the "essentials," defined by Bruner as the logical coherence in disciplines. The Isaacses, on the other hand, speak of response to a child's attempt to understand reality, his engagement with the physical and social world. The genetic process is viewed with different emphasis and "essentials" are defined dissimilarly.

But in fact the compatibilities are strong and Bruner's argument for curriculum and instruction is never separated from a child as knower. His work stood as a critique of the "usual" school. Thus, he is aware that the problem about learning

> . . . exists not so much in learning itself, but in the fact that what the school imposes often fails to enlist the natural energies that sustain the spontaneous learning—curiosity, a desire for competence, aspiration to emulate a model, and a deep-sensed commitment to the web of social reciprocity.[10]

Social reciprocity is stressed but its meanings in relationships other than that of tutor or learner are not particularly elaborated as they are in Isaacs.

"Contrast" is another word used by Bruner that seemed a link with English formulations. Used creatively by the teacher, "contrast" can further learning. Nathan Isaacs, too, discussed possibilities for the teacher's use of "discrepancy," but for the most part the Isaacses discussed the correc-

[10] *Ibid.*, p. 127.

tives—from adults, other children, or extended experiences—to the discrepancies in a child's understandings arising from his limited reference frame. They stressed a child's own question, though the teacher's employment of stimulating "contrast" was by no means ruled out.

Bruner talks of different styles of learning. As a consequence of these the teacher must support a child with responsive and individualized teaching.

> There is no unique sequence for all learners, and the optimum in any particular case will depend upon a variety of factors, including past learning, stage of development, nature of the material, and individual differences.[11]

> The fact of individual differences argues for pluralism and for an enlightened opportunism in the materials and methods of instruction . . . no single ideal sequence exists for any group of children. . . . A curriculum, in short, must contain many tracks leading to the same general goal.[12]

But again, for Bruner, it is the *same* general goal and that goal is the inner structure of the disciplines, the essentials, the basic concepts. These essential ideas are the inheritance, and the pluralism he refers to exists within the predetermined curriculum.

The dissimilarities in emphasis are obvious: the English emphasis was on learning and Bruner's—through 1966—was on curriculum, on the critique of triviality, and on teaching. But since the English were similarly preoccupied with better teaching, better curriculum, and a critique of triviality, they seized eagerly on Bruner's work in spite of its dissimilarities.

The Nuffield work, the work of the Schools Council, and the present discussion in England of goals, adult role, environment, and thinking (see chapter 6) bear witness to the English parallel critique and search. The Froebel Institute discussion of goals for teaching and for a child's growth within the curriculum of the school acknowledges its debt to Bruner, as well as to Piaget and the Isaacses.[13] Absorbing not only the obvious agreements on early learning process, the Froebel analysis accepts from Bruner the obligation, in teacher education, to help the teacher understand more clearly and deeply the inner structure of the disciplines so that she in turn can recognize, affirm, and extend a child's insights.

Like Bruner, the Froebelians accept the need for less trivial content, for a more aware planning of the environment. But their planning for less trivial environment focuses on the development of a child's mental struc-

---

11 *Ibid.*, p. 49.
12 *Ibid.*, p. 71.
13 Molly Brearley (ed.), *The Teaching of Young Children.*

tures, on his active growth away from egocentricity.[14] The stress is always on the *internal* nature of the development, accepting that it is active, individual, and personal. Nevertheless, while internal, this essential process of development takes place in an outer reality—physical, social, and cultural —and so of course bits of the "essentials" of the inner logical relatedness of one thing or another are perceived as a child grows in understanding. The planning of environment supports this.

The teacher must work with awareness of a child's growing understanding and with awareness that his understanding of the disciplines may be a later result. The Froebel use, led by Molly Brearley, suggests:

> The wise teacher joins this forward thrust and helps a child to define, fix and organize his responses, genuinely preparing for more structured approaches in later work.[15]

The stress is on *later*. The essential *content* of Bruner's preoccupations must wait for the essential *process* of development of understanding. Organized, serious study of a subject may follow from earlier interests that are sustained, but it must wait until a child reaches the level of systematic thinking. This analysis, stressing interests and a child's personal and individual path of development of understanding, precludes a core curriculum representing a supposed statement of "essentials." Thus for the English, pluralism exists not only in the different learning patterns and necessary, different instructional strategies; it exists also in the content, in the inheritance.

Bruner's was a positive approach, a heuristic view of instruction and curriculum, building on curiosity, on what is inherent in the knowing. He was quoted often—in support of better teacher education, less trivial content, reconstitution of curricula, a more aware planning of the environment. He was quoted to sustain those who argued for a base of concrete experience and discovery method, and to sustain those examining the role of the adult in instruction. All of these were areas of English concern, and Bruner's work in no sense could be taken as a critique of formulations of informal education. It was not critique of English formulations in its original purpose or in its applications. Certainly there are dissimilarities with English formulations but, even with these dissimilarities in emphasis and in focus, Bruner's questions, raised in the context of a search for better teaching and curriculum in the United States, applied also in the English context. They generated further refinements of the informal solution. His analysis was accepted as contribution.

---

[14] For further discussion of the English struggle against trivialty, see chapter 6.
[15] Brearley, *The Teaching of Young Children*, p. 9.

BASIL BERNSTEIN [16]

Bernstein, an English sociologist, did not write specifically on educational curriculum or teaching. Bernstein's highly technical description of language pattern differences, analyzed for social and class factors, pointed out that such differences in the learner have been ignored in school practice and that instruction and curriculum have not matched the learner's context of use. Bernstein's work is critique but it could be absorbed by the English informal educators because its descriptions were evocative of and even sharpened observations already made. His work was linked with their search for continuity, for better connection with a child's individual background and need. It is this link that places Bernstein's work within the major tradition of the ideas of English informal education.

In the United States, however, the study of Bernstein's work has resulted in different emphases and derivations though some emphases were similar. Thus, in some programs in the United States, as in England, Bernstein's description of alienation was taken as a rationale for a strengthened support of a child's self-image. But in the United States Bernstein's speculations on lack of curiosity [17] were used to justify orderly programming or "structuring." Some programs,[18] in accepting his description of a lack of curiosity in children whose language showed deficit, provided for the language deficit, *not* the curiosity deficit.

Bernstein was analyzed in the United States in a way that linked language and the mother-child communication system as *cause* and perpetuator of poverty. His description of restricted language use in the lower

[16] Sources for my analysis:
"A Socio-Linguistic Approach to Socialization: with some reference to Educability," in *Research in Socio-Linguistics*, J. Gumperz, D. Hymes, (eds.) (New York: Holt, Rinehart & Winston, in press).
"A Socio-Linguistic Approach to Social Learning," in *Social Science Survey* (London: Pelican Books, 1965).
"Social Class and Linguistic Development," in A. H. Halsey and C. A. Anderson, (eds.), *Education, Economy and Society* (New York: Free Press, 1961).
"Social Structure, Language, and Learning," *Educational Research*, Vol. 3, June 1961 (Sussex, England).
"A Critique of the Concept of 'Compensatory Education'," in *Education for Democracy*, Rubinstein & Stoneman (eds.) (London: Penguin Books, Ltd., 1970).
Denis Lawton, *Social Class, Language and Education* (London: Routledge, Kegan Paul, 1968).
[17] Martin Deutsch, see note 51.
[18] Carl Bereiter and Siegfried Engelmann, *Teaching Disadvantaged Children in the Pre-School* (Englewood Cliffs, N.J.: Prentice-Hall, 1966).

class was taken as description of deficit in concept formation; in other words, as a description of extremely limited thinking.[19] The remedy proposed for the limited thinking—the limited language—was language teaching, using the method of direct drill. In these programs *language* was all-important, and experiential encounters could be eliminated or severely limited.

My reading of Bernstein, on the other hand, does not support the emphases given his work in the United States. Bernstein himself discusses these derived meanings and disowns them.

> I have taken so much space discussing the new educational concepts and categories because, in a small way, the work I have been doing has inadvertently contributed towards their formulation. It might, and has been said that my research through focusing upon the subculture and forms of familial socialization has also distracted attention from the conditions and contexts of learning in school.[20]

He disowns the term "compensatory education" and urges serious and systematic consideration of the educational environment.

> I do not understand how we can talk about offering compensatory education to children who in the first place have not, as yet, been offered an adequate educational environment.[21]

He disowns the use made of the term "restricted code."

> The concept "restricted code" has been equated with "linguistic deprivation" or even with the non-verbal child.[22]

> Because a code is restricted it does not mean that a child is non-verbal, nor is he in the technical sense linguistically deprived for he possesses the same tacit understanding of the linguistic rule system as any child. It simply means that there is a restriction on the *contexts* and on the *conditions* which will orient the child to universalistic orders of meaning and to making those linguistic choices through which such meanings are realized and so made public. It does not mean that the children cannot produce at any time elaborated speech in particular contexts.[23]

About dialect, he says, "There is nothing, but nothing, in the dialect as such which prevents a child from internalizing and learning to use uni-

[19] R. D. Hess and V. C. Shipman, "Early Experience and the Socialization of Cognitive Modes in Children," *Child Development*, December 1965.
[20] Bernstein, "A Critique of the Concept of 'Compensatory Education'," in *Education for Democracy*, p. 114.
[21] *Ibid.*, p. 111.
[22] *Ibid.*, p. 114.
[23] *Ibid.*, p. 118.

versalistic meanings." [24] The fight against alienation must respect not only a child's dialect; it must respect the experience a child already possesses.

> We should start knowing that the social experience the child already possesses is valid and significant, and that this social experience should be reflected back to him as being valid and significant. It can only be reflected back to him if it is part of the texture of the learning experience we create.[25]

For the English use of Bernstein, based on earlier writings, these disavowals are confirmation. The English had already analyzed that central to Bernstein's position is preserving for a child what he already has and extending for him new possibilities. The English could use Bernstein's work in the context of informal education because his position was also theirs.

Their commitment (in idea) had long been to meet the developmental needs of all children, accepting that children were individually different. However, Bernstein's research in social class and language raised many serious questions about whether schools were, in *fact*, properly relating to these differences. His questioning of the performance of the schools follows the historic tradition of Robert Owen in its concern for a better life for working-class children, and is in the context also of the developmental tradition of English informal education. His research forces a look at the reality of an alien school culture that devalues a child's prior pattern of development, that insufficiently meshes with his past, and then creates neither sufficient continuities for his "natural" language development nor bridges to the school language. Furthermore, Bernstein's work forces a sharper, more focused implementation of English thinking on *how* to maintain continuity with prior-to-school development. It has resulted in a renewed commitment to make better connections with a child's background, to use his "natural" language in his first learning, and then to extend the language to cope with a child's experience of new contexts and new roles. Mindful of the history of the English working class, Bernstein does not rule out the possibility of mobility because of restricted language. Changes in the form of social relations, he writes, modify speech systems, and possibilities for such changes exist in each language code.

Courtney Cazden,[26] one of the few American research workers in

---

24 *Ibid.*, p. 120.
25 *Ibid.*
26 Sources for my analysis:
"On Individual Differences in Language Competence and Performance," *Journal of Special Education*, Vol. 1, no. 2, 1967.
"Some Implications of Research on Language Development for Pre-School Education," in *Early Education: Current Theory, Research and Action*, R. D. Hess and R. M. Bear (eds.) (Chicago: Aldine, 1968).

linguistics who has concentrated on Bernstein's views on change, derives as a possible conclusion that

> . . . in the short run, struggles by groups of people to improve their own lives may have an indirect effect on their language more powerful than direct educational efforts.[27]

She quotes Bernstein on the American scene:

> Apart from attempts of the school which so far have not been outstandingly successful, the most important influence upon change of linguistic code is probably the Civil Rights Movement. This movement and its various organizations is bringing about a change in the Negro's view of both his own sub-culture, his relation to the white culture and his attitude towards education. This movement has produced powerful charismatic leaders at both national and local levels, who are forcing Negroes to reassess, re-examine their structural relationship to the society. This confrontation (despite the violence) is likely to make new demands upon linguistic resources and to challenge the passivity of the old sub-culture and its system of social relationships. The language of social protest, with its challenging of assumptions, its grasping towards new cultural forms, may play an important role in breaking down the limitations of subculturally bound restricted codes.[28]

Her own interest in Bernstein's analysis leads her to arraign American primary classrooms in a way that reads like a sequel to Nathan Isaacs's indictment of formal classrooms (p. 186).

> Here, especially in the cities and more especially in the urban slums, the prevailing climate is more like the climate in which the restricted code is presumably generated in the first place: order and discipline are valued above all, and exploration—both physical and verbal—virtually prohibited.[29]

"Three Sociolinguistic Views of the Language and Speech of Lower Class Children —with Special Attention to the Work of Basil Bernstein," *Developmental Medicine and Child Neurology*, Vol. 10, no. 5, October 1968, London.

"Evaluating Language Learning in Early Childhood Education," in B. S. Bloom, T. Hastings, and G. Madaus, *Formative and Summative Evaluations of Student Learning* (New York: McGraw Hill, in press).

Cazden, J. C. Baratz, W. Labov, and F. H. Palmer, "Language Development in Day-Care Programs," chapter for a "State of the Art" document on day-care, October 1970.

"Social Class Differences in the Effectiveness and Style of Children's Coding Ability," in *Project Literacy Reports*, 1968 (mimeographed).

[27] Courtney B. Cazden, "Three Sociolinguistic Views," p. 610.

[28] *Ibid.* Quotation is from Bernstein, "A Socio-Linguistic Approach to Socialization."

[29] *Ibid.*, p. 609.

Of course, Bernstein did make speculations that are *not* used by English educators. The informal educators view these speculative extrapolations from Bernstein's early research as rather wide-ranging, insufficiently hedged in with the modifications he is otherwise so careful to make about the potentialities of restricted language. They view these speculations on working-class character as additions to his basic description of language differences that can be considered separately. Thus, analyzing lower socioeconomic language and finding few expressions of guilt, Bernstein speculates on its lack, perhaps insufficiently differentiating between guilt and its expression. On the basis of the limited research on curiosity and the very limited indication that children, given a meaningful discovery kind of curriculum, respond with limited curiosity, Bernstein speculates that people using restricted language have limited curiosity, an orientation to a "low order of causality."[30] He says they may have "an inherent passivity."[31] His analysis indicates that there may be poor verbalization of tender feelings. However, in this case, he qualifies his speculation on the verbalization of tender feelings.

> Again, it is important to add that this does not imply that tender feelings are not subjectively experiences, but that the form and implications of their expression are modified. . . . Further, it is probable that 'tough' terms will be used to characterize situations or objects rather than the articulation of tender feelings in an individually discrete way.[32]

His qualifications, however, do not restrain him from a conclusion: "This in its turn modifies the individual's ready entertainment of such feeling."[33]

It is in such speculative fashion, inconsistently pressed, that Bernstein makes some generalized attacks on informal education,[34] halfway suggesting that it be blamed for the nonlearning of working-class children and the lack of mesh between the experiences these children had in and outside of school. A case, of course, might well be made for blaming nonlearning on the *lack* of the rich experiential context of informal education, and Bernstein might well agree, but his comments are not a detailed critique of what informal schools are doing. His criticisms perhaps stem from an unclear blending in his considerations of present and desired education. The poor results of today's formal education somehow become equated with the small spread of informal education into the junior schools, and it is unclear what is being asked or criticized.

[30] Bernstein, "Social Class and Linguistic Development," p. 302.
[31] *Ibid.*, p. 301.
[32] *Ibid.*, pp. 302, 303.
[33] *Ibid.*, p. 303.
[34] Bernstein is currently engaged on work with infant school children. These earlier studies (1961–65) were not of young children and not focused on infant education.

Bernstein goes on to more specific questioning of informal education with his speculations on use of the concrete.

> To make the educational experience happy and contented is not necessarily to solve the problems of learning, if this is achieved by by-passing the problem and playing directly into a concrete perceptual set—as is done by much use of concrete and visual material.[35]

English educators, of course, agree, but they feel this is half the description. They would agree with the first half and argue that the second half describes a part while implying a whole. The use of the concrete in informal education does not exist in a vacuum. The whole is a child learning not *only* in encounters with the concrete environment, but *also* in interaction, and in discussion of his experiences, with adults and with other children. Indeed the freer organization of informal education *allows* more discussion, more mesh with a child, more help to a child in extension of his learning and his thinking. Descriptions of informal education make this *whole* abundantly clear.

Bernstein questions use of the concrete. Then, not quite on the same plane, he speculates that drill methods are required.[36] But he himself sees difficulties in this reasoning about drill:

> However, there is a possible conflict between such techniques and the need to encourage insightful generalization and to facilitate active exploration of relationships.[37]

Though he questions the applicability of Piaget-based methods to children with restricted language, the same difficulties beset his own speculative propositions. Fertile as these speculations may be, they would not seem to be conclusively confirmed by present research.

Thus, his speculations on drill are ignored by English educators. After all, discussion on language restriction in the poor was not new to these infant educators. Susan Isaacs had described the limited language of the poor and E. R. Boyce's work is a classic on this, full of illustrations of the paucity of language in very poor children and of great differences between children and teachers in the sound, construction, and complexity of language used. She said that "the majority of children who enter the schools at four or five years come with distorted, inarticulate speech habits." [38] The infant educators had already tried drill, and language

[35] Bernstein, "Social Structure, Language and Learning," p. 165.
[36] Bernstein, "Social Class and Linguistic Development," p. 305.
[37] *Ibid.*
[38] E. R. Boyce, in C. Sturmey (ed.), *Activity Methods for Children Under Eight*, pp. 87, 88.

"lessons" and language "training" were not at all new to infant schools. Educators had used and discarded them after they had been found far less useful in stimulating free and rich use of language than their present teaching. They found: "Speech training lessons in formal schools sometimes defeat their ends by cramping the natural flow of language and inhibiting continuous, verbal expression." [39] And they found that "no amount of speech training replaces the simple method of just talking freely." [40] The pioneer infant educators emphasized dramatic play, or acting. Boyce understood very clearly the relationship of role playing to speech: "A royal road to clear speaking, and one which belongs essentially to activity methods, is by way of dramatization." [41] Much of the present infant school "way" may be said to be response to the task of setting up an environment that encourages *communication,* an environment where children *talk* naturally and easily with adults in a free social situation with possibilities for rich experience.

Thus, English educators do not take Bernstein's work as an attack on the best of infant school practice but use his criticisms to reinforce their own search for better and more conscious work on language. They take Bernstein's work as urging greater understanding of the children he is describing and therefore more apt support of them in their development. They take it as support for extension and for continuity of method. Greater structure can only mean, these educators think, more careful planning of the mesh between school and nonschool experiences so that the context in which a particular individual child learns is not lost. Bernstein's work, in fact, as well as the Plowden Report (with indebtedness to Bernstein), call for greater awareness of a child's background to prevent his alienation and his defeat in the different linguistic context of the school.

Clearly Bernstein's own speculations on character and on the use of the concrete *allowed* the emphases in the United States that took these as research conclusions rather than speculations. His expanded discussion of his basic description of class language differences sheds additional light on why it was possible to derive the different emphases.

Bernstein has described the more restricted kind of language, as he calls it, of the lower socioeconomic group, and asserts that there is in this restricted code a "common cultural identity which reduces the need to verbalise." [42]

In a restricted code, the limitation on the expression of complex experience is traced to social relationships Bernstein considered typical of the lower class, indeed to the original social relation between mother

[39] *Ibid.,* p. 90.
[40] *Ibid.,* p. 88.
[41] *Ibid.,* p. 91.
[42] Bernstein, "A Socio-linguistic Approach to Social Learning," p. 9.

and child, which "exerted little pressure on the child to make his experience relatively explicit in a verbally differentiated way." [43] The result is that for those sharing the restricted code less abstraction, less precise formulation, is needed and used.

> This is not to say that the speakers of this language interact in a completely uniform manner, for the potential of a public language allows a vast range of possibilities, but it provides a language use that discourages the speaker from verbalizing his relationships with the environment. The individual qualification is realized . . . by expressive symbolism, together with a linguistic form that orients the speaker to a relatively low causal order, to descriptive concepts rather than analytic ones.[44]

This formulation has sometimes been recast in the United States as an "intrinsic" view of limitation, but Bernstein denies that the difference or limitation is intrinsically intellectual.[45] He denies the equation of "restricted" with "deprived" or "nonverbal." The speaker using a restricted code will, in some contexts, use a "universalistic" order of meaning.[46] In Bernstein the language limitation is fitted into its setting of social function, its function in strategies necessary for school success. The restricted language thus can be problem solving within its own framework, and very vividly and clearly so. Over and over again Bernstein modifies his description of adequacy to ensure understanding that

> . . . one code is not better than another; each possesses its own aesthetic, its own possibilities. . . . Variations in behaviour found within groups who fall within a particular class (defined in terms of occupation and education) within a mobile society are often very great.[47]

But common cultural identity results in less need for translation such as is necessary between individuals of two different social classes or even between the middle class amongst themselves. For instance, though the restricted code is typical of the first relationships of any child with its mother, the individualism and privacy of the middle-class family forces extension of language if a child is to go even one step beyond the mother-child nexus. The extended family of a lower-economic level child, on the other hand, may communicate in *almost* the same common code and only slight translation is needed. Translations result in an elaborated code and verbal explicitness, rather than an implicit meaning within a common identity.

---

[43] *Ibid.*, p. 15.
[44] Bernstein, "Social Class and Linguistic Development," p. 300.
[45] Bernstein, "A Critique of the Concept of 'Compensatory Education'."
[46] *Ibid.*, p. 118.
[47] Bernstein, "A Socio-linguistic Approach to Social Learning," p. 16.

Bernstein points out that all such descriptions of use of language codes that can be called "restricted" or "elaborated" or "universalistic" must be modified and therefore that difficulties in translation are relative, not absolute. He points out that most people have some access to several modes of speaking (one is, for example, a standard product of a job), and that users of a restricted code will in some context use universalistic expression.[48] Equally he makes clear that all individuals, no matter what the class, use a restricted code at some time or other, as between very good friends and for very personal things.

But the school problem *is* translation, that is, a growth towards "universalistic" meanings. Translation is more difficult for a lower-class child because his teacher does not meet his first expressions with comparable expressions or understanding. Thus, while separateness and difference from others, the experience of alienation, is a common initial school experience, class differences determine how these qualities are received. From the first moment at school a middle-class child will find understanding and guidance for his use of language, for his extensions and translations, because his teacher, through her own living, feels a kinship for at least the outward trappings of his experience. And so, without being made self-conscious about his group or general modality, he enters the language of the school subjects, retaining his private restricted language, or languages, as a modality for home, mother, his school fellows. School for him is an extension of the mother-child frame of reference. For a lower-class child, the social distance from home to school is greater and may even be a *denial* of his home, or group, or extended family language. The stimulation to language from the initial school experience of having something to communicate to home, and in reverse *to* school, may not occur if *total* translation is involved. A lower-class child may, as a result of this "social distance" from home to school, develop in much lesser degree the linguistic forms strategic for school and career success.

Therefore the task is to ease the difficulties of translation and to avert alienation. This was and is the central focus of Bernstein's work. For a child, the point is whether the differences between school and home and class have been experienced in a negative way and whether access to the other mode was prevented. Bernstein feels the teacher must bear the first burden of translation.

> If the culture of the teacher is to become part of the consciousness of the child, then the culture of the child must first be in the consciousness of the teacher. This may mean that the teacher must be able to understand the child's dialect, rather than deliberately attempting to change it.[49]

[48] Bernstein, "A Critique of the Concept of 'Compensatory Education'," p. 118.
[49] *Ibid.*, p. 120.

It is only where the mode of particularism and implicit meaning is the *only* one, or where alienation occurs, that extreme educative difficulties result. If the teaching situation exposes a child to a persistent attack on his language, his normal mode of orientation, and his social experience, then this—rather than his language differences—may be the source of the hindrances to his thinking. Bernstein's mode of coping with alienation would certainly not be to supplant a child's restrictive code with direct teaching of the structure of the elaborated code. The task is not to change or supplant the language.

> The task would seem to be to preserve for the speaker the aesthetic and dignity which inheres in his language . . . but to make available the possibilities inherent in a *formal* language.[50]

It is this, says Bernstein, to which education must bend itself, and the English informal educators agree. His more recent formulations are re-affirmation of this point.

AMERICAN FORMULATIONS

But there *was* latitude in Bernstein's earlier formulations for different emphasis and application and indeed in the United States very different applications did claim derivation from Bernstein. These came back to England in writings proposing a different kind of teaching that followed from an analysis in which the assumption of curiosity was put aside. Curiosity was considered an attribute of language development rather than synonymous with the active growth thrust of a human child leading to his exploration and interaction in the social and physical world. From this analysis it becomes less important, even unimportant, to provide the environment that will encourage the continuity of the exploration and interaction.

These American writings took their perspective from the crisis of failure in American schools, the low mastery of the skills necessary for school progress. Aspects of this crisis, of course, existed in England, but in a different configuration of possibilities for solution. Consequently, the English, as they reexamined their own ideas, weighed the American writings only as these related to English possibilities and to the different world of English polemic, both educational and political. The following discussion centers only on the impact of the American writings on the English reexamination of their developmental formulations.

It was a flood of writings, a flood of action proposals and research

[50] Bernstein, "Social Structure, Language and Learning," p. 176.

studies all deriving from and applying the more intensive earlier studies on the critical nature of early learning and on social and class language differences. Focused on the solution of school failure, they proposed compensation for the deprivation that was supposed to be the root of school failure, and they proposed intervention, a different kind of teaching based on their different analysis of the significance of curiosity and experiential encounter. What was of significance for the English, however, was that the proposals moved in a progression away from the developmental formulations—in fact, armed the attack against informal education—and could hardly be ignored.

The questioning of how schools were in fact serving children from the lower socioeconomic class came from many sources, within and without the educational world. But while the English could accept the questioning as they had done before when Bernstein raised these questions, they could not absorb a solution that discarded developmental formulations. Such a solution would have to be rejected as an invalid conclusion from the research, as not *necessary* solution.

Drawing implications from an analysis of the bits and pieces of premises embedded in the various intervention proposals, a full-blown position could be constructed. Underlying all else seems to be the analysis of what is considered the failure of curiosity. Thus, apathy or the failure of curiosity is attributed to linguistic deprivation, and the task of the schools is to meet a child's needs for competence in linguistic skills. A child's own curiosity cannot be trusted to result in learning. His language deprivation becomes so definitive of his difference from other children that the very way of child learning is considered changed. A deprived child must be handled differently from other children to produce necessary further changes. He must be guided towards the needed specific learnings.

As to alienation, it is considered the result of the poor match linguistically deprived children make to schools that are based on language skills. The *quicker* a child learns the needed school language, the less the alienation.

Time, too, is a factor in this analysis because of the lost time of early deprivation. And so, in the compensatory programs time cannot be wasted, time cannot be allowed for learning in the ordinary, "unplanned" way. There will even be less of a time loss if a child's previous langauge ways, so weak anyway, are ignored altogether and he is taught the right way at the start. The needs of the next step of the school curriculum, as it exists, determine the program, and it can be figured out by working backwards. Deprivation, lacks, define aims for the program. The aim is intervention in order to *change* a child.

The break with the developmental definitions and the divergence from English thinking seem complete. Of course the discard of the developmental formulations was not immediately fully developed. It had antecedent and incipient forms. Chief examples are in Deutsch, at one end of the scale, and the Bereiter-Engelmann prescriptions on the other end.

Martin Deutsch [51]

Deutsch, predecessor of Bereiter and Engelmann, referred in his work to Bernstein's description of alienation and of language limitation, and accepted, as did Bernstein, developmental formulations. As a logical consequence from the description of alienation, Deutsch's solutions included tuning-in, response to a child, preservation and extension of a child's "natural" language, the need for variety and richness of experience, the need for continuity. A child's emotional life was not left outside the school door.

Nevertheless, even in Deutsch, there were elements that made possible the progression to the later discard of the developmental formulations. The determining factors in school programming were the *deprivations of a child* and the needs of school progress. The program was determined by working backwards.

> What program content will be most effective can be determined in part by a careful examination of where the cultural discontinuities are most evident in first grade performance. . . .[52]

It was a child who must change.

> It might be that some changes in the curriculum would help in establishing a continuity between the child's previous experience and the demands of the school, but essentially, it is the child who is going to have to make the major adjustment in order to handle the school materials.[53]

[51] Sources for my analysis:
"Early Social Environment and School Adaptation," *Teachers' College Record*, Vol. 66, no. 8, May. 1965.
"Facilitating Development in the Pre-School Child: Social and Psychological Perspectives," *Merrill-Palmer Quarterly of Behavior and Development*, Vol. 10, no. 3, 1964.
"Nursery Education: The Influence of Social Programming on Early Development," *The Journal of Nursery Education*, Vol. 18, no. 3, April 1963.
"The Role of Social Class in Language Development and Cognition," *American Journal of Orthopsychiatry*, Vol. 35, no. 1, January 1965.
"Some Effects of Social Class and Race on Children's Language and Intellectual Abilities," Minneapolis, Minn.: Society for Research in Child Development, March 1965. (Mimeographed)
[52] M. Deutsch, "Nursery Education: The Influence of Social Programming on Early Development."
[53] *Ibid.*

Thus, the pieces tying Deutsch's position to the developmental formulations *could* be dropped. From research on auditory discrimination it was speculated that the distraction in a free setting was a factor to be considered. From such speculation it was possible to suggest constriction and limitation of the rich school environment, to a "more school-like organization for the nursery school at least for such functions as auditory training." [54]

The constriction and limitation do not in fact occur in the Deutsch programs but these suggestions arm the Bereiter-Engelmann position. Play, experience, and social interchange, still important for Deutsch, are dislodged as the necessary avenues of a child's learning. If not necessary, they could even be eliminated.

It is in this progression that all consideration of the active dynamics towards learning in a child could be swallowed up, and produce the chief weapon used for the attack on informal education, the Bereiter-Engelmann prescriptions,[55] as described in *Teaching Disadvantaged Children in the Pre-School.*

Carl Bereiter and Siegfried Engelmann

Characteristic of the Bereiter-Engelmann use of Bernstein formulations is the absence of all the modifications Bernstein himself made on his research conclusions. Their statement asserts that thinking, or concept formation, *rests* on the tools and skills of language. Cognition as a process of building and rebuilding the frame of conceptual understanding of reality, or of the disciplines, has no place in the discussion. Instead, the focus is on cognitive skills, skills necessary for cognition—discrete words, sentence formation, sentence statements, grammatical form, enunciation, word endings, verbal clarity. For these skills specific language training is necessary and becomes the program.

The Bereiter-Engelmann formulations insisted that a child's deprivation made so specific a program necessary. Because a child spoke in such a limited way and his ability to *think* was so limited,

> . . . many disadvantaged children of preschool age come very close to the total lack of ability to use language as a device for acquiring and processing information.[56]

[54] C. Deutsch, "Auditory Discrimination and Learning: Social Factors," *Merrill-Palmer Quarterly*, Vol. 10, no. 3, 1964, 283.

[55] Carl Bereiter is now involved in work that modifies his approach and it is Engelmann who now speaks for the pragmatic position developed in *Teaching Disadvantaged Children in the Pre-School.*

[56] *Ibid.*, p. 39.

Moreover, this limitation, in their opinion, was so great that Bereiter and Engelmann could talk about *ignoring* the language the child comes with— "the safest program is one that assumes no prior mastery." [57]

The deprivations were so great that the teacher had to compensate by imparting, with no time loss, the skills supposed to be preliminary necessities for cognition. A child's "giant word" way of handling sentences must be changed so that he can speak in sentences "composed of discrete words." [58] This change is best accomplished as a highly controlled injecting process that uses drill, rote, mnemonic devices, devices a child enjoys. To make sure that all efforts focus towards this end of compensation and intervention, the teacher is to follow specific step-by-step instructions.

For these purposes and as compensation for these deprivations, rich environment is meaningless. Bereiter and Engelmann focus on language deprivation, not sensory deprivation, and for them the attachment of meaning to word in experience and discussion is less important than use of words in the grammatical and logical form of their drills. Thus, Bereiter and Engelmann prescribe minimal environmental stimulus. This kind of stimulus is to be treated as distraction, and the need for *variety* of experiential interaction is dismissed. Play can be relegated to a bit of change of pace or relaxation. Emotional development of a child can be ignored and, since maladjustment for these deprived children is seen as a result of insufficient competence, teaching for competence *may* produce adjustment. Social development is equally secondary. Therefore, emotional development, social development, can be left outside the classroom. The deprivation of a child is considered to be of such severity that the frame of reference a child has formed from home and street encounters prior to school entrance, what he has learned up to school entrance and the ways of his learning this, can be ignored.

Imposed on a child with energy and demanding of that child energetic participation the Bereiter-Engelmann program remained external to that child; it was discontinuous with his already existent frame. It represented a *complete* discard of the developmental formulations, and, as such, its prescriptions could be dismissed as misreadings of the Bernstein formulations, publicly now disavowed by Bernstein. They could be dismissed as inapplicable to the context of infant school ideas and organization. They could be dismissed as an unnecessary solution.

However, answers to the most critical questions raised by those who advocated direct drill language teaching and curtailed experiential encounter could come *only* from an analysis of the relationships between language and experience and from an analysis of the adult role in lan-

[57] *Ibid.*, p. 138.
[58] *Ibid.*, p. 36.

guage formation and language comprehension. Such an analysis had been made by Susan Isaacs and Nathan Isaacs, drawing upon Jean Piaget's. Thus, for the English, the answers already existed. But additional bulwarking for their answers came from linguistic research, largely from the United States.

The Linguistic Position [59]

Exploring the deepest questions of language comprehension and language acquisition, the linguists reexamined Bernstein's questions on language use differences.[60] Was difference deficit? What, if any, was the relationship of language deficit to deficit in thinking? What, actually, *were* the deficits? What intervention could help remedy deficit? The linguists' discussion stressed the large number of unknowns but no linguist assessed the situation in Bereiter-Engelmann terms equating limited language with limited thinking.[61]

Language acquisition as such was described as a universal human process.[62] Following a unique and still largely unknown, perhaps biological

[59] Sources for my analysis (in addition to Cazden, pp. 199–200.):

Chomsky, Noam, "Language and the Mind: II," *Columbia University Forum*, Vol. 11, no. 3, Fall 1968.

———, "The Formal Nature of Language," in *Biological Foundations of Language*, E. H. Lenneberg (ed.) (New York: John Wiley & Sons, Inc., 1967).

Hymes, Dell, "On Communicative Competence," in *Proceedings of Research Planning Conference on Language Development in Disadvantaged Children* (New York: Teachers College, ERIC, No. EDO27 346, June 1966).

Labov, William, "The Logic of Non-Standard English," in Frederick Williams (ed.), *Language and Poverty*, Institute for Research on Poverty Monograph Series (Chicago: Markham Publishing Co., 1970).

Lavatelli, C. B. (ed.), "Problems of Dialect," Washington, D.C.: U.S. Department of Health, Education, and Welfare (mimeographed).

McNeill, David, "How to Learn a First Language," in *Proceedings of Research Planning Conference on Language Development in Disadvantaged Children*.

———, "Developmental Psycholinguistics," in F. Smith and G. A. Miller (eds.), *The Genesis of Language* (Cambridge: Massachusetts Institute of Technology Press, 1966).

Moskovitz, Sarah T., "Some Assumptions Underlying the Bereiter Approach," *Young Children*, Vol. 24, no. 1, October 1968.

[60] Hymes, "On Communicative Competence," p. 2. Chomsky, "The Formal Nature of Language." McNeill, "Developmental Psycholinguistics."

[61] See articles by Arthur R. Jensen and answers to these in *Harvard Educational Review*, Winter, Spring, and Summer, 1969. Since the low I.Q. clustering in the lower socioeconomic group is, in large measure, a reflection of different or limited language use, the linguistic argument is particularly relevant to the Jensen controversy. It is interesting in this connection that Jensen turns to the prescriptions of Bereiter and Engelmann and not to the thinking of Bernstein or the linguists.

[62] See note 60.

path, hypothesizing, selecting, generalizing, synthesizing, a child was said to be the *active agent* in linguistic acquisition:

> There is evidence that the child *derives* sentence structure from the complex utterances of the surrounding adults who do *not* require complete sentences from him.[63]

Pointing to the many unknowns, Chomsky questioned "the belief that a language is simply a very complex system of habits or fabric of disposition to respond, established through conditioning and association." [64] Mechanistic explanation, mechanistic intervention, was rejected.

Whether reacting directly [65] to Bereiter or exploring the general questions,[66] linguists questioned whether drill on syntactic cues could *produce* comprehension, could *produce* concept formation, could *produce* acquisition.

Regardless of how language was acquired, however, regardless of the underlying competences, differences existed, the differences that led to the preoccupation with language deficit. Linguists were led, very much like Bernstein, to discuss social and class differences, verbal repertoire, the social function of language.[67]

Whether these differences are related to *thinking* remained a moot point for the linguists, as it had for Bernstein. Rather, the argument stated that the relationship of language difference to thinking had yet to be proved.[68] McNeill speaks for this view:

> . . . I would like to suggest the possibility that the differences in dialect associated with differences in socioeconomic status are, cognitively speaking, marginal and slight. One grammar is as good as another, and one grammar, is as demanding as another when being learned. This is true across languages. It would be remarkable indeed if it were not true within languages. Problems of prejudice (such as dialect rejection) aside, it is at least possible that there are not important cognitive deficits associated with the *language* of disadvantaged children. The step of examining their language may be, in this case, a step in the wrong direction, for the deficit may exist elsewhere.[69]

[63] Moskovitz, "Some Assumptions Underlying the Bereiter Approach," p. 26.
[64] Chomsky, "Language and the Mind: II," p. 23.
[65] Moskovitz, "Some Assumptions Underlying the Bereiter Approach."
[66] Hymes, "On Communicative Competence," Chomsky, "The Formal Nature of Language," McNeill, "Developmental Psycholinguistics."
[67] Hymes, "On Communicative Competence."
[68] Lavatelli (ed.), "Problems of Dialect," p. 3 and Jane W. Torrey, "Illiteracy in The Ghetto," *Harvard Educational Review*, Vol. 40, no. 2, May 1970, 253.
[69] McNeill, "How to Learn a First Language," p. 31.

Certainly, linguists, investigating all sorts of usage, questioned whether dialects were simpler, *substandard*, or *different* and therefore nonstandard.

Bernstein had similarly discussed the differences as not better or poorer, standard or substandard, but as *different* codes, each with rich possibilities. Nevertheless, his analysis did point to the restricted code as a less favorable one for school progress. Decisions on intervention still might have to be made. Hymes, commenting on intervention, had this to say on the course it should take:

> In the complex circumstances of our own society it is hard to see how children can be expected to master a second system, complementing or replacing their own, if the process is not perceived as intrinsically relevant, or enjoyable (preferably both).[70]

Cazden, too, searches for the ways to replicate the kinds of environment that foster language development. Bernstein called for preservation and extension, and in a similar vein Cazden recommends the "expatiation" process,[71] the response which enlarges on the ideas, on the context.

> My recommendation is that pre-school teachers concentrate on enlarging the child's linguistic repertoire and not do anything about altering his nonstandard form beyond the provision of models of standard English. With young children, language for social mobility is far less important than language for learning, and the danger that correction will extinguish verbal behavior in general outweighs any possible gains.[72]

The linguists were relevant beyond their own discipline. Their investigations touched on questions fundamental to human development. The questions had recurred persistently, unanswered by the solutions offered for dealing with language deficit. The linguistic analysis supported solutions which converged on the developmental approach and bolstered its definitions.

In the examination of ideas what became apparent was the recurrence of the developmental questions. The questions could not be bypassed. The descriptive picture of a child that raised such questions could be added to but not displaced or discarded. Central to the process was examining ideas for any displacement or discard of the developmental descriptions. The reception and later examination of the ideas of Bruner and Bernstein are illustrations of this process.

[70] Hymes, "On Communicative Competence," p. 12.
[71] Cazden attributes this term to David McNeill.
[72] Cazden, "Some Implications of Research on Language Development," p. 139.

The Bruner and Bernstein formulations, drawn from descriptions of somewhat different phenomena, were not *offered* as relating in any direct fashion to informal method, and their direct focus was certainly not on the infant school. They were not congruent with the ideas of informal education nor were they expected to be. They were read selectively and read with great eagerness for new insights into questions of relevance to informal educators.

As these formulations were circulated and discussed in one intellectual circle after another, they were sometimes applied to the whole analysis of learning, to the analysis of informal method, and were suggested as displacements for previous formulations. Such suggestions, which were more often a feature of American rather than of English discussions, did finally arrive in England. It was only as this happened that it became important to examine more closely the new American ideas for adequacy and completeness of explanation, to ask whether, in addition to their contribution in new areas, these formulations were in fact adequate explanation of the process of child learning. It became important to examine the ideas for any limitation, for any loss or discard of essential elements of previous explanation.

The rationale of such examination was to ask whether the previous older descriptions of a developing child had been accounted for and the previous questions recognized, to ask for an accounting of the old data with the new. Those educators working in the developmental tradition had a similar obligation in *reexamination* of their own formulations—an obligation not to discard the new data or the new questions, not to ignore the problems that had led to the new questions. Thus, reformulations also had to submit to the test of adequacy and completeness.

Using the yardstick of compatibility with a developmental view of a child as a minimum, *all* studies and findings on child growth had to be absorbed as contributions to an increasingly whole view of a child—whether they revealed factors previously ignored or hidden from observation or brought the added weight of a sharpened focus on material already observed. If accepted as valid observation, the new view and the new phenomena had to be added to the many previous partial views. Reformulation had to and would always have to—in still newer reformulations—account for both new and old observational studies. The inherent limitation in any formulation spelled out the constant need for reformulation.

What then, in fact, was the response to the barrage of new ideas? What reformulations, if any, resulted from reexamination of the body of ideas on informal practice? What happened to the coherent idea? What was the effect of reexamination on the actual infant school organization and practice?

chapter 6

EXTENSIONS
AND REAFFIRMATION

The whole time I was in England I was aware of a struggle over the course education should take in planning for its next steps, a struggle that used ideas to either affirm or attack informal education and that, of course, resulted in reexamination of the ideas underlying informal work in the schools. Certainly it was not just the barrage of new ideas that made reexamination *necessary*. The impact of an idea is not entirely dependent on its logic or the adequacy of its explanation. The sociopolitical setting is the context in which organizational change is projected. This setting affects the reception of ideas too; indeed, it is even reflected in the data used to support the ideas.

Thus, the study of a child's development was not *all* that was reflected in the ideas of informal education. The ideas also reflected an historic sociopolitical context of concern for betterment, and they were bedded in the realities and adaptive possibilities of the organizational web in which informal education had to grow. Impetus for reexamination of the ideas came not only from observing children in a specifically defined social and class context and from interaction with the ideas about these ob-

215

servations, but also from exploring the *possibilities* for changing the organization of practice.

These possibilities were explored in the course of the Plowden Committee's investigation of primary education. Preliminary reports and studies considered changes in points of transition, size of classes, and home-school relations; proposals were made to guide the Committee's recommendations for next steps. The reports used, and were sensitized by, the new research and new formulations. But their concentration was not on idea *per se*, but rather on organizational adaptation *within* the accepted framework of informal education. Similarly, the Plowden Report affirmed the existing framework of idea and practice, and made recommendations for the correction of imperfections and for extension and continuity.

Criticism by the Report, on the one hand, of this or that practice and by informal educators, on the other, of this or that specific recommendation, did not dilute the general atmosphere of accord. Plowden recommendations for spreading the best of informal methods to infant schools with inadequate implementation were already broadly accepted within infant education. The infant schools had already changed and had even shaped the change. But the polemic on the future of education was broader than the discussion on infant education. It was when the Plowden Report spoke for continuity, for the *spread* of infant methods into the junior school, that those apprehensive of change challenged the Report's underlying assumptions about informal education and suggested that it offered too incomplete an analysis of the proper goals of primary education.[1]

The apprehensions aroused by the Report, even though it did not extend its recommendations beyond primary education, existed in the context of the concurrent battles over 11+ exams, comprehensive secondary education, and university reform.[2] Planning for organizational change in education had to be carried on in the midst of complex interaction between groups with vested interests in certain organizational forms and therefore in the social and economic ideologies used to give rationale to these forms. So much was this true that plans for further organizational change even became the platforms of political parties, and arguments backing educational planning became the party ideology.

It is within the context of this contest over the future course of education, with the clear need of infant school educators to defend the recommendation for continuity that reexamination was *necessary*, that

---

[1] Richard Peters (ed.), *Perspectives on Plowden*.

[2] *Ideas*, the organ of the Curriculum Laboratory of Goldsmith's College, University of London, edited by Charity James, regularly reports on new ideas for school organization and curriculum for children of the postprimary years. Terms like IDE (Interdisciplinary Inquiry), Three Dimensional Studies, Creative Flow, Open System, Block Teaching, Clustering, Four-Fold Curriculum, Collaborative Studies, indicate the new paths of these reports.

extensions resulted, and that the accepted base of informal thought was reaffirmed.

Historically, changes in infant school organization towards informality reflect what had been observed about children. By *allowing* children to function in these observed ways, the school organization provided the setting for further confirming observations. More than anything else these observed differences in individual patterns of learning and the observed wholeness of a child's functioning—what Susan Isaacs described as the inextricable mesh of his emotional, social, and intellectual development— were key to the organizational adaptations of infant school practice. Individual pace of development, as noted earlier, was first provided for with use of Montessori materials and methods. The individual *pattern* of development and the "coexistence of disparate functioning," discussed by Susan Isaacs, were provided for by overflow, the open school, family grouping, and the undifferentiated day. The unique individuality of the cognitive-synthesizing process was provided for by nonprescribed offerings centered around a mesh with a child's own purpose, by free access to a rich environment, and by discussion with adults and children in a free social setting. All these provided a child with the tools for correcting the discrepancies of his first thinking. Throughout the long history of development in the infant school, the links forged between observation, clarifying idea, and organizational adjustments were inextricable.

Individual Differences: *IQ* and Streaming

In current proposals for organizational adjustment, provision for individual differences again looms large. The challenge this time is what is taken to be the limited opportunity for the disadvantaged. Continuing and extending the old concern for betterment, a better match is demanded for the individual needs of *all* children.

Many new adaptations of infant school organization were formulated to meet this challenge. But the correction of imperfections in the infant school was not enough. Indeed it seemed clear that more than informality on the infant level was needed, that transition was difficult, that for too many the change of methods from informal to formal was defeating, that continuity was needed. The proposal for the continuity of infant methods into junior school was a major response to the challenge of better match.

The implications of this organizational change established the battleground. Since the proposal carried with it a definite stand against the streaming which had arranged children according to the individual differences revealed by their IQ, everything that had carried the infant school away from formalism and away from streaming was reexamined, including the political-philosophic value discussion. Studies specific to streaming and the research specific to the IQ were used to attack or bolster organizational positions.

The whole context in which the English educators had responded to IQ as a reminder of individual difference was resurrected as part of re-examination. The IQ test had been accepted as an indicator of a basic individual difference and was used to aid the teacher's perception of this individual difference.[3] In other words, it was used as a tool, and related to the old search for adequate match with individual need and difference. But all of the unique individuality of a child could not be defined by a test for intellectual function, and in the infant school the provision for intellectual function was only a small part of the provision for individual difference.

The informal school's role in support of the real individuality of a child had been broadly defined. No matter what his IQ, the school was committed to support the continuity and process of a child's development, its uneven and individual pace and pattern, its wholeness—emotional, social, and intellectual. The organizational adaptations made to support this development led to the truly individualized and flexible infant school program which did not need streaming by IQ to provide for individuality.

Acceptance of the fact of individual difference is, indeed, so much a part of present informal school practice that, even without the reminder of this fact from IQ test measurement, nothing would lead the English to what has been called a "naive" environmentalism, an expectation of a common product, common goal, prescribed or core curriculum, or pre-scribed standard. In their broad context, the IQ is only a peripheral tool, basically irrelevant to helpful school organization.

Nathan Isaacs had described the traditional class-organized formal school as a static, inflexible situation that tends to deflate learning and produce apathy and failure. It was not IQ limitations that produced failure of the mass of children in the formal school but the constriction and starvation of whatever forces a child had for learning. The infant school's duty was to maintain and extend these forces in whatever degree they existed. For this purpose Susan and Nathan Isaacs stressed "optimal" environment, the importance of environmental stimulation, the role of the adult in opening new avenues of possibility. Their beliefs implicitly challenged any absolute concept of IQ stability.

Nathan Isaacs's critique of the traditional formal school was also a critique of the organization of the school into streams differentiated by IQ. Streaming was an attempt to achieve, within a formal school, a measure of adjustment to individual differences. Streaming, organized

[3] The accuracy and relevance of the test could be questioned, however. "It is only within a common field of equal experience that individual differences due to intelligence alone can be seen." (Susan Isaacs, *Intellectual Growth*, p. 72.)

around one aspect of individual difference and providing for little mobility from the level on which a child is streamed, offered too partial an adjustment, and reflected a stabilized view of a child's capabilities. This measure of adjustment, infant school educators urge, can no longer be considered pertinent in a situation where the formal school is moving toward informal organization.

Furthermore, additional studies specific to IQ and to streaming in school organization have added strength to these older positions. These studies again question IQ stability, its accuracy or relevance, its possible social bias in the use of language alien to lower socioeconomic groups. They also described, as did Nathan Isaacs, the organization into streams as tending to be fixed as well as one-dimensional, as tending to lock a child on the level in which he has been placed.[4] Moreover, the studies state, a teacher's perception of a child tends also to be fixed on the level of streaming, and the reciprocal effect of a teacher's perception and expectation and a child's response succeeds in further "fixing" the level.[5] The research, however, is by no means ended. Research on the effects of streaming on children's learning seems at this point simply to be inconclusive.[6]

The battle was reopened in the winter of 1969 by publication in the United States of a paper massing arguments to prove that the lower IQ of the bottom socioeconomic group is linked to intrinsic intellectual difference.[7] Speculations are made about the accommodation of educational provision to such "facts." Old views supportive of streaming are revived. Controversy rages on the validity or lack of validity of the evidence. Many social scientists argue that the statistical generalizations of this discussion offer no guides that can be applied to the individual.

> High or low heritability tells us absolutely nothing about how a given individual might have developed under conditions different from those in which he actually did develop.[8]

Those upholding this view join the informal educators who, believing that the concern of education should be with an individual child, consider the "research" irrelevant. They feel the obligation of the public educational apparatus remains "to do everything in our power to maximise each child's

---

[4] Brian Jackson, *Streaming: An Education System in Miniature,* and Brian Simon, *Non-Streaming in the Junior School.*
[5] Robert Rosenthal and Lenore Jacobson, *Pygmalion in the Classroom* (New York: Holt, Rinehart & Winston, Inc., 1968); and B. Jackson, B. Simon (see note 4).
[6] Joan C. Barker Lunn, *Streaming in the Primary School.*
[7] Arthur Jensen, "How Much Can We Boost I.Q. and Scholastic Achievement?" *Harvard Educational Review,* Vol. 39, Winter 1969.
[8] J. Hirsch, *CSSRS Bulletin* (Cambridge, England: Cambridge Society for Social Responsibility in Science), July 18, 1970.

use of his gifts—whatever those gifts happen to be." [9] In addition they feel that lower IQ clustering in the bottom socioeconomic group need not always be discussed in this context of possible intrinsic or genetic intellectual difference. It can be discussed as the reflection in the IQ of the different or limited language use described by Bernstein. These Bernstein descriptions have led informal educators away from all that produces alienation and thus away from the streaming that locks a child at the level of his language difference.

Obviously, what informal educators react to in this debate is not only the research *per se* but their own values and goals. Now underscored with new vehemence, the arguments for extending informal infant school methods into the junior school are in essence no different from those used to support the development of these methods in the first place. In other words, it is not new research that is reflected in these arguments but acceptance of Piaget's and the Isaacses' view of how children learn.

It seems paradoxical that a *finer* attention to individual difference should lead to recommendations for *less* division in organization, a less segmentalized approach to children's learning, but the English organization that recognizes unevenness also recognizes the inextricable mesh of all aspects of a child's development. His individual differences cannot be compartmentalized, infant school educators assert, because it is through *his* active integrative process, in which his learning is "continuous and of one piece," that his uniquely individual mental synthesis is formed.[10]

Thus, it is precisely the recognition of individual differences in learning that leads to the drive for more continuity in *all* aspects of a child's life, that in fact has led in the infant school to a blurring of *all* artificial points of division in the education process. The campaign against streaming is an extension of the drive against artificial division. There is even a campaign to blur the division between home and school, using a new British awareness of the importance of involving parents in their children's education. This trend has been encouraged by Plowden recommendations and by many studies.[11] More parental support for their children's progress in school is considered crucial to this progress. A closer link to home, it is felt, can help the school match more accurately the individual needs of all children. In fact, characteristic of the beginning changes towards informal method in junior schools are more informal parent-school relationtionships.

[9] L. Hudson, *CSSRS Bulletin,* July 18, 1970.

[10] Nathan Isaacs, *What is Required of the Nursery-Infant Teacher in this Country Today?,* p. 5.

[11] Michael Young and Patrick McGeeney, *Learning Begins at Home,* and Patrick McGeeney, *Parents are Welcome.*

The Commitment to All Children

As each implementation of the informal school idea is evaluated for success and for areas in which it has fallen short, a new commitment, a new implementation, follows. And the extensions and reaffirmation of the idea are considered in the context of *all* children, not just in the context of compensatory education for the deprived. The English would say that this commitment to support the development of all children follows inevitably from any serious consideration of the meaning of compulsory education. Even their narrower response to need had always encompassed *most* of the children. Though the origin of the infant school is rooted in work with the poor, since *most* of the children in state schools were poor, the focus from the beginning was on *children*, not on poor children only.

As an example, planning nursery schools for all those who want it, as was recommended in the Plowden Report, goes far beyond the compensatory approach in education. Rather it is a compensatory approach to the problems of urban living and the circumstances of home life in this century. The English reacted to high-rise living by emphasizing society's obligation to provide a human environment in which children can be close to the materials of learning, the visible connections of cause and effect. In line with this approach, Nathan Isaacs's analysis of the traditional school held that *most* of the children suffered, *most* of the children failed.

In the historic continuity of English infant school educators' analyses, good compensatory education would be *good* education, based on a mesh with a child's own functioning. Activity methods and rich experience were not associated in their minds with private, progressive, middle-class education. Their state schools had been in the slums, and the methods had been developed there and adapted to the reality of large groups without loss of aim. The variety of rich environment and individual pace and relationship were meant to allow for many possible starting points and different ways and paces of development.

When the education of economically deprived children became a matter of international concern, the majority of English infant school educators reacted by reaffirming the applicability of informal education to these needs. They reaffirmed the unique concentration on the individual of their own ways of education, not in ignorance of different ways (the Plowden Committee reports on wide travels), but in serious consideration of their specific suitability to their own national scene and in accord with their study and thinking. By reaffirming such applicability to the needs of "Bernstein's children," English teachers were not insisting on any simplistic "informalism"; their commitment to the children could not tolerate false rigidities. Whatever their study convinced them was usable within the basic framework of informal education, they used. So it is that, here and there in England, American structured programs are being tried out as additions or mild modifications to the informal setting of free social interaction and free access to experience.

The Adult Role in Language Growth

The American structured programs have not been left simply to be tried out. In fact, the American Bereiter-Engelmann programs, as well as the international preoccupation with economically deprived children and Bernstein's thought, have stimulated one of the most intense reexaminations underway in English circles: the attempt to refine what is understood of the adult role in language growth. Attention has been focused on whether language growth is related to (a) experience, and/or (b) direct provision by the adult, and/or (c) the fostering presence of adults discussing a child's experience with him.

In their discussion, the English informal educators do not separate language growth from experience and the growth of understanding. Meaning is stressed. They reject teaching that is built around lessons with little base in direct experience. They reject the verbalizing that may be solicited from a child before the experiencing is sufficient. Stressing the importance of discussion of experience, they do not advocate an automatic verbal underlining or interpretation of each experience as the equivalent of discussion. Such automatic verbal reinforcement or "feedback" may indicate to a child that the teacher has heard him or has seen his work, or it may tell a child the teacher's understanding of the experience, but it may not properly match the actual understanding achieved by a child or be the proper response to his implicit question. It may demand of the child's understanding too quick a step out of haziness. It may be an overeager tuning-in to what a child *could* have been aware of, rather than what, in fact, he *is* aware of. Thus English teachers reject the confirmation of only "essential points." They see it as possibly blocking their perception of what a child *did* perceive, of what *he* needed for confirmation or correction, and of the bridges he is building of his own insights into "essentials."

The stress on experience is not meant to negate the adult role in language formation and development. Any oversimplification of the process that ignores this role is criticized. Infant school teachers are reminded of Susan Isaacs's account of the mother-child conversational interaction. They are reminded of her discussion of adult role, crucial in language growth (p. 178). Passive waiting for verbalization before offering confirmation or suggestions is being questioned. Attention, it is felt now, must be focused on the verbalization that is too weak, too limited, and too reluctant in young children—or in immigrant children, or in deprived children—to be *waited* for. For verbal interaction to occur the teacher *must* be familiar with a child's circumstances—his context—and must be able to anticipate, to catch context barely expressed. A child cannot pin vocabulary to his new experience, cannot spurt ahead with new power of vocabulary, and cannot sort confusions, unless he has an adult *nearby* who *knows* his experience. The child needs an adult who tries to see with what piece of reality he is grappling and what insight he has had, in effect, who tries to see with a child's eye. An adult must be able to see what discrepancy in a child's past perception has challenged him. Does another child or the teacher argue for a different perception? If so, this difference has to be discussed. And such discussions—adult with child and child with child—are necessary, in the English infant school analysis, for learning.

Ideally there would be smaller classes than now exist and enough adults to talk often enough with each child about his own unique reactions and experiences. The Plowden recommendations, with careful examination of economic possibility, spoke to this point. But the English were not overly apologetic about their large groups. In spite of large groups they *had* made progress in setting up classrooms that implemented what they knew about children's learning. These changed classrooms fed additional progress and they hoped for yet more.

"What is a perfectly sized group?" they ask—and the answer is still unknown. The smaller group is desired but *how much* smaller may be a variable, dependent on the situation—school organization and teacher. A class could be too small to provide for the learning that children get from and give to each other. It could have too many adults to allow for the development of a child's responsibility and independence. The English do not seek tutorial organization or an adult-child relationship in which a child's experience is constantly with the adult. Concomitantly with smaller classes and a closer and qualitatively better relationship to adults, they continue to stress and plan for a child's active and independent learning in free social situations.

Thus, not only smaller classes and more teachers are recommended. More urgent is the search for sensitive teachers who are careful not to interact in any way that cuts *across* a child's purposes. What is stressed is the sensitive verbal interaction between parent and child, and teacher and child, which Susan Isaacs described over and over—the fostering of the conversation and discussion that brings out judgment, discrimination, and analysis, even as it reinforces and provides vocabulary. In other words, the present plea is for better implementation of already known and accepted purposes, for more of what has already been described as the basic English vision.

A free situation fosters spontaneous use of language. Only a free situation allows the flow of the essential conversation among children about things important to them; and only in a free situation can there be the multiple teacher-child discussions directed to the particular needs of a particular child. Experience that leads to a need of the word is essential. If a child lacks vocabulary and experience, the first essential is to fill in the missing experience, the second is the word for the experience. Obviously that is a limited view, for there is need also for discussion of experience and for enlarging vocabulary *at the time* of the experience.

The English verdict, then, is that the catalytic agent that turns a child's experience into language is the fostering presence of adults discussing that experience with him. They continue to feel that the experience most effective for vocabulary stimulation occurs during spontaneous play. They continue to question direct provision by the adult, the efficacy of passive take-in, of specific structuring. In response to the needs of "Bernstein's children" they press for more time, for more continuity, for greater implementation of a child's purposes and, therefore, even greater breakthrough of the old classroom structure. The renewed intent is to use the school to keep continuous—in other words, to maintain, extend, and restimulate if necessary—a child's forces for learning.

The Adult Role in Environment Provision

Inevitably any aspect of implementing the informal school idea implied all the others. Major points that could be separated out for concentrated reexamination with some advantage could not remain separated. The whole school life of a child was affected by the finer response to individual difference. Observation of individual differences in language use resulted in an analysis of language development, and again almost the whole web of what was known of children's learning was rewoven. Indeed the whole discussion of environment provision took on new meaning in the light of this analysis of language growth and in the light of the examination of the adequacy with which the infant school had met individual needs. Again the teacher's role and the problem of the school's mesh with a child's life were reconsidered.

With all the richness of environment described earlier, the English still worried about finding "starting points" with sufficient relevance and meaning for immigrant children. They worried about whether they had made a mesh with the children's background.

Although many schools had made beginnings towards stretching the environment in this way, in only one or two schools had the children's background been included easily and richly. Perhaps schools assumed that immigrant children had the same experiences as other children, and an insufficiently individualized approach resulted. Perhaps the enrichment of school environment was developed in a certain fixed way. Perhaps for *this* particular child school held little pertinence to the specific experiences of his own life in his neighborhood. Perhaps he could find no obvious connections that meshed school with home and so there were no starting points for him. In the informal infant classroom it was *possible* for children to bring their lives to school, and this was what they did—when they counted how many cars passed in their neighborhood, when they told about their holidays and their grandmother, when they played at house and at working like father, when they acted, and when they set up shops or even went to neighborhood shops or asked local workmen about the sewer. But the same question asked about the teacher's role in cases of weak verbalization was asked again: Did the teacher do the necessary outreaching that could make a mesh with the experience of an inarticulate child, with the experience that was different, with the experience of a child who did *not* contribute it on his own, through discussion, for use in the school environment?

The English infant school teacher is certainly not, at this point, content with a role that presumes provision of a standard environment. She has taken that further step of accepting *responsibility* for making the mesh that produces continuity. School environment is now examined for this mesh with home background. Nor do English teachers today stand back and arrange the environment just for use and social interaction. They had already accomplished this and assessed that such arranging ensures the release of the will to learn and that the will to learn be unimpeded. And indeed the children I observed in infant schools seemed interested in the world and in people. Reassessing their achievement, the English educators considered this success minimal and preliminary.

In addition to provision and arrangement of the environment, the teacher takes a still further step when she helps a child pursue his questions, invests what he experiences with importance and extension, and discusses with him the implications of his questions so that he realizes his power to deal with and adapt to the realities of the environment. The English teacher accepts the responsibility of adapting and extending the environment in response to what she *observes* of a child's use. Such extension supports the growth of a child's understanding.

Fostering Thinking

Accepting this responsibility, with what materials, and in what environment, does the teacher meet her responsibility to the children? What is to be the guide for first choice, for extension? The examination takes place not only in Bernstein's context of mesh, but in Bruner's context of content, and in the Piagetian context of analysis of a child's mental structures and his accommodative-reaccommodative process. Since it is considered that a child's encounters in his living, his firsthand experiences, are and remain the prime source for his learning, the teacher's choice for starting points is the material from the surrounding environment, the ordinary material. It is this material from a child's life—outside, before, and after school—that Isaacs and Boyce urged as sources for intellectual development *in* school. It is urged again by the Nuffield group. In this material can be found the insurance against the discontinuity of a child's life experience, insurance against interference with the forces for learning already within a child. This mesh with the level of a child's use and understanding is considered *first* in importance. But the further responsibility of the teacher is to choose material that provokes questions, that fosters exploration, that suggests new possibilities as a child uses it. The extension of the environmental provision is based on a child's interests, his questions, the path of his already expanding, independent understanding. The teacher *observes* a child's use and, as she discusses with him the implications of his questions, she adds materials, adapts, extends, offers new alternatives. The material is meant to help carry children into deeper concentration; it is meant to "assist them in making new connections between previously organized ideas." [12]

Thus, the teacher is now urged, as she selects materials, to go beyond any preoccupation with "activity." The teacher observes how material is *used*. The adult in the classroom is "a mediator of experience who looks on every aspect of children's living as a means of learning." [13] The teacher seeks to encourage thinking, and material is therefore selected with this purpose of developing good *thinking*.

Exploring the implications in Piaget for curriculum and school studies and for choice of environment, a Froebel Institute group under Molly Brearley's direction reaffirmed the need to maintain continuity with the prior-to-school learnings. The teacher joined the path of a child's independent drives, the Froebelians stated, "supporting, extending and continuing purposes from within." [14] The teacher was *behind* a child with support of his own independent drives and *ahead* of him with offerings that extended the continuing purposes of these drives. For each child this path was different. The Froebelians described as a proper goal for school and teacher that of assisting each child to be "a good thinker." [15] This meant supporting a child's growth in ability to concentrate and to estimate, his growth in confident expectation that questions *have* answers, his growth in ability to *imagine*, to form images, to seek analogies, to synthesize.

[12] Molly Brearley (ed.), *The Teaching of Young Children*, p. 166.
[13] *Ibid.*, p. 184.
[14] *Ibid.*, p. 168.
[15] *Ibid.*, p. 11.

In this analysis the fostering of thinking through discussion takes precedence over the old demand for a quick automatic recording of experiences. Furthermore, the teacher responds to children's differences in pace and patterns of synthesis by accepting a wide range of responses and modes of expression. The goal is to help a child in all the ways *possible* to that child, to develop his power to deal more and more objectively with experience.

The Froebelian analysis makes even more pointed what I had observed in the infant schools: the English do not have a single model for "a good thinker." In other words, they do not feel that by assisting each child to be a good thinker, and by making a better, finer connection with each child, they will eliminate difference. Instead their drive is *to help each child pursue to the fullest the potentiality of his difference.* Of course they know he will need skills to pursue his purposes. But they continue to feel he will best develop the skills and meanings as *he* needs them, for *his* purposes, defined by him, and they think material can be thought about well in *different* ways. They think that a child can be helped to develop deep implications using all *sorts* of material.

Moreover, the use of all *sorts* of material is not intended to minimize the importance of material and content—social and cultural. In their discussion the Froebelians link material, environment, and social and cultural content with a description of the internal development of mental structures. The inextricable link of inner and outer reality had been described by the Isaacses. A child's mental structures are not *empty* structures. His development of mental structures is about the world and himself, and he grows in understanding of the outer reality, the environment, the materials, the relationships. His thinking is in a social and cultural context and inevitably his understanding of this cultural context grows, but in growing it follows the personal path of its own independent expansion.

The curriculum that is implied by the teacher's offerings of environment, material, and experiences must offer possibilities for the free play of this personal path of development. It must offer choice and selection. Its commitment to good thinking in *all* children precludes prescription of a specific core curriculum, though *all* offerings are in the social and cultural context. The skills of writing and reading are needed, but no specific set of facts or specific syllabus for a specific subject can be considered essential. Thus content is not analyzed for essentials that would then be presented in more focused fashion to ensure their intake. A spiraling grasp of essentials marks the growth and development of a child's understanding, but when he understands one aspect or another, he does not yet relate these aspects to a distinct discipline or even to each other.

The trivial, the ephemeral, the cumulative, on a static level of understanding, are rejected in this analysis. The growth of an understanding of the world is ineluctably a growth out of an egocentric view. At some point, as a child reaches the level of systematic thinking (somewhere in the early teens) his *interests* may sustain him in serious study of a subject in its inner logical relatedness, as Bruner has described. It is at that point that the essential content, as in Bruner, and the essential process of development of understanding, as in Isaacs and Piaget, merge.

For English infant school educators the task for the teacher of young children is not the "teaching" of a set of specifics; however they know that it is certainly useful, even *necessary*, that the teacher understand as much and as deeply as possible the content of the environment she has provided. Certainly the teacher must see relationships, connections, alternative possibilities. It is with this understanding that the teacher plans for the possibility and potentialities of exploration. She must of course understand how children progress into understanding aspects of the world and the time this takes, but she must herself understand these aspects of the world if she is to recognize and foster understanding. Only then can she tune in to the implications of a child's question, and, in this way, help resolve the discrepancies of that child's understanding.

To support a child's growth of understanding or thinking makes new demands on the teacher. Certainly, fostering thinking through experience, and through discussion with a child *as* he experiences, is of a much different order from only the releasing of the will to learn, prime as this is. It is a step further, a deeper conception of interaction with the environment than is implied even in "making contact." In order to implement this kind of environment, the teacher *also* is forced to look at the world. "The environment is the world in which [children] live, so the best advice a teacher can be given is: 'Go out and see what is there'." [16] The teacher is forced, in looking at the world, to reexamine her past labelings, her past stereotypes. She cannot "behave as if the word were really all there is to the object which it designates." [17] She tries not to use language that "bars the access to the world, obscures the objects." [18] The word, if it does not illuminate what a *child* has seen, may shut off all further question and mask with verbalism a lack of understanding.

To see with a "child's eyes" is to free perception from only the schematic *essentials* of the storehouse of accepted "namings"—the conventions, in other words—of adult vision. The broader a teacher's vision of possibility, the more certain is it that a good mesh will be made with the piece of possibility a child has perceived. So the teacher herself becomes involved in discovery and thinking and an endless experimentation to find better and better ways of feeding a child's inquiry. She stretches

[16] *Mathematics in Primary Schools*, p. 3.
[17] Ernest Schachtel, *Metamorphosis* (New York: Basic Books, Inc., 1959), p. 189.
[18] *Ibid*.

her empathy for potential, she *thinks with* a child as he discusses. The "tuning in," the thinking "with," the seeing with a "child's eyes," are part of the response to a child's *own* question. It is this question, which a child must follow to further the development of his thinking, that is prime to the teacher—not her own preconceived questions or answers.

Curiosity and Continuity

This then is the way the English extended and reaffirmed infant school theory and practice. Reexamination of goals in environment provision led not only to a refinement in the definition of the adult role but also to reexamination of the drives within a child that determine his use of what is provided and his active participation in his own development. Given the mesh that is recognizable within his own purposes, the English found, a child *will* ask his own questions and will learn from these. But his trust in his *own* perceptions must be kept continuous. The English teacher could accept this imperative, could accept a child's curiosity as a trustworthy motive and as sufficient power for learning because she had watched children; she had watched especially a child's intense and whole absorption in any problem he has set for himself. By the same token, she could examine the questions raised by Bernstein on curiosity in lower-class children and not accept their relevance, being loath to discard her long experience with "poor" children in nursery and infant schools, where rich experiences and free access to these experiences allowed the play of curiosity or succeeded in restimulating it. Perhaps the question, for the English teacher, came down to who, and how many, are the "poor" whose curiosity you cannot trust?

Research on learning in the preschool years stressed its *basic* character, underpinning all further learning, and emphasized these years as possibly a "critical" (irreversible?) period for such learning. The English interpreted this as a clarion call to support the spread of nursery education and the deepening of a teacher's concept of her role. But awareness of what might constitute a critical period did not eliminate the English teacher's faith in restimulation or reversibility. (The possibility of reversibility or restimulation is the act of faith of all educators.) Rather it underlined the necessity for *time*, for *many* exposures to experience, for a blurring of the lines in transition, for *continuity* of the methods that engage a whole child in exploration of his environment. If it is the learning in early childhood that is basic, the English asked, *how* was it learned, *when* was it learned? To restimulate a child, they answered, he must be allowed *time* to use all his sensory powers in the unsegmentalized way of his earliest learning, certainly the way still most familiar to him. All the ways of extending the conception of environmental setting—the positive use of a child's street and neighborhood life to form recognizable links with formal learning—were found also to be ways of restimulating, of opening or keeping open, the paths of learning most accessible to a child. The object, the English came to accept, is to maintain possibilities.

Thus, time and continuity are key standards in the present discussions. The English question *any* program, no matter how good, that is discontinuous with what has been offered previously or will be offered next. They question any program, even one in a "perfectly-sized" group, that provides experiences for only a *short* time. They would question expecting children to be ready in any certain way for a preplanned curriculum. Griffiths questioned "preparing" children a long time ago.

> The present movement to establish schools for children as young as 18 months of age is open to the same danger, should they become widespread, for the primary schools many come to regard these as institutions from which they may expect a continuous stream of children partially broken in to school life as they conceive it.[19]

Time and continuity, moreover, are considered important questions in their own right—not only as arguments triggered by a discussion of "crash" programs. For the English have seen that the same child will pose questions of the environment on many levels of varied complexity and concentration and go *back* to problems again and again, and not necessarily in an obvious *sequence* of development. They take seriously Susan Isaacs's discussion of the coexistence of disparate functioning. On this rests their organization for "wholeness" of the infant school experience, for family grouping, and a good part of their argument for continuity. Their present struggles are for *more* continuity—for continuous implementation of a child's own drives to learn, for the application in his learning of the *wholeness* of involvement seen in his play. In fact, the commitment to implement learning in this way is being projected as desirable for *all* the years of childhood —not only for infant school, but for junior school and possibly beyond, for as long as a child needs it.

Passage of the 1944 Education Act was prompted by a vision of a new Jerusalem in England, rising out of the ruins of World War II bombings.[20] It was a vision of gardens and beautiful new schools. Teachers had come back with their children from the evacuation placements. They had come back with new insights, new improvisations, and new stimulation after working with teachers from many different areas. They were ready to make new and further applications of the ideas that were already rooted in

[19] Ruth Griffiths, *Imagination*, p. 337.
[20] "Till we have built Jerusalem / In England's green and pleasant land," from "Milton" by William Blake, music by Hubert Parry—during my stay in England I often heard this song.

English tradition and already extended and deepened in uniquely English ways. That they were unable to do this in any complete way had more to do with the budgetary and political situation than with any want of effort. Buildings were not too easily had (though many were built), and circumstances had to be bent, adapted to problems of buildings, of size, of supply of teachers. But the effort *was* made, and given the extra-educational difficulties, it succeeded beyond one's wildest dreams.

Now Plowden has recommended a vast expansion of nursery education in priority areas for all who want it. Funding for this, too, will have to be fought for. But the evidence of continued commitment can be found in the way Plowden recommendations on continuity, on age of transfer, on parent involvement, are being implemented, even without funding, and in the continued willingness to bend circumstances.

The heart of the English vision was a vision of *how* children learned. Granted that vision, commitment to carry it out followed. If the traditional school organization violated and impeded a child's learning, then no circumstances could justify its continuation. English educators had, like Susan Isaacs, a concern, an obligation, a responsibility to make things better in terms of what they knew about children, and the obligation and responsibility encompassed all children.

Because of this concern, the English infant schools changed, and the change resulted in "a successful, though very gentle, revolution." [21]

[21] W. A. L. Blyth, *English Primary Education: A Sociological Description* (London: Routledge and Kegan Paul, 1965), p. 49.

SUMMARY THOUGHTS
Turning to America

By the time I returned to America it had become clear to me that the whole fabric, not just pieces, of the entity I've described, English publicly maintained infant education, was different from the longstanding institutional forms on which American public school systems were built.

The American primary school, also a recognizable entity, is characterized (with notable and shining exceptions) by class teaching and by a reliance on the teacher as central, controlling and imparting information in a classroom in which there is little provision for active learning from the environment.[1] The contrast is with the active, individual, unsegmentalized, continuous, and gradually cumulative learning in the English school in which prescribed curriculum and prescribed standard have no part. Though the syllabus in the United States is not quite as prescribed as is imagined, there usually is a grade standard—even for first and second grade. Courses

---

[1] John Goodlad, "The Schools vs. Education," *Saturday Review*, April 19, 1969. See also Goodlad and M. F. Klein, *Behind the Classroom Door* (Worthington, O.: Chas. Jones, 1970).

of study are still state mandated. This situation is summarized by *The New York Times* (January 5, 1969).

> The ultimate control over curriculum in the city lies with the State Department of Education on the basis of some programs it proposes and others that are mandated by the State Legislature. It produces teacher bulletins in many subject areas for over-all curriculum development.
>
> State law requires as a minimum course of study on the primary level instruction in 11 subject areas (including English, mathematics, reading and history).
>
> The city course of study is prepared by committees of teachers, principals and specialists in the subject area, all of whom work out of the Bureau of Curriculum of the Board of Education.
>
> Within this framework, there are as many approaches to teaching children as there are people with ideas on the subject. In New York City, there seems to be almost as many plans in operation.

Thus, it was the total context of discussion that was different and the extension of the differences was systemwide on both sides.

In the very same way that the English practice differed from the traditional American institutional forms, it differed also from our new compensatory programs. Concern for the alienation and nonlearning of economically impoverished children could be common to both cultures, but the practice that met these shared concerns was fundamentally different; it was actualized in systems with fundamentally different conceptions. The English concentrated on learning; Americans concentrated on teaching—an intensified and "improved" form of the longstanding view of the teacher as central. The key words of discussion in the United States and the key words of English discussion were different, specific to the different systems. In each case the whole focus of solution was different.

One broad aspect of difference is that the American institutionalized form has had less impetus within it for change in its basic structure. Our system evolved as a response to pressures of an earlier history, its model an earlier model. For us the formulation of our compulsory state education, which started to take shape in the 1840s, was *itself* the reform. Occurring at an earlier date than England's Compulsory Education Act of 1870, the organizational forms of our compulsory education owed more to Lancaster's adaptation of industrial procedures (see p. 162) than to either Robert Owen or the new developments that were beginning to be felt in the late nineteenth century. For our many purposes of Americanization of those fleeing external oppression, the state system seemed to work. We ignored those historically oppressed *within* our system. Their mass migrations and struggles had not yet forced us to confront the failures. Except at certain periods of great social pressures—from the unemployed, from immigrants, from "cold war" competitive tensions, or as today from our racial minorities—we could look away from state education, assuming that it worked, or, if we felt helpless to change it, we could establish private schools that incorporated for us what we wanted.

We have no history, as England does, of attempting to define and codify the freedom of the head to decide on school curriculum or of struggling to free schools and educators from "payment by results." We have no history of loosening the specific regulatory, prescriptive power of the central authority, even while it continues to confer its umbrella of standard and common aim and idea. We have no history of *continuous* evolution of idea in association with practice. We have no history of inspectorate reports serving to disseminate illustration and suggestion among the schools and thus to spread a varied but recognizable entity nationwide, without prescription. Our post-World War II period was not a period filled with the vision of rebuilding the bombed and scarred fabric of the countryside with new schools and social institutions. On the contrary, the history of educational development in the United States is of a development of local and state authority that left little decision to individual schools, school heads, or teachers.

Ours is a big country and our educational systems are set up by state and local governments. There is great diversity of level, of monies spent, of standards of teacher education, of character of teachers colleges, of education departments in universities, of offerings in curriculum—a potpourri of programs. Nevertheless, the public authority in all our separate states has acted in directions that created an entity as though the system was unified. The examining bodies, such as the testing services, have acted as unifier of standards that perpetuate the present forms of the institution. Far more decisive than the spread of a vague Deweyism was the much wider spread of administrative adjustments to correlate with business practices, described most provocatively by Callahan in *Education and the Cult of Efficiency*.[2] Such changes simply made *more efficient* the earlier, already accepted, model.

Thus, in contrast with the *standard* of English informal education constantly evolving in reciprocal effect from theory and application, the process by which American education became describable as entity, as system, can be characterized as *standardization*. It is a standardization of administration that perpetuates the organizational modes of the "usual" school. Whatever change takes place in such a system goes through the channels of the organization, of the bureaucracy—certainly not through

---

[2] R. E. Callahan, *Education and the Cult of Efficiency* (Chicago: University of Chicago Press, 1962).

the teacher. The very nature of the prescribed syllabus, the prescribed standard, the supervision of plan books for teachers' lessons, produces a lesser freedom for American teachers and a lesser involvement in "idea." Class teaching with stress both on lessons and on the control necessary to ensure intake has been the standard expectation from the young teacher leaving our teachers colleges. Certainly it is not the American teacher who is the initiator of experiments. The teacher and principal can be freer than they may realize, but the teacher is not often encouraged to work out new variations, new ideas. Without connection to a coherent nexus of constantly reexamined idea and examples of applications that extend idea, the teacher has adapted to the *systematization* of the American school, and the teacher as an individual feels helpless to produce change.

But the *major* difference was that the basic teacher-child relationship in American traditional classrooms reflected very little of American developmental theory, in contrast with England where developmental theory was the basis of the development of method in the compulsory infant school. Influenced by Froebel and others, we did make *some* applications of developmental thinking in our public education. We, too, had a kindergarten philosophy which spread in the late nineteenth century and was admired and influential in England. As a matter of fact these kindergartens spread widely in the atmosphere of the early twentieth century interest in child development, and their philosophy spread outside public education as well as within it. Some of the best of the experimental independent schools started in this way as free kindergartens for the poor and only later became fee paying and exclusive. Lochhead contrasted English and American education in the late 1920s, and spoke of kindergartens and Dewey schools as covering the land.[3] This may well have been Lochhead's wish, but it does not represent the reality even for kindergartens. The statistics of kindergarten extension [4] do not confirm the Lochhead vision. In the system of state education, continuity from the kindergarten into first grade was never developed. Kindergarten philosophy remained isolated from all that went after. The kindergarten and nursery school were never *models* for the first grade.

Dewey's critique came on *top* of the already formed and standardized state system. A vague Deweyism, filtered through administrative bureaucracy as rules, as a surface of "conditions" without the implementing intent of the teacher's creative understanding, did spread from the teachers colleges and influenced some local practice. Unit work and projects may have spread, but they did not spread very widely, and certainly not in our inner city schools. Some midwestern cities and a number of suburban

---

[3] Lochhead, *Education of Young Children.*
[4] Schloss, *Enrollment of 3-, 4-, and 5-year olds in Nursery Schools and Kindergarten.* See note 4, Introduction.

schools may have made more effort to provide environment and curriculum more related to a child's interests, but there were *few* such Dewey programs in public education, and even fewer were ever really fully developed. For most schools that were part of the public system, real experiential learning and activity around a development of the communal life of the school remained only an idea.

The republication of *The Dewey School* in 1966, with its richness of curriculum and intellectual learning, revealed how little we had ever implemented Dewey ideas.[5] The dream of the twenties and thirties was frozen. English infant schools, especially after 1944, developed their own versions of what Lochhead had described as better in American kindergartens and Dewey schools. But in the United States the traditional classroom structure had hardly been disturbed by Dewey's influence.

The few All-Day Neighborhood Schools and After-School Play Centers for deprived children in New York tried to retain the experiential content, the work-play connections for learning. But only a small number of children benefited from these efforts to apply the ideas that came from the study of children's growth—the ideas developed in and applied to situations of deepest poverty and nonlearning in England.

Nevertheless activity, experience, interest programs have been blamed for all faults of performance, as though Lochhead's account was reality— as though such programs had really existed in the schools. It was implied that such programs were failures, though strangely the *children* in the suburban schools with even diluted Dewey programs were not failures. The experimental private schools that had in fact embraced experience programs, each in a way specific to that school, had for the most part applied these with success. So successful were they that, even when their beginnings had been with the poor, the more well-to-do demanded this kind of education for their own young. (An interesting case, in fact, might be made for such takeovers as being the pattern of education for the middle class. First, activity methods in the early "free" workingmen's kindergartens were so completely adopted that the schools became fee-paying independent institutions, and it came to be the received wisdom after awhile that such methods *belonged* to the middle class. Then Montessori methods, used successfully first with the poor, proliferated in middle-class schools. Now "structured" methods, meant for the deprived, are following the same pattern of takeover. In the competitive race for place, anything said to be successful is "taken over.")

Child development thinking, however, remained isolated from application in the major mass institutions. While it influenced nursery schools, university demonstration schools, experimental private schools, and parent

[5] K. C. Mayhew and A. C. Edwards, *The Dewey School.*

education, developmental thinking within state education—in kindergartens or in the few Dewey schools—suffered from restriction, narrowness of application, and lack of influence.

An aura of theoretic coherence guiding application in the schools resulted from the fact that Dewey's was the most talked about, the most widely known idea. But Dewey's own school was a small demonstration school, limited in influence on the public schools by its size and its special conditions. Since the Dewey applications in public school were so diluted and so slight, and their effect on changing the traditional class organization so minimal, the Dewey impact as idea must also be said to have been diluted and slight. Without real application in the major public institutions Dewey's ideas were cut off from their necessary nourishment. Dewey had spoken of the "adequate facilities" needed for development of theory, the "continual union of theory and practice" needed "to modify, to build up" the theory.[6] There was no such union, however, and the influence of Dewey's ideas on change in the schools was illusory.

Further, the *main* body of university research on child development in this pre-World War II period did not attempt the extended critique directed at school application that characterized Dewey's thought. What was attempted was directed to the development of more and more studies of special traits, of segmentalized aspects of a child's development. Physical function and IQ had to be measured. Achievement had to be tested too, and this, of course, further standardized expectations and curriculum. From its very nature, the university focus on separate studies led in other directions than to the development of a coherent or integrated view of a child's development applicable to school life.

At no time did the university (nor for the most part does it today) organizationally serve to create bridges of influence from its research or from its teacher education programs to the practice in the schools. There is in fact nothing analogous to the English system of University Institutes, each of which serves as a center for a group of teachers colleges which consult with the Institutes on matters of program and participate in a system of external assessment of each other. The correlation of ideas from the schools, colleges, and Institutes with administrative and organizational plans of local authorities, and with Parliamentary committees and reports, certainly does not exist in the United States. University and teacher college influence in this country is exerted in the formulation of state programs, but it is not a unified influence; rather it is separated into this opinion or that.[7]

[6] John Dewey, "Pedagogy as a University Discipline," *University Record*, University of Chicago, Vol. 1, no. 26, September 25, 1896, 263. (This discussion by Dewey was called to my attention by Charles Silberman.)
[7] Conant in his historic study, *The Education of American Teachers*, attempted to create a unifying rationale for teacher education.

In any case, no coherence of ideas developing in close relationship to application in the public schools really exists in teacher education. Each individual independent private college may implement its thinking in a self-operated demonstration school and, with no attempt to spread the methodology it has developed in the demonstration school, also place students in public schools for a period of practice teaching. The teachers colleges included in universities have a similar framework. Thus their demonstration schools have served as testing grounds for theory and have influenced practice in experimental schools with equally special conditions, but they have not really influenced practice in the public schools. The tone is similar in the teacher education institutions set up by public authority. For the most part each one operates individually, and teacher education, though sharing theory with the private colleges, relates to the public school in the terms of the forms and relationships that perpetuate the existing institution. Assigned to public schools, teachers who have been educated in this way have no support to help them change practice. On the whole, they "adjust" to the "system" or assume that, without the special circumstances of the demonstration school, application from developmental theory is impossible. For most of these teachers the traditional classroom organization remains unexamined, unchallenged—a necessary and accepted premise.

By contrast, extension of the implications of English theory into practice followed naturally from the fact of its having been developed in a state frame in the first place, having adapted to state conditions, having come to count on the state umbrella for support of its premises. The English struggle for their beliefs never relinquished the connection between theory and practice, between theoretician and practitioner. Theory developed in continuous extension along with, and in support of, a practice that, far from being isolated to infancy and earliest childhood, related at least to the age range of children in the state infant schools and even to children of the whole age range of primary schools.[8] The extensions and clarity of statement about the wholeness of childhood, the mesh of social and emotional and intellectual functioning, were part of a long history of applications, of testing and extending theory in state schools, and the growth of theory from these applications and from this testing.

In every instance, examination of differences uncovers a different history. For example, the integration of English thinking on early childhood into the practice of the state system reflected the fact that very young children were in the English state schools. The infant school admitted babies; it cared for the young children (even two-year-olds) of the vast number of working mothers whose living conditions reflected greatest poverty; it worked out its methods specifically to meet the needs of these

[8] Susan Isaacs, *Children We Teach.*

situations. Only with the turn of the century reports on mind-dulling routine (discussed in chapter 3) was the school population of babies reduced and the nursery school developed as a separate institution. But some very young children remained and still remain (even as nursery classes) in the infant school, included along with children past kindergarten age.

In our earlier history, we did not have or need to have babies in the school in such numbers. We did not need to care for the children of such vast numbers of working mothers from densely settled areas of great poverty. Schooling of very young children was not included as an obligation for public planning. It was not considered essential to include kindergarten programs in compulsory education, and our nursery schools and even our day care programs were offered as small optional programs, not as mass programs. The limited number of people who used these services did so with few demands on the public. The public school institutions, in turn, felt no compunction to consider the rationale of nursery school and day care, either for planning transitions or extending provisions in their own planning.

This very restricted application from the thinking of those concerned with early childhood in the United States provided a context for the development of such thought very different from the context in which English thought developed.[9] Applied for the most part to young children in the nursery schools and in day care centers or in *private and experimental schools*, it existed isolated—precisely where its English counterpart stood connected—from the main institutional forms. It had created few bridges of continuity to the next level of public education and had little base in compulsory education.

Thus, when the new compensatory programs came along, they had a more devastating impact on early childhood thinking in America than on this thinking in England. Those leading the new programs could insist on the irrelevance of observations and theoretic formulations that had, in their light, such small and narrowly "middle-class" reference.[10] The new programs could brush aside developmental theory with scathing remarks, could simply bypass and ignore it and develop new channels within the public school organization in a way that represented nothing more than a tightening and intensification of already existent relationships.

Clearly, reconstitution of American developmental thinking depended on a new base of function and the growth of a new fund of observations on

[9] Hartley, Frank, and Goldenson's tremendously perceptive discussion of day care children's play was much used in the preparation of early childhood teachers.
[10] The experience of those trained in American developmental thinking with day care, All-Day Neighborhood Schools, and after-school Play Centers, was ignored, and indeed the extent of this experience was small.

which it could draw for its reaffirmations. It had to establish a relation to the large mass who were outside the small framework of its original application. This need, in effect, was what was fulfilled by the experiences and observations of the early childhood teachers who rallied to staff the Head Start programs. The observations they made of the deprived gave them confidence in reaffirming much of their developmental thinking. A deprived child, they saw, was nonetheless a child and, even with specific needs, learned in the ways of all children. The answer to deprivations was certainly not giving *less* in a more restricted environment and for a shorter time.[11] A child's developmental process, they could see, must not be "short circuited." Slowly, painfully, and laboriously, developmental theory was reconstituted in the terms of American sociopolitical problems.

The common frame I had assumed for American and English developmental thought indeed existed—based on the reciprocal influence of the common fund of research—but American developmental research in the period between World War I and World War II never concentrated on the continuity *from* infancy and the preverbal, preschool life *to* the later school life. It was preoccupied with earliest childhood development and with problems of sequence in the development of the infant psyche, the inner "reality." The implications to be drawn from discussions of emotional life were separated from discussions of intellectual development. The direct connection of play with intellectual development was left unstressed. The role of the adult ranged from "unimpeding provider of environment" to "aware understander." With a later focus on adjustment difficulties and in a psychodynamic context, the adult's role became creative "enabler" or active "intervener." [12] Of course the concept was that the adult's role was to *support*, and to restart if necessary, the active force in a child. But, with all these assumptions about active role for school and teacher, real awareness of the active force of a child sometimes became blurred in practice. And because of these blurred formulations, accusations about nursery school programs as "de-intellectualized" and "stress-free" met with weak rebuttal.[13] Seeming similarities in the use of the word "intervention" in different contexts sometimes delayed the sharp definition of basic dissimilarity.

Under the pressure of criticism, reexamination of the whole context of American developmental thought resulted not only in restatement but also in reexamination of old material, as well as examination of the new research and the new situations. This led in turn to clearer statements

[11] Rose Mukerji, "Roots in Early Childhood for Continuous Learning."
[12] Lili Peller and, later, Sylvia Brody and Milton Schwebel were among many who discussed this point.
[13] M. Deutsch, "Early Social Environment and School Adaptation," *Teachers College Record*, Vol. 66, no. 8, May 1965, 706.

and extensions of past positions. New formulations in State bulletins [14] were able to integrate cognitive emphasis with the older developmental terms. Research confirming a child's drive to explore, to play, to master, appeared. Not only play but curiosity, a child's *active* learning, had to be reasserted.[15] The individual and uneven character of a child's learning, the integration and necessary connection between development of a child's inner emotional reality with the cognitive processes, was reaffirmed.[16] Still operating in the context of early childhood practice, and still without the bridges to continuity on the next level in the public sector, the developmental formulation was at least reaffirmed—and in American terms congruent with the English terms.

Reformulation in theory of course is not enough to change the course of American education. It is only preliminary, reasserting the base of native context for our wider application. What has yet to be accomplished by American developmentalists is the forging of an essential, inextricable link between theory and practice. In the past, only a narrow range of organizational possibility in support of developmental theory had been explored. Thus, developmental applications to school organization that follow of necessity from theory are either not yet established or are still in their beginning.

It is from the perspective of our failure, so far, to establish a dynamic relationship between theory and application that the history of the English commitment to continuity of a child's experience in state schools commends itself as a source from which to cull clues for application to our own possibilities.

Possibilities do exist now for at least some challenge to the old system. Changes have been set in motion, this time *directly* concerned with practice in the public sector, and the perpetuation of existing bureaucratic practice is threatened. Some of the changes may seem to offer nothing more than a tighter, more efficient performance of old ways. They may only replace the old bureaucracy with a new one. But they inject new elements and, therefore, new possibilities.

Thus national influence, previously offered only in very broad suggestion, is felt in the funding of research and in the funding of programs and creation of guidelines, all of it in response first to Sputnik, later to integration pressures, and then to the crisis of learning in our cities. Research began to focus on *essential* curriculum and on classrooms organized for more efficient learning. Class teaching, with its one-dimensional "lockstep" insufficiently differentiating between differences in children's pace,

[14] Ruth Flurry, *The Five-Year-Old and His Thinking*, and D. H. Cohen, *Learning in the Kindergarten*.
[15] Millie Almy (ed.), *Early Childhood Play*.
[16] B. Biber, in Almy (ed.), *Early Childhood Play*.

came under criticism. Keeping within the realities of the several ideas contending for dominance, the national influence helped set standards for Head Start and Follow Through programs in terms wider than response only to local pressures and local opinions.

Of course, while these new forces stimulated new thinking, their challenge to the system lacked continuity with past research on child development. New programs were often prefaced with a critique of the imagined Deweyism in our schools. In its concern for the deprived, the new research often discarded or ignored ideas from the past because examples of application of these ideas were located in the middle-class experimental schools.

Furthermore, the learning disaster of the inner city was so great that discussion of emotional factors, of need for "adjustment" (all considered outside the life of the school and classroom) seemed to evade the need for finding positive direct ways of coping within the situation. It was felt that in the presence of such learning disaster and such deprivation, problems of "adjustment" had to be treated as all-pervasive, a given from which one proceeds to other factors.

Direct grappling with the classroom could be an enormous prod to classroom reorganization, but in fact none of this new analysis was at first an attack on the basic standardization of traditional classrooms. Indeed the startling account of learning failure in the poor tended to divert criticism from the school organization as such. The "reasonable" success of middle-class children (in comparison with ghetto children) seemed to vindicate the schools, even with the Sputnik kind of criticism still spurring reconsideration and updating of curriculum, and in spite of the shallow success for *all* children in the "usual" school.[17] With so many children "successful," the problem seemed less one of school organization than one of "lack" in those who could not succeed. The failing children had to be "fitted" for the schools, and might need to be taught in "special" ways.

What was presumed was the "inevitable" character of the existing school organization. The situation was analyzed simply as requiring more efficient and focused instruction based on an analysis of the sensory deprivations that blocked intake of ordinary instruction in poor children. Instruction, in other words, would be compensatory. The reasoning, I think, went this way: "Now, given this child in this school we have, how can we organize the intake for greatest efficiency, for least distraction and dispersion of effort?" There was, in some of this first grappling, little effort to consider the school as anything but a given necessary premise, into which some more efficient plan of learning would help a child fit. Denigrating the necessity for direct experience, the reasoning suggested that since in

[17] Nathan Isaacs, "Memorandum for the Plowden Committee," and *Piaget: Some Answers to Teachers' Questions.*

this school, which must be accepted, there is so little equipment, that too is a "given premise." And since it is language that is so defective in a deprived child, the reasoning continued, "let us, therefore, *teach* it to him most directly." Finally, "since he has already lost so much time as a consequence of his deprivation, we cannot trust to chance intake but must *focus* presentation to ensure intake."

The system itself was to be accepted. The prescribed standard imposed on a child could not be questioned. A child had to be helped to cope with what could not be controlled. Once past the nursery school— the education that precedes compulsory education—and inside the state system, there could be no demand for time for a child's *own* pace, for continuity, for *his* way of learning. Such demands were proper only for private education. It seemed proper and necessary for a child to be made to adapt once he became part of mass education. This viewpoint was a clear consequence of the teacher's own adaptation and her individual helplessness to act in any other way within the "system."

The new programs and new thinking were bent to fit the old shape of the system, but they contained new elements that in turn bent the system into evident contradictions or into possibilities that were not the first intent of the programs.

The programs assumed that perhaps a whole group (the deprived) needed similar "specific" methods and "specific" help from the teacher in order for them to learn. The programs, in fact, proposed a homogeneity more defined than the usual. Tutorials would help prepare for the transition back to the usual homogeneous class grouping; assistants would help ensure the intake of the specific. Yet the logic of individualization in tutorials moved in another direction—toward breaking the bounds of any specific methodology applied to the whole group of the deprived. Thus, the deprived community's demand for good schools pulled in contradictory ways—toward the existing homogeneous grouping and, at the same time, toward the methods that would recognize individual difference.

There is further contradiction. Since the attack on poverty, the inclusion of assistants, and the attack on nonlearning all go hand-in-hand, we have witnessed simultaneous and parallel proposals that take contradictory positions: tremendous prescribed structure for children on one hand, and, on the other hand, proposals from those living in the poverty areas for self-definition and self-management of their own programs. Because it is in fact obvious that children's adaptability is great (it has been called a "fatal adaptability"),[18] it is assumed a child's needs can be prescribed and that he will adapt to whatever is prescribed. But nonlearning and apathy are the situations where even the half-successes [19] and shallow learning

[18] D. E. M. Gardner, lectures at Institute of Education, University of London.
[19] Nathan Isaacs, *New Light on Children's Ideas.*

produced by adaptability and amenability did not or could not operate. In any case, these contradictions—between proposals for community and proposals for children—remain unresolved, creating their own unease and need for reexamination.

The Head Start program is an illustration of this. Contradiction, modifications, new possibilities were characteristic of the operation of Head Start in the standardized institution. The concession to a program "like" nursery school, but with stronger *focused* language learnings, was meant to be made for only a *short* time, to "fit" a child *quickly* for coping with the "usual." The effort for that short time was meant to focus on matching and being responsive to the level of a child's development, on enriching environment, and on adding adults. And a child *did* change —he was more responsive, he showed less apathy and a burgeoning curiosity. However, within the short time allocated, a child was *not* made ready for the old, for the usual, for the prescribed.

So, on the heels of the summer Head Start came year-round programs and then the call for follow-through, continuity programs. *Within* the old school structure a new entity was formed. The kindergarten next door could see it, as could the first grade. Enrichment could overflow from this intrusive new thing, included *within* the old. The motivation to experiment may have been the concentration on specific disability, but the experiments represented changes. The environment may have been enriched only to ensure that content areas be presented in more focused fashion, not really to satisfy a child's curiosity or restimulate and extend it—but nevertheless the environment *was* enriched. Similarly, even though the motivation for the assistants' program may have been jobs for people in poverty areas rather than children's needs, the program did create a new unthreatened feeling that the teacher and perhaps even the children can be helped by forging links, recognizable to a child, between home and school. With this same mixed motivation—concentrating on more efficient ways of *teaching*—professionalization and career progression for the aides are considered. But, whatever the reason, the presence of assistants produces, or can produce, further changes.

In actual practice there are many missed opportunities and one sees classrooms with two, or even three, adults where whole-classroom "teaching" style still rules. But the inevitable logic of the changed situation begins to make clear that the closed-door classroom, with one teacher central, dominant, and alone, is on its way out. Student teachers have to be trained to work with paraprofessionals, in a small-group or individual way, and the closer individual relationships will require that the *effort* be made to make a mesh, a recognizable link. One of the possibilities of this is that prescribed methods and prescribed curriculum will begin to go by the board. As in the individual tutoring and voluntary programs, standardization no longer operates. The commitment is to make impact however one can, to help the learning in whatever way—and all sorts of ingenuities begin to operate. Prescribed curriculum or not, a child's *interests* and his *active* learning begin to be used, and though such "daring" is only intermittent and teachers continue to dash back to "essentials," the contradictions produced by the operation of the new elements within the old structure have begun to produce change.

Unfortunately the "usual" remained unchanged for the most part, waiting there for a child as he finished with Head Start. The next level was *not* continuous with Head Start; there was no continuity for a child's development. The original premise that he *could* be "fitted" to the "usual" failed and within the "usual" there was little improvement.

The feeling of total impasse about change within the structure of public education that was reinforced by this experience with Head Start is now pervasive and spreads.[20] *Change* is demanded and very little change has occurred. The administrative stranglehold itself seems to make change in the public institution hopeless. The result has been a turning to other possibilities which are neither private nor public. Private is not the proper term for the new speculations. Public *funding* is asked for; open admission and no tuition are seen to be necessities of the situation. Issue is taken with bureaucratic control, with the structure and system itself, with its fixed and rigid character.

> But it does not seem likely the changes necessary for increased efficiency of our urban public schools will come about because they should. Our urban public school systems seem muscle-bound with tradition.[21]

Kenneth Clark suggests using such parallel developments as *levers* in the public sector, as "Alternatives—realistic, aggressive, and viable competitors—to the present public school systems." [22]

Clark further suggests:

> With strong, efficient, and demonstrably excellent parallel systems of public schools, organized and operated on a quasi-private level, and with quality control and professional accountability maintained and determined by Federal and State educational standards and supervision, it would be possible to bring back into public education a vitality and dynamism which are now clearly missing.[23]

[20] A whole literature of critique reinforced the spread of disillusionment with the schools—Kozol, Herndon, Kaufman, Leacock, Wasserman, and others.
[21] Kenneth Clark, "Alternative Public School Systems," *Harvard Educational Review*, Vol. 38, no. 1, Winter 1968, p. 110.
[22] *Ibid.*, p. 111.
[23] *Ibid.*, p. 113.

Thus a call is made for the competition of different systems to be funded in a way which will permit parent choice. Espoused by Christopher Jencks, the voucher system proposes the *principle* of alternatives—whether or not such parallel developments serve to lever change in the public sector.[24] And the qualities sought in the parallel systems stem from what was condemned—the bureaucracy, the impotence, the poor human relationships. Even within the large educational parks' concept, the small unit is built in for this need.[25] "Localism," local control, is offered as an answer to both political impotence and the need for human dimension.[26] "Voluntarism"—for parents in selection of school and also for students in a new individualism that maximizes potential—makes strange bedfellows of the ideas of many different theorists.[27]

And so, stimulated in part by the human and humane environment of the English infant school, some trial ventures of parallel systems, some of these plans for a whole new structure, some small attempts to set in motion a first step toward such education, some replanning of already existing independent schools, appear in many areas. But the ventures remain ventures, and parallelism and voluntarism remain, as Clark sees, prods to the public sector, but not the solution needed for mass public education. The system itself cannot be bypassed.

On the other hand, despite the mood of "impasse" and the reality of a "bureaucracy" that limits change to possibility, not probability, the old attitude of accepting and adapting to the system is passing. Our "standardization," if it ever existed, is cracking. Fissures appear in what has seemed so solid. New shapes and new configurations are becoming possible. Supported by new research on classroom organization, on ways of creating a "climate" of learning, more call is being made for general reconstruction of the school. There is renewed encouragement to try out many new things, to break through "administrative stranglehold" and "lockstep." The new possibilities and relationships unfolding within a still unchanged structure encourage a new attitude. No longer masked by acceptance of the unchanged context, the new possibilities are beginning to be explored for even newer possibilities. All sorts of experiments, local and national, are going on.

In the present climate some teachers, despite administrative discouragement, are no longer passive and are experimenting. Even a few

---

[24] Christopher Jencks, "Education Vouchers," *New Republic*, July 4, 1970.
[25] Max Wolff, *Educational Parks: A Guide to their Implementation* (New York: Center for Urban Education, 1970).
[26] Peter Schrag, *Village School Downtown* (Boston: Beacon Press, 1967).
[27] Kenneth Clark's criticisms, Melvin Tumin's "Teaching in America" (*Saturday Review*, October 21, 1967), Milton Friedman, *Capitalism and Freedom* (University of Chicago Press, 1962) and Paul Goodman, *Compulsory Mis-Education*— all seem to follow similar paths.

principals have begun to shift from placing their administrative function first to educative leadership of their school in the manner of the English head.[28] The mood for some has become one of "commitment to try," for different reasons and in different ways, but with some analogy to the commitment of the English facing the discrepancy of the traditional school method with what they knew of how children learn.

Our discrepancies are still to be faced and we now confront our state school system with the limited tools of our past restriction of application. We have hardly explored the possibilities; and the school models that would support a child's active learning do not exist in our system. The history of English practice, tested within the context of state education, has relevance and should be studied for this very reason. Even the variations of English practice due to differences in the way heads realized the "idea," differences in capacities, experience, and supply of teachers, differences in local conditions and need, have importance for us. They can give us important clues to the rationale and process of development. They can help us, as we make changes, endure the various and uneven character of change. The changes in English state education that resulted in the successful application of American as well as English premises of child development— for the most part never tried in our state education—should encourage us to search for possibilities and steel us against polemic that rejects these premises as inapplicable or as failures without permitting any real trial.

We Americans search for human dimension and we find in English formulations—in their acceptance for school practice of the conditions within which a human child learns—the clear bulwark for the definition of such a dimension. In England what was defined as necessary conditions for a human child were also conditions for an economically impoverished child. The idea and the methods were never separated from problems of mass education, from problems of large classes, from application to the needs of the deprived. Deprived children also, and perhaps especially, needed continuity in school for their own way of learning, whatever that had been, when they had learned at all. Deprived children needed even more time, a special bulwarking of whatever is in them, a restarting and restimulation of any and all of their internal drives. The present extensions of English practice, like fingers from a base, are refinements of application, and represent even *more* response to the needs of the new poor—the immigrants or "language handicapped."

---

[28] Dr. Ewald B. Nyquist, Commissioner of Education of New York State, urged that principals who were so convinced act independently to begin to develop informal education in their schools. (*The New York Times*, December 7, 1970.) Within the same month, Harvey B. Scribner, Chancellor of the New York City public schools, also spoke for administrators' acting independently in support of informal education (see Bibliography).

We search, in particular, for clues to organization and there seem to be special clues in the *active* participation of English heads and teachers in the extension of implications from theory, their active participation in the development of method and curriculum. There seems to be a special clue in the fact that English heads remain teachers—actively participating in the educational life of the school. There seems, too, to be a special clue in the English focus on schools rather than classrooms. The schools are small enough for teachers to learn from each other and from the guidance of the headmistress, small enough for children to use the environment of the school in a freely interacting social setting and in their own active individual way.

Small and obvious bits, with similarities to English practice, are already in evidence or may soon be. We are using assistants and training them. Recognizing individual and uneven development, we *might* move to make our ungraded sequences and heterogeneous groupings more flexible in ways analogous to English mixed-age grouping.[29] A gradual admission system is certainly possible. Some colleges working in collaboration with cooperating public schools are trying to create model situations. Using the administrative "elbow room" created by community pressures, the model situations are trying to reverse the contradiction that has existed so long between the theoretical presentation of how children learn and the facts of the traditional classroom.[30] They are trying to develop in student teachers the ability to organize classrooms that permit the teacher to relate to small groups and even to individuals. They are trying to help teachers reshape their classrooms so that children have access to material they can explore in their own way. They are trying to create situations where adaptation, adjustment, knowledge of the "system" will no longer be primary for survival. They are urging students to try, urging that at least some space and some time be found, even within the system, for the ways of a child's learning.

All this is still *within* the system and only fissures are being explored. But such classroom organization *is* possible; it is possible, within present thinking, to enrich environment in all classes, at least for children up to age 8, and to give these children a chance to use this environment sometime during the day. It is possible to afford some experiments with smaller units housing children through age 8. If any new smaller units were built, I would hope they would be built in ways that allow the overflow move-

---

[29] Research on ability grouping—by Goodlad and by Goldberg, Passow, and Justman—had already created the setting for questioning homogeneous grouping.
[30] On my return from England, I proposed to City College reorganizing classrooms in order that this discrepancy between the theoretical presentations in college lecture halls and the practice situations in public schools be eliminated. I am thankful that the College felt it was useful to their students for me to begin to do this.

ment I have described as in-and-outness (for indoors as well as outdoors). The decentralization of the large City Boards of Education into smaller community units is encouraging such experimentation in the use of school plant, in planning for and in constructing school buildings. There is interest in the design of open plan schools.[31]

But when I look at all the *old* buildings, the old unquestioned and accepted organization and regulations, I think that even within the *old* buildings and even without college-sponsored model situations, the new "commitment to try" makes change possible. The "commitment to try" even leads to a trial of new flexibilities for old regulations on the use of schools; it leads to the "bending of circumstances" of old buildings built for old closed classrooms. We can test new *uses*, extending learning space, finding possibilities for in-and-outness in areas unused before. Roof courtyards used in private schools and unused in public schools can be explored. Corridors between classes, now unused except for passage through the school, can be examined for other uses, perhaps uniting classes. Large schools can be examined for possible reorganizing into smaller, more livable, self-contained units. More manageable, more intimate units can be sought within the old mammoth buildings. For it is not enough to reorganize the classroom. The English changed *schools*, not classrooms. There have always been "good" teachers who tried to defeat the system behind the closed door of their own classroom. A further step would help teachers who think in these ways to work together so that they are not eventually lost in isolation and discouragement. By clustering such classes around a corridor, the whole unit can be considered living, learning space —a space with more possibilities for children and for teachers' continuous development than exist in the enclosed classroom.[32] In such a cluster and in such a space, continuity is possible, more spontaneous relationships might be allowed, richer experiences can be offered. Around the needs and workings of such a cluster other personnel of the school, from custodians to supervisors, can begin to redefine how they can help. In these small ways perhaps we can begin to change the traditional "teaching" classroom so that instead of "fitting" a child to it, the classroom space grows to more closely fit the needs of a child.

These are first steps—applications from my "seeing," specific to the situations in which I work. All over the country others are making applications to their own specifics and vision. These are *all* small first steps, and all within the context of *our* history and possibilities.

[31] Education Facilities Laboratories, *Schools Without Walls*.

[32] In exploring how we could reorganize our mammoth schools to be more supportive of children's growth, I created this design for classrooms and corridor, variously referred to as the "Open Door," the "Open Corridor," and the "Open-Door Corridor." See *Open Door*, a Report by the Program Reference Service, Center for Urban Education, New York, 1971.

These steps that are possible within the situation we now have do not imply "informal" education, English-style. Our prescribed curriculum, our fixed standard for grades established by tests, our supervision of teachers —judgmental and evaluative—by administrative rule book, and our mammoth schools, would all have to change before we could get education English-style. We lack in our organization anyone who is like a headmistress; and the undifferentiated day and a child's own purposes, as guiding principles, are far along in the continuum of development even for English schools. They are points of principle, parts of theory, implemented through the understanding of a particular head, of particular teachers, and they represent absorption of theory in a more integral way. They follow from accepting the developmental view of a child as guide, from the English vision of learning, not teaching. I make no recommendations about that. It makes its own case through the details of the illustrations, through the case studies on practice, through what I have said on ideas.

Nor *should* there be an attempt to establish an English context in this country for "English" ideas. I have not come back to America with *English* ideas. In the first place, English thinking found stimulation in many American writers; ideas from American writers were used in the building of the English concept—as were ideas from Switzerland, Italy, *and* England. Everywhere I went in England I was told, "But we read of things like this in your books," and indeed our books were in use in England; our descriptions of experimental and demonstration schools were familiar to the English. Guidelines from these schools were used along with much else to provide the implementing force, under state conditions, for an education fitted to a child. We had not so used them but the English had, revamping them for their own use. I return with ideas that have suffered no sea change, that are my own, as an American—ideas that I understand better for having seen them in new reference. I return with hope about the applicability of such ideas in state education here.

The experimental programs of today, whether for child or adult, find the passivity and apathy of poverty constant stumbling blocks to any real coping. Yet it is in the context of today's demands by poor communities for self-management and self-definition that the educational words, "activity," "active agent," "own questions," "own purposes," begin to have meaning.[33] Perhaps, as we explore these meanings we will again revive the strong tradition of our own past for activity and involvement in the classroom. Our involvement in the needs of deprived children, at this point, contains the commitment and concern, the urgency and experimental in-

[33] Fantini, Gittell, and Magat, *Community Control and the Urban School* (New York: Praeger Publishers, 1970); also Fantini and Weinstein, *Toward Humanistic Education*.

ventiveness that characterized England's 1944 Education Act, when a new Jerusalem was to be built out of the ruins of the bombing. Out of the ruins of our ghettos a new education can be built and revitalized in our own terms. It can be an education to meet all the positive forces within our ghetto children—yes, using the ghetto homes, the ghetto street life, the ghetto neighborhood—using all the things the children know, and expanding from there. Fitting children to the "usual" school is too small an idea to meet the problem. The question posed by Nathan Isaacs holds for us:

> . . . how far [might we have] to go if we were resolved to adapt our practice to our problem instead of our problem to our practice? [34]

[34] Nathan Isaacs, "What is Required of the Nursery-Infant Teacher in This Country Today?" p. 2.

BIBLIOGRAPHY

The references listed here were selected for their pertinence to informal education. American and English sources are arranged alphabetically under each heading. Other listings appear in the extended footnotes found in Chapter 5.

The Bibliography has been arranged in seven sections, as follows:

    I. Descriptions
    II. Curriculum
         General
         Art
         Math
         Music and Movement
         Reading
         Science
         Writing
    III. Theory
         John Dewey
         Jean Piaget
         On Piaget
         Susan Isaacs

On Susan Isaacs
Nathan Isaacs
On Nathan Isaacs
Others
IV. Special Aspects
V. Analysis
VI. Guidelines
VII. Publications and Films of Special Interest

I. DESCRIPTIONS

BAZELEY, E. T., *Homer Lane and the Little Commonwealth.* New York: Schocken Books, Inc., 1969.

BIBER, B., L. B. MURPHY, L. P. WOODCOCK, AND L. S. BLACK, *Child Life in School.* New York: E. P. Dutton & Co., Inc., 1942.

BLACKIE, J., *Inside the Primary School.* London: HMSO, 1967. (In U.S., British Information Services, New York, N. Y. 10022.)

BOYCE, J., *The First Year in School.* London: Nisbett & Co., 1953.

————, *Play in the Infants' School.* London: Methuen & Co., Ltd., 1938. (New York: Agathon Press, Inc., 1971.)

BROWN, MARY, AND NORMAN PRECIOUS, *The Integrated Day in the Primary School.* London: Ward Lock Educational Co., Ltd., 1968. (New York: Agathon Press, Inc., 1970.)

CAZDEN, COURTNEY B., AND S. M. WILLIAMS, *Infant School.* Newton, Mass.: Education Development Center, 1968.

CHANNON, GLORIA, *Homework.* New York: Outerbridge & Dienstfrey, 1970.

Children and Their Primary Schools, A Report of the Central Advisory Council for Education (England), Lady Plowden (Chairman), *Volume 1: Report, Volume 2: Research and Surveys.* London: HMSO, 1967. (In U.S., British Information Services, New York, N. Y. 10022.)

Children at School, G. Howson, ed. London: Heinemann Educational Books, Ltd., 1969.

COOK, A., H. MACK, AND W. KERNIG, *The Open School.* New York: Frederick A. Praeger, Inc., in press.

CULLUM, ALBERT, *Push Back the Desks.* New York: Citation Press, 1967.

DANIEL, M. V., *Activity in the Primary School.* Oxford: Basil Blackwell & Mott Ltd., 1962.

DENNISON, GEORGE, *Lives of Children.* New York: Random House, Inc., 1969.

FEATHERSTONE, JOSEPH, *The Primary School Revolution in Britain.* (Reprint of four articles published in *The New Republic,* 1967, Washington, D.C.)

————, "Report Analysis: Children and Their Primary Schools," *Harvard Educational Review,* Vol. 38, No. 2, Spring 1968.

————, *Schools Where Children Learn.* New York: Liveright Publishing Corp., 1971.

FLURRY, RUTH, "How Else," *Young Children,* January 1970.

GAGG, J. C., *Common Sense in the Primary School*. London: Evans Brothers, Ltd., 1968.

GARDNER, D. E. M., *Education of Young Children*. London: Methuen & Co., Ltd., 1956.

———, *Education Under Eight*. London: Methuen & Co., Ltd., 1949.

———, *The Children's Play Centre*. London: Methuen & Co., Ltd., 1937. (New York: Agathon Press, Inc., 1970.)

GORDON, JULIA WEBER, *Country School Diary*. New York: Dell Publishing Co., Inc., 1946.

GORDON, VIOLET E. C., *What Happens in School*. Elmsford, N. Y.: Pergamon Press, Inc., 1965.

Hadow Report. *(Report of Consultative Committee of the Board of Education on Infant and Nursery Schools, 1933; Report of Consultative Committee on The Primary School, 1931.)* London: HMSO

HAWKINS, FRANCES, "The Logic of Action," *From a Teacher's Notebook*, Elementary Science Advisory Center, Boulder, Colo.: University of Colorado, 1969.

HOLLAMBY, LILLIAN, *Young Children Living and Learning*. London: The Longman Group, Ltd., 1962.

How to Form a Play Group, Eileen Molony, ed., BBC, London, 1967.

HULL, W. P., "Leicestershire Revisited." Newton, Mass.: Education Development Center, 1964.

KOHL, HERBERT, *36 Children*. New York: The New American Library, Inc., 1967.

LOCHHEAD, JEWELL, *The Education of Young Children in England*. New York: Teachers College, Columbia University, 1932.

MACKINDER, JESSE, *Individual Work in Infant Schools*. London: London Educational Publishing Co., 1925.

McMILLAN, MARGARET, *The Nursery School*. (Rev. ed.). London: J. M. Dent & Sons, Ltd., 1930.

MARSH, LEONARD, *Alongside the Child in the Primary School*. London: A. & C. Black Ltd., 1970.

MASON, S. C., *The Leicestershire Experiment and Plan*. Birmingham, England: Councils and Education Press, 1963.

MAYHEW, KATHERINE C., AND ANNA C. EDWARDS, *The Dewey School: The Laboratory School of the University of Chicago 1896–1903*. New York: Atherton Press, Inc., 1966.

MELLOR, EDNA, *Education Through Experience in the Infant School Years*. Oxford: Basil Blackwell & Mott, Ltd., 1950.

MITCHELL, LUCY SPRAGUE, *Our Children and Our Schools*. New York: Simon & Schuster, Inc., 1950.

MURROW, CASEY, AND LIZ MURROW, *Children Come First*. New York: American Heritage Press, 1971.

NEILL, A. S., *Summerhill: A Radical Approach to Child Rearing*. New York: Hart Publishing Co., Inc., 1960.

Open Door: Informal Education in 2 New York City Public Schools. New York: Center for Urban Education, 1970.

PHILIPS, H., AND F. J. C. McINNES, *Exploration in the Junior School.* London: University of London Press, 1967.

PICKARD, P. M., *The Activity of Children.* London: The Longman Group, Ltd., 1965.

PLOWDEN REPORT *(see Children and Their Primary Schools).*

Plowden Two Years On. London: Council for Education Advance, 1969.

POCOKE, S. E., *Children of Today.* London: The Longman Group, Ltd., 1966.

PRATT, CAROLINE, *I Learn from Children.* New York: Simon & Schuster, Inc., 1948.

PRESTON, LAURA A., "London Venture—A Look at England's Nursery Schools," *Young Children,* Vol. 22, No. 1, October 1966.

PRESTON, P., "Plowden for Parents," *Where,* Supplement 8. London: Advisory Centre for Education, 1967.

Primary Education. London: HMSO, 1959.

RASBERRY, S., AND R. GREENWAY, *Rasberry Exercises.* Santa Barbara, Calif.: The Freestone Publishers, c/o *New Schools Exchange Newsletter,* 1970.

RATHBONE, CHARLES H., ed., *Open Education: The Informal Classroom.* New York: Citation Press, in press.

RAZZELL, A., *Juniors: A Postscript to Plowden.* London: Penguin Books, Ltd., 1968.

REPO, SATU, ed., *This Book Is About Schools.* New York: Pantheon Books, Inc., 1970.

Report of Central Advisory Council for Education, Lady Plowden (Chairman) *(see Children and Their Primary Schools).*

RICHARDSON, ELWYN S., *In the Early World.* Wellington, N. Z.: New Zealand Council of Educational Research, 1964. (New York: Pantheon Books, Inc., 1969.)

RICHMOND, W. KENNETH, *The Teaching Revolution.* London: Methuen & Co., Ltd., 1967.

RIDGWAY, LORNA, AND IRENE LAWTON, *Family Grouping in the Infants' School.* London: Ward Lock Educational Company, Ltd., 1965. (New York: Agathon Press, Inc., 1969.)

ROGERS, VINCENT R., *The Social Studies in English Education.* London: Heinemann Educational Books, Ltd., 1968. (New York: Fernhill House, Ltd., 1968.)

————, *The English Primary School.* New York: The Macmillan Co., 1970.

ROWE, A. W., *The Education of the Average Child.* London: George G. Harrap & Co., Ltd., 1959.

SCHLESINGER, J., "Leicestershire Report 1965." Newton, Mass.: Education Development Center, (Mimeographed).

————, "Leicestershire Report—The Classroom Environment." Newton, Mass.: Education Development Center, 1966, (Mimeographed).

SILBERMAN, CHARLES E., *Crisis in the Classroom.* New York: Random House, Inc., 1970.

SIMPSON, D., AND D. M. ALDERSON, *Creative Play in the Infants' School.* London: Sir Isaac Pitman & Sons, Ltd., 1968.

STEVINSON, E., *The Open-Air Nursery School.* London: J. M. Dent & Sons, Ltd., 1923.

Story of a School. London: HMSO, 1949.

STURMEY, C., ed., *Activity Methods for Children Under Eight.* London: Evans Bros., Ltd., 1950.

TOBIER, ARTHUR J., "The Open Classroom: Humanizing the Coldness of Public Places," *The Center Forum,* Vol. 3, No. 6, May 15, 1969. New York: Center for Urban Education.

VAN DER EYKEN, WILLEM, *The Pre-School Years.* London: Penguin Books, Ltd., 1967.

WEBB, LESLEY, *Modern Practice in Infant Schools.* Oxford: Basil Blackwell & Mott, Ltd., 1969.

WEBER, LILLIAN, "The Infant School in England," in *Encyclopedia of Education.* New York: The Macmillan Co., 1971.

Your Child and School, Christopher Price, ed. London: Cornmarket Press, Ltd., 1970.

II. CURRICULUM

General

BREARLEY, MOLLY, ed., *The Teaching of Young Children: Some Applications of Piaget's Learning Theory.* New York: Schocken Books, Inc., 1970.

CHEESERIGHT, M. L., *Understanding Young Children.* London: Thomas Nelson & Sons, Ltd., 1968.

The Curriculum of the Junior School. Report of a Consultative Committee Appointed by the Executive of the National Union of Teachers. London: The Schoolmaster Publishing Company, Ltd., 1958.

GAGG, J. C., *Beginning the Three R's.* London: Evans Bros., Ltd., 1969.

HOLT, JOHN, *What Do I Do Monday?* New York: E. P. Dutton & Co., Inc., 1970.

Integrated Studies in the Primary School, D. N. Hubbard, J. Salt, eds. Sheffield, England: Institute of Education, University of Sheffield, 1970.

KOHL, HERBERT, *Open Classroom.* New York: Random House, Inc., 1970.

List of Equipment and Materials for Workshops on the Integrated Day. (Mimeographed.) National Association of Independent Schools, 4 Liberty Square, Boston, Mass. 02109.

The New Curriculum. London: HMSO, 1970.

SEALEY, L., AND V. GIBBON, *Communication and Learning in the Primary School.* Oxford: Basil Blackwell & Mott, Ltd., 1962.

WEST, R. H., *Organization in the Classroom.* Oxford: Basil Blackwell & Mott, Ltd., 1967.

YARDLEY, ALICE, *Reaching Out.* London: Evans Bros., Ltd., 1970.

————, *Discovering the Physical World.* London: Evans Bros., Ltd., 1970.

————, *Exploration and Language*. London: Evans Bros., Ltd., 1970.

————, *Senses and Sensitivity*. London: Evans Bros., Ltd., 1970.

Art

COLES, NATALIE R., *The Arts in the Classroom*. New York: The John Day Co., Inc., 1948.

————, *Children's Art from Deep Down Inside*. New York: The John Day Co., Inc., 1966.

KELLOGG, RHODA, AND SCOTT O'DELL, *Psychology of Children's Art*. Del Mar, Calif.: CRM Books, 1967.

MARSHALL, SYBIL, *Aspects of Art Work—5 to 9 Year Olds*. London: Evans Bros., Ltd., 1970.

————, *Experiment in Education*. Cambridge, England: Cambridge University Press, 1963. Paper, 1966. (New York: 32 East 57th Street, New York, N.Y. 10022.)

READ, HERBERT, *Education through Art*. New York: Pantheon Books, Inc., 1945.

ROWLAND, KURT, *Learning to See, Book 1 & 2*. London: Ginn & Co., Ltd., 1968.

SAUNDERS, EVERETT, ed., *Whitman Creative Art Books*. Complete list available from Albert Whitman & Co., Chicago, Ill.

SPROUL, ADELAIDE, *With a Free Hand*. New York: Van Nostrand Reinhold Company, 1968.

Mathematics

BIGGS, EDITH E., AND JAMES R. MACLEAN, *Freedom to Learn: An Active Learning Approach to Mathematics*. Reading, Mass.: Addison-Wesley Publishing Co., Inc., 1969.

CHARBONNEAU, MANON P., *Learning to Think in a Math Lab*. Boston: National Association of Independent Schools, 1971.

CHURCHILL, EILEEN M., *Counting and Measuring*. London: Routledge & Kegan Paul, Ltd., 1961.

Mathematics in Primary Schools. Curriculum Bulletin No. 1. London: The Schools Council, HMSO, 1965.

New Math in Junior Schools, Advisory Centre for Education, Forum 3, London: Ginn & Co., Ltd., 1967.

Notes on Mathematics in Primary Schools. Association of Teachers of Mathematics. London: Cambridge University Press, 1968.

Nuffield Mathematics Project. Complete listing from John Wiley & Sons, Inc., New York.

Primary Mathematics. A further report for the Mathematical Association. London: G. Bell & Sons, Ltd., 1970.

SEALEY, L. G. W., *Learning about Decimals*, 2nd edition. Oxford: Basil Blackwell & Mott, Ltd., 1962.

————, *The Creative Use of Mathematics in Junior School*. Oxford: Basil Blackwell & Mott, Ltd., 1960.

————, *More Mathematical Ideas*. Oxford: Basil Blackwell & Mott, Ltd., 1962.

————, *Facts to Discover and Learn*. Oxford: Basil Blackwell & Mott, Ltd., 1967.

————, *Finding Mathematics Around Us*. Oxford: Basil Blackwell & Mott, Ltd., 1967.

————, *Some Important Mathematical Ideas*. Oxford: Basil Blackwell & Mott, Ltd., 1967.

WILLIAMS, E. M., AND HILARY SHUARD, *Primary Mathematics Today*. London: The Longman Group, Ltd., 1970.

Music and Movement

BAILEY, E., *Discovering Music With Young Children*. London: Methuen & Co., Ltd., 1958.

CAMERON, W. McD., AND M. CAMERON, *Education in Movement in the Infant School*. Oxford: Basil Blackwell & Mott, Ltd., 1969.

LABAN, RUDOLF, *Modern Educational Dance*. London: Macdonald and Evans, Ltd., 1963.

Moving and Growing, Physical Education in the Primary School, Part One. London: HMSO, 1967.

RUSSELL, JOAN, *Creative Dance in the Primary School*. London: Macdonald and Evans, Ltd., 1965.

Teaching Music in the Primary Schools, Advisory Centre for Education, Forum 2. London: Ginn & Co., Ltd., 1967.

THORNTON, S., *Movement Prospective of Rudolf Laban*. London: Macdonald & Evans, Ltd., 1970.

Reading

ASHTON-WARNER, SYLVIA, *Teacher*. New York: Bantam Books, Inc., 1963.

GODDARD, NORA L., *Reading in the Modern Infants' School*. London: University of London Press, 1964.

"Learning to Read," from *Report on Education No. 64*, Department of Education and Science. London: HMSO, 1970.

MACKAY, D., B. THOMPSON, AND P. SCHAUB, *Breakthrough to Literacy*. London: Longman for the Schools Council, 1970.

MOYLE, DONALD, *The Teaching of Reading*. London: Ward Lock Ltd., 1968.

Reading Skills. United Kingdom Reading Association. London: Ward Lock Ltd., 1968.

SIMPSON, M. M., *Suggestions for Teaching Reading in Infant Classes*. New Zealand: Department of Education, 1962.

TANSLEY, A. E., *Reading and Remedial Reading*. London: Routledge & Kegan Paul, Ltd., 1967.

Teaching Reading in Junior and Secondary Schools, Advisory Centre for Education, Forum 4. London: Ginn & Co., Ltd., 1967.

THOMPSON, BRENDA, *Learning to Read.* London: Sidgwick & Jackson, Ltd., 1970.

Science

A *Working Guide to the Elementary Science Study (ESS).* Newton, Mass.: Education Development Center, 1971. Complete listing of *ESS Teachers Manuals* available from McGraw-Hill Book Company, Webster Division, Manchester, Mo.

BAKER, ROBERT M., "A Study of the Effects of a Selected Set of Science Teaching Materials (ESS) on Classroom Instructional Behaviors," listed in A *Working Guide (see above).*

BLACKWELL, F. J., *Starting Points for Science—1.* Oxford: Basil Blackwell & Mott, Ltd., 1968.

DeSHIELDS, SHIRLEY MANSON, "A Comparison of Student Achievement in Fifth Grade Science Classes Employing Traditional and Discovery Approaches," listed in A *Working Guide (see above).*

Environmental Studies, American Geological Institute, Boulder, Colo., 1970.

The ESS Reader, Elementary Science Study, Newton, Mass.: Education Development Center, 1970.

HAWKINS, DAVID, "Messing About in Science," *Science & Children,* Vol. 2, No. 5, Washington, D. C., February 1965.

LAWRENCE, EVELYN, NATHAN ISAACS, WYATT RAWSON, *Approaches to Science in the Primary School.* London: The Educational Supply Association, Ltd., 1960.

Nuffield Junior Science Project. Complete Listing from William Collins Sons & Co., Ltd., London. (SRA, Don Mills, Ontario, Canada.)

Science in the Primary Schools. London: HMSO, 1966.

SMERAGLIO, ALFRED, AND FRED K. HONIGMAN, "Examining Behavioral Differences Between 'New' and 'Traditional' Methods of Elementary Science Instruction," listed in A *Working Guide (see above).*

Writing

CLEGG, A. B., *The Excitement of Writing.* London: Chatto & Windus (Educational), Ltd., 1966.

HOLBROOK, DAVID, *English for the Rejected.* London: Cambridge University Press, 1965.

———, *Children's Writing.* London: Cambridge University Press, 1967.

HOPKINS, LEE BENNETT, *Let Them Be Themselves: Language Arts Enrichment for Disadvantaged Children in Elementary Schools.* New York: Citation Press, 1969.

KOHL, HERBERT, *Teaching the Unteachable.* New York: The New York Review of Books, 1967.

LEWIS, RICHARD, *Miracles: Poems by Children of the English-Speaking World.* New York: Simon & Schuster, Inc., 1966.

MIRTHES, CAROLINE, *Can't You Hear Me Talking to You?* New York: Bantam Books, Inc., 1971.

Teachers and Writers Collaborative Newsletter, Pratt Center for Community Improvement, 244 Vanderbilt Avenue, Brooklyn, N.Y. 11205.

III. THEORY

John Dewey

The Child and the Curriculum. Chicago: University of Chicago Press, 1956.
Democracy and Education. New York: The Macmillan Co., 1965.
Experience and Nature. LaSalle, Ill.: Open Court Publishing Co., 1958.
The School and Society. Chicago: University of Chicago Press, 1915, rev. 1943.
AND EVELYN DEWEY, *Schools of Tomorrow.* New York: E. P. Dutton & Co., Inc., 1962.

Jean Piaget

The Construction of Reality in the Child. New York: Basic Books, Inc., Publishers, 1954.
The Language and Thought of the Child. New York: Humanities Press, Inc., 1962.
The Moral Judgment of the Child. New York: The Free Press, 1965.
The Origins of Intelligence in Children. New York: International Universities Press, Inc., 1966.
Play, Dreams and Imitation in Childhood. New York: W. W. Norton & Co., Inc., 1962.
The Psychology of Intelligence. Totowa, N. J.: Littlefield, Adams & Co., 1968.
Science of Education and the Psychology of the Child. New York: Grossman Publishers, Inc.—Orion Press, 1970.
AND BARBEL INHELDER, *Psychology of the Child.* New York: Basic Books, Inc., 1969.

On Piaget

ALMY, MILLIE, *Logical Thinking in Second Grade.* New York: Teachers College Press, 1970.

————, E. CHITTENDEN, AND P. MILLER, *Young Children's Thinking: Studies of Some Aspects of Piaget's Theory.* New York: Teachers College Press, 1966.

BREARLEY, MOLLY. (See "Curriculum—General.")

————, AND ELIZABETH HITCHFIELD, *A Teachers' Guide to Reading Piaget.* London: Routledge & Kegan Paul, Ltd., 1966.

CHURCHILL, EILEEN M., *Piaget's Findings and the Teacher*. London: National Froebel Foundation, 1960.

ELKIND, DAVID, AND JOHN H. FLAVELL, eds., *Studies in Cognitive Development: Essays in Honor of Jean Piaget*. New York: Oxford University Press, Inc., 1969.

FLAVELL, J. H., *The Developmental Psychology of Jean Piaget*. New York: Van Nostrand Reinhold Co., 1963.

FURTH, HANS G., *Piaget for Teachers*. Englewood Cliffs, N. J.: Prentice Hall, Inc., 1970.

———, *Piaget and Knowledge: Theoretical Foundations*. Englewood Cliffs, N. J.: Prentice-Hall, Inc., 1969.

HUNT, J. McVICKER, *Intelligence and Experience*. New York: The Ronald Press Company, 1961.

———, *The Psychological Basis for Using Pre-School Enrichment as an Antidote for Cultural Deprivation*. (Reprint from the *Merrill-Palmer Quarterly of Behavior and Development*, Vol. 10, no. 3, 1964).

SIGEL, IRVING E., AND FRANK H. HOOPER, eds., *Logical Thinking in Children; Research Based on Piaget's Theory*. New York: Holt, Rinehart & Winston, Inc., 1968.

Susan Isaacs

Childhood and After. London: Routledge & Kegan Paul, Ltd., 1948. (New York: Agathon Press, Inc., 1970.)

The Children We Teach. London: University of London Press, 1963. (New York: Schocken Books, Inc.,©1971.)

The Educational Value of the Nursery School. London: Nursery School Association of Great Britain and Northern Ireland, No. 45.

Intellectual Growth in Young Children. London: Routledge & Kegan Paul, Ltd., 1930. (New York: Schocken Books, Inc., 1966.)

The Nursery Years. London: Routledge & Kegan Paul, Ltd., 1929. (New York: Schocken Books, Inc., 1968, with an Introduction by Millie Almy.)

Social Development in Young Children. London: Routledge & Kegan Paul, Ltd., 1937.

On Susan Isaacs

GARDNER, D. E. M., *Susan Isaacs: The First Biography*. London: Methuen Educational, Ltd., 1969.

Nathan Isaacs

"Children's 'Scientific' Interests," in *First Years in School, Studies in Education*. London: University of London, Institute of Education, Evans Brothers, Ltd., 1963.

"Children's 'Why' Questions," Appendix to S. Isaacs, *Intellectual Growth in Young Children*. London: Routledge & Kegan Paul, Ltd., 1936.

Early Scientific Trends in Children. London: National Froebel Foundation, 1958.

The Growth of Understanding in the Young Child. London: Ward Lock Ltd., 1961. (New York: Agathon Press, Inc., 1971, N. *Isaacs: A Brief Introduction to Piaget.*)

"Memorandum for the Plowden Committee," *Froebel Journal,* No. 2, London: June 1965.

The Nathan Isaacs Papers, (tentative title), Mildred Hardeman, ed., New York: Teachers College Press, in press.

New Light on Children's Ideas of Number. London: Ward Lock Ltd., 1960. (New York: Agathon Press, Inc., 1971, N. *Isaacs: A Brief Introduction to Piaget.*)

Piaget: Some Answers to Teachers' Questions. London: National Froebel Foundation, 1965.

Some Aspects of Piaget's Work. London: National Froebel Foundation, 1955.

What is Required of the Nursery-Infant Teacher in This Country Today? London: National Froebel Foundation, 1967.

On Nathan Isaacs

WEBER, LILLIAN, "Nathan Isaacs—An American Appreciation," *The New Era,* Vol. 49, No. 3, March 1968, Sussex, England.

Others

ALMY, MILLIE, ed., *Early Childhood Play: Selected Readings Related to Cognition and Motivation.* New York: Associated Educational Services Corporation, 1968.

BIBER, BARBARA, *Preschool Education.* New York: Bank Street College of Education Publications. (Reprint from *Education and the Idea of Mankind,* Robert Ulich, ed., Council for the Study of Mankind, 1964.)

———, AND MARGERY B. FRANKLIN, "The Relevance of Developmental and Psychodynamic Concepts to the Education of the Pre-School Child," in Almy, ed., *Early Childhood Play.*

Children Learning through Scientific Interests. London: National Froebel Foundation, 1966.

ERIKSON, ERIK H., *Childhood and Society.* New York: W. W. Norton & Co., Inc., 1950. Rev. ed., 1964.

FANTINI, MARIO, AND GERALD WEINSTEIN, *Toward Humanistic Education.* New York: Frederick A. Praeger, Inc., 1970.

FRANK, LAWRENCE K., *On the Importance of Infancy.* New York: Random House, Inc., 1966.

FREIRE, PAULO, *The Pedagogy of the Oppressed.* New York: Herder and Herder, Inc., 1970.

FREUD, ANNA, *Normality and Pathology in Childhood.* New York: International Universities Press, 1966.

GATTEGNO, CALEB, *What We Owe Children: The Subordination of Teaching to Learning.* New York: Outerbridge & Dienstfrey, 1970.

GOODLAD, J. I., AND R. H. ANDERSON, *The Non-Graded Elementary School.* New York: Harcourt, Brace & World, Inc., 1963.

GOODMAN, PAUL, *Compulsory Mis-Education.* New York: Horizon Press, 1964.

GRIFFITHS, RUTH, *Imagination in Early Childhood.* London: Routledge & Kegan Paul, Ltd., 1945.

HAWKINS, DAVID, "Childhood and the Education of Intellectuals," *Harvard Educational Review,* Vol. 36, No. 4, Fall 1966.

————, "I, Thou, It." (Leicestershire, 1967). Newton, Mass.: Education Development Center. (Mimeographed.)

HOLT, JOHN, *How Children Fail.* New York: Pitman Publishing Corp., 1964.

————, *How Children Learn.* New York: Pitman Publishing Corp., 1967.

ILLICH, IVAN D., *Celebration of Awareness.* Garden City, N. Y.: Doubleday & Company, Inc., 1970.

JACKSON, PHILIP W., *Life in Classrooms.* New York: Holt, Rinehart & Winston, Inc., 1968.

LAWRENCE, EVELYN, *Froebel and English Education.* London: National Froebel Foundation, 1952. Reprinted 1969.

LECKY, PRESCOTT, *Self-Consistency: A Theory of Personality.* Garden City: Doubleday & Co.—Anchor Books, 1968.

LEWIS, M. M., *Language and the Child.* London: National Foundation for Educational Research, 1969.

MCLELLAN, JOYCE, *The Question of Play.* London: Pergamon Press, Ltd., 1970.

MASLOW, A. H., "Perceiving, Behaving, Becoming," in *Yearbook,* Association for Supervision and Curriculum Development, 1962.

————, *Toward a Psychology of Being.* New York: Van Nostrand Reinhold Company, 1962.

MILLER, S., *The Psychology of Play.* London: Penguin Books, Ltd., 1968.

MOFFITT, M., AND E. OMWAKE, *The Intellectual Content of Play.* Washington, D. C.: National Association for the Education of Young Children.

MONTESSORI, MARIA, *The Absorbent Mind.* New York: Holt, Rinehart & Winston, Inc., 1967.

————, *Spontaneous Activity in Education: The Advanced Montessori Method.* New York: Schocken Books, Inc., 1965.

MUKERJI, ROSE, "Roots in Early Childhood for Continuous Learning," in *Teaching the Disadvantaged Child.* Washington, D.C.: National Association for the Education of Young Children.

MURPHY, L. B. et al, *The Widening World of Childhood: Paths Toward Mastery.* New York: Basic Books, Inc., 1962.

NAVARRA, J. G., *The Development of Scientific Concepts in a Young Child.* New York: Teachers College Press, 1955.

RAMBUSCH, NANCY, *Learning How to Learn.* Baltimore, Md.: Helicon Press, Inc., 1962.

READ, HERBERT, *The Redemption of the Robot.* New York: Simon & Schuster, Inc., 1969.

ROGERS, CARL, *Freedom to Learn.* Columbus, O.: Charles E. Merrill Books, Inc., 1969.

RUSSELL, BERTRAND, *Education and the Good Life*. New York: Liveright Publishing Corp., 1931.

SIMMS, J. A., AND T. H. SIMMS, *From Three to Thirteen*. London: The Longman Group, Ltd., 1969.

WALL, W. D., AND ANNA FREUD, *The Enrichment of Childhood*. Nursery School Association. London: Kenyon House Press, Ltd., 1960.

WANN, K. D., M. S. DORN, AND E. A. LIDDLE, *Fostering Intellectual Development in Young Children*. New York: Teachers College Press, 1965.

WHITEHEAD, ALFRED N., *Aims of Education and Other Essays*. New York: The Free Press, 1967.

WINNICOTT, DONALD W., *The Child, The Family and The Outside World*. London: Penguin Books, Ltd., 1964.

————, *The Maturational Processes and the Facilitating Environment*. London: The Hogarth Press and the Institute of Psycho-Analysis, 1965.

IV. SPECIAL ASPECTS

ABRAHAM, ENA, "Young Children in High Flats," *Froebel Journal,* June 1967.

BARKER LUNN, JOAN C., *Streaming in the Primary School*. London: National Foundation for Educational Research, 1970.

BENJAMIN, J., *In Search of Adventure. A Study in Play Leadership*. London: The National Council of Social Service, 1966.

BLACKIE, JOHN, *Inspecting and the Inspectorate*. London: Routledge & Kegan Paul, Ltd., 1970. (In U.S., British Information Services, New York, N. Y.)

BOWLBY, J., *Child Care and the Growth of Love*. London: Penguin Books, Ltd., 1953.

BURLINGHAM, D., AND A. FREUD, *Infants without Families*. London: George Allen & Unwin, Ltd., 1944.

————, *War & Children*. New York: International Universities Press, 1943.

CLEGG, A. B., AND B. MEGSON, *Children in Distress*. London: Penguin Books, Ltd., 1968. (In U.S., British Information Services, New York, N. Y.)

COOK, A., AND H. MACK, *The Head Teacher's Role, The Teacher's Role*. New York: Citation Press, in press.

DERRICK, JUNE, *Teaching English to Immigrants*. London: The Longman Group, Ltd., 1966.

DOUGLAS, J. W. B., *The Home and the School*. London: MacGibbon & Kee, Ltd., 1964.

GOLDSWORTHY, G. M., *Part-Time Nursery Education*. London: The Nursery School Association of Great Britain and Northern Ireland, No. 75, 1964.

GRANNIS, JOSEPH G., "The School as a Model of Society," *Harvard Graduate School of Education Association Bulletin,* Vol. 12, No. 2, Fall 1967.

GREEN, LAWRENCE, *Parents and Teachers*. London: George Allen & Unwin, Ltd., 1968.

HAWKES, NICHOLAS, *Immigrant Children in British Schools*. London: Pall Mall Press, Ltd., 1966.

JACKSON, BRIAN, *Streaming: An Education System in Miniature*. London: Routledge & Kegan Paul, Ltd., 1963.

JAMES, CHARITY, *Young Lives at Stake*. London: William Collins Sons & Co., Ltd., 1968.

LADY ALLEN OF HURTWOOD, *Design for Play*. London: The Housing Centre Trust, 1961.

———— et al, eds., *Space for Play*. Copenhagen: OMEP (World Organization for Early Childhood Education), 1964.

Eveline Lowe Primary School, London. Building Bulletin No. 36, Department of Education and Science. London: HMSO, 1967.

MARSHALL, SYBIL, *Adventure in Creative Education*. London: Penguin Books, Ltd., 1968.

MAY, DOROTHY E., *Children in the Nursery School: Studies of Personal Adjustment in Early Childhood*. London: University of London Press, 1963.

McGEENEY, PATRICK, *Parents Are Welcome*. London: The Longman Group, Ltd., 1969.

National Union of Teachers, *First Things First*. London: National Union of Teachers, 1964.

————, *The Financing of Education*. London: National Union of Teachers, 1964.

————, *The State of Nursery Education*. London: National Union of Teachers, 1964.

NEWSON, JOHN, AND ELIZABETH NEWSON, *Four Years Old in an Urban Community*. London: George Allen & Unwin, Ltd., 1968. (Chicago: Aldine Publishing Co., 1968.)

Parent Teacher Relations in Primary Schools, Education Survey 5, Department of Education and Science. London: HMSO, 1968.

Periods of Stress in the Primary School. London: National Association for Mental Health, 1962.

PRINGLE, M. L. KELLMER, *Deprivation & Education*. London: The Longman Group, Ltd., 1965.

RASMUSSEN, M., ed., *Space, Arrangement, Beauty in School*. Washington, D. C.: Association for Childhood Education International, 1958.

The Role of the Primary Head, Advisory Centre for Education, Forum 1. London: Ginn & Co., Ltd., 1969.

Schoolboys of Barbiana, *Letter to a Teacher*. (With postcripts by Robert Coles and John Holt.) New York: Random House, Inc., 1970.

Schools Without Walls. New York: Education Facilities Laboratories, 1965.

SIMON, BRIAN, *Nonstreaming in the Junior School*. Leicester, England: PSW (Educational) Publications, 1964.

Slow Learners at School. London: HMSO, 1964.

The State of Nursery Education. Report of a survey conducted by the National Union of Teachers, 1964. London: National Union of Teachers, 1964.

Streaming and the Primary Teacher, Gabriel Choron, ed. London: National Foundation for Educational Research, 1970.

Studies in Education: First Years in School. University of London: Institute of Education. London: Evans Bros., Ltd., 1963.

TANNER, J. M., *Education and Physical Growth*. New York: International Universities Press, 1970.

TANSLEY, A. E., AND R. GULLIFORD, *The Education of the Slow Learning Child.* London: Routledge & Kegan Paul, Ltd., 1960.

TIZARD, JACK, *Survey and Experiment in Special Education.* London: George G. Harrap & Co., Ltd. (for the University of London Institute of Education), 1967.

————, M. RUTTER, AND KINGSLEY WHITMORE, *Education, Health and Behaviour.* London: The Longman Group, Ltd., 1970.

UTZINGER, ROBERT, *Some European Nursery Schools and Playgrounds.* Ann Arbor: University of Michigan, 1970.

WHITE, EIRENE, et al, *The Forgotten Two Million: Why Nursery Schools?* London: The Nursery School Association of Great Britain and Northern Ireland, 1964.

————, *Two to Five in High Flats.* London: The Housing Centre Trust, 1961.

YEOMANS, EDWARD, *The Reeducation of Teachers for the Integrated Day.* (Mimeographed.) Boston, Mass.: National Association of Independent Schools, 1970.

————, *The Wellsprings of Teaching.* Boston, Mass.: National Association of Independent Schools, 1969.

YOUNG, M., AND P. McGEENEY, *Learning Begins at Home.* London: Routledge & Kegan Paul, Ltd., 1968.

————, AND M. ARMSTRONG, "The Flexible School—The Next Step for Comprehensives," *Where.* London: Advisory Centre for Education, Ltd., 1965.

YUDKIN, SIMON, *0-5 A Report on the Care of Pre-School Children.* London: George Allen & Unwin, Ltd., 1967.

————, AND A. HOLME, *Working Mothers and their Children.* London: Sphere Books, Ltd., 1969. (First published in 1963 by Michael Joseph, Ltd.)

V. ANALYSIS

Analysis of an Approach to Open Education, Interim Report, A. M. Bussis and E. A. Chittenden. Princeton, N. J.: Educational Testing Service, 1970.

CARINI, PATRICIA, JOAN BLAKE, AND LOUIS CARINI, A *Methodology for Evaluating Innovative Programs,* from The Prospect School, Title 3, Project 825. Bennington, Vt.: Supervisory Union, June 1969, (Mimeographed).

CHITTENDEN, EDWARD A., "What Is Learned and What Is Taught," *Young Children,* Vol. 25, No. 1, October 1969.

CLARK, MARGARET M., *Reading Difficulties in School.* London: Penguin Books, Ltd., 1970.

COX, C. B., AND A. E. DYSON, eds., *Fight for Education: A Black Paper.* London: The Critical Quarterly Society, 1968.

————, *Black Paper Two: The Crisis in Education.* London: The Critical Quarterly Society, 1969.

Evaluations of ESS (See "Curriculum—Science").

GAHAGAN, D. M., AND G. A. GAHAGAN, *Talk Reform.* London: Routledge & Kegan Paul, Ltd., 1971.

GARDNER, D. E. M., *Experiment and Tradition in Primary Schools*. London: Methuen & Co., Ltd., 1966.

———, "The Plowden Report on 'Children and Their Primary Schools'," *Froebel Journal*, January 1968.

———, AND JOAN E. CASS, *The Role of the Teacher in the Infant and Nursery School*. London: Pergamon Press, Ltd., 1965.

GULLIFORD, R., *Backwardness and Educational Failure*. London: National Foundation for Educational Research in England and Wales, 1969.

JACKSON, B., AND B. McALHONE, eds., *Verdict on the Facts*. London: Advisory Centre for Education, 1969.

MINUCHIN, P., B. BIBER, E. SHAPIRO AND H. ZIMILES, *The Psychological Impact of School Experience*. New York: Basic Books, Inc., 1969.

PETERS, R. S., ed., *Perspectives on Plowden*. London: Routledge & Kegan Paul, Ltd., 1969.

Plowden Report (*see Children and Their Primary Schools*, under "Descriptions").

Progress in Reading 1948–1964, Department of Education & Science. London: HMSO, 1966.

RAVENETTE, A. T., *Dimensions of Reading Difficulties*. London: Pergamon Press, Ltd., 1968.

Reading: Problems and Perspectives, J. C. Daniel, ed., United Kingdom Reading Association. London: Partisan Press, Ltd., 1970.

RESNICK, LAUREN B., *Teacher Behavior in an Informal British Infant School*. Paper Presented at American Educational Research Association, 1971. (Mimeographed.)

WALBERG, HERBERT J., and SUSAN CHRISTIE THOMAS, *Characteristics of Open Education: Toward an Operational Definition*. Newton, Mass.: TDR Associates, Inc. for Education Development Center, 1971.

VI. GUIDELINES

COHEN, D. H., *Learning in the Kindergarten*. Albany, N. Y.: The University of the State of New York, Bureau of Child Development and Parent Education, 1968.

Curriculum Is What Happens, L. D. Dittman, ed. Washington, D. C.: National Association for the Education of Young Children, 1970.

FLURRY, RUTH, *The Five-Year-Old And His Thinking*. Albany, N. Y.: The University of the State of New York, Bureau of Child Development and Parent Education, 1967.

Hadow Report (*see* "Descriptions").

Half Our Future. Report of the Central Advisory Council for Education. London: HMSO, 1963.

LAW, NORMA, et al, *Basic Propositions for Early Childhood Education*. Washington, D. C.: Association for Childhood Education International, 1965.

Living and Learning. The Report of the Provincial Committee on Aims and Objectives of Education in the Schools of Ontario. Toronto, Ontario: Department of Education, 1968.

Nyquist, Ewald B., "The British Primary School Approach to Education: Time for Reform in the Elementary Schools." (Remarks made at Conference on British Infant School, December 7, 1970.) Albany, N. Y.: State Education Department.

———, "The State's Responsibility for Early Childhood Education." (Remarks made at Superintendents' Work Conference, Teachers College, Columbia University, July 14, 1970.) Albany, N. Y.: State Education Department.

Plowden Report (*see* "Descriptions").

Scribner, Harvey B., "The Process of Learning." (Text of Talk at Chancellor's Conference on Educational Alternatives in Elementary Schools, Teachers College, Columbia University, January 29, 1971.) New York City Board of Education, *Staff Bulletin,* February 11, 1971.

Spodek, B., *Open Education,* Proceedings of a Conference sponsored by the National Association of the Education of Young Children, Washington, D. C., 1970.

Vermont State Department of Education, *Vermont Design for Education,* May 1968. Office of the Commissioner of Education, Montpelier, Vt., 05062.

Yeomans, Edward, *Education for Initiative and Responsibility.* Boston, Mass.: National Association of Independent Schools, 1967.

VII. *PUBLICATIONS AND FILMS OF SPECIAL INTEREST*

BBC publications. *Discovery and Experience,* 1965, *Mother Tongue—Study Notes,* 1967. BBC, 35 Maryleborne High Street, London W. 1, England.

Big Rock Candy Mountain, Portola Institute, Menlo Park, Calif. 94025.

Department of Education and Science pamphlets. London: HMSO.

Forum. Leicester, England: PSW (Educational) Publications.

Froebel Foundation pamphlets. National Froebel Foundation, 2 Manchester Square, London, W. 1, England.

Froebel Journal, National Froebel Foundation.

Harvard Educational Review, Harvard University, Cambridge, Mass.

Ideas, Goldsmith's College, University of London.

Insights, New School, University of North Dakota, Grand Forks, N. D. 58201.

London Times Educational Supplement, London.

National Association of Pre-School Playgroups pamphlets. London.

National Campaign for Nursery Education, *Newsletter,* London.

Nursery School Association of Great Britain and Northern Ireland pamphlets, 89 Stamford Street, London.

Outlook, Mountain View Center for Environmental Education, University of Colorado, Boulder, Colo.

Schools Council Publications. London: HMSO. (In U.S., British Information Services, 845 Third Avenue, N.Y., N.Y. 10022.)

The Teacher Paper, Fred L. Staab and Robin B. Staab, eds., Portland, Ore.

This Magazine Is About Schools, 56 Esplanade Street, E., Toronto, Ontario.

Trends in Education. London: HMSO.

Where, Advisory Centre for Education, 32 Trumington Street, Cambridge, England.

FILMS:

Available from Time-Life Films, New York:
    BBC: *Discovery and Experience*.
    ————: *Mother Tongue*.
    ————: *Springs of Learning*.

Available from Education Development Center, 55 Chapel St., Newton, Mass.
    Felt, Henry, *Battling Brook Primary School (Four Days in September)*.
    ————, *Choosing to Learn*.
    ————, *Medbourne Primary School (Four Days in May)*.
    ————, *Westfield Infant School (Two Days in May)*.
    Leitman, Alan, *I Ain't Playin' No More*.
    ————, *I Am Here Today*.
    ————, *They Can Do It*.
    Weber, Lillian, *Infants School*.

INDEX

Accidents, responsibility, 41–42
Acting, 82, 117
Activity cards, 106
Activity methods, 236
Activity period (see Timetable)
Adult role, 177–78 (see also Environment; Language; Teacher, English)
Age of entry, 78, 140
Aggression, handling of, 41–42
Alienation, 205, 208
Alternatives, 245
Art School Service Committee, 117 note
Assimilation-accommodation-reaccommodation (see Learning)

B.B.C. programs:
  on music, 84
  on Plowden, 159

Beginning points (see Learning)
Bell, Andrew, 162
Bereiter, Carl, 208–12, 242
Bereiter-Engelmann program, 209, 210, 211, 242
Bernstein, Basil, 191, 197–208, 211–14, 220, 225, 229
"Bernstein's children," 221
Big Hall, 64, 82–88
  in communal life, 95
  design (illus.), 83
  disadvantages, 85
  as shared area, 82, 84, 99, 133
  side hall, 88
Birmingham schools, 7, 8, 17, 47
Blackie, John, 138
Board of Managers, 45, 100
Boyce, E. R., 160, 202–3
Brearley, Molly, 196, 226 (see also Froebelian position)

Bristol schools, 7, 8, 17, 47, 91
Bristol Teachers' Centre, 154
Brooks, Marian, 10 *note*
Brown, Mary, 92
Bruner, Jerome, 191–96, 213–14, 225, 228
Buildings:
  infant schools, 68
  nursery schools, 19–20
Burlingham, Dorothy, 166

Callahan, R. E., 234
Cazden, Courtney B., 199–200, 213
Child, active (*see* Curiosity)
Children and Their Primary Schools (*see* Plowden Report)
Children's behavior, 134–37 (*see also* Aggression)
Child's own question, 109, 111, 183–84, 194, 195, 250
Child study, 46, 149, 170, 225 (*see also* Learning; Development stages)
  behaviorism, 172–73
  observation, 165, 172–73
Child's whole day (*see* Timetable)
Chomsky, Noam, 211 (*see also* Linguists)
Churchill, Eileen, 122
Circular 8/60, 56, 57, 58 (*see* Notes on Usage)
City College, 9 *note*, 10 *note*, 248
Civil Rights Movement, influence of, 2–3
Clark, Kenneth, 5, 245
Classroom plan (*illus.*), 116
Class size, 223
  in infant schools, 69–71
  in nursery schools, 17, 18, 43
Class teaching, 232
Communal life:
  lunch period, 98
  participation in work of school, 100
  role of head, 94–97
  shared areas, 99
  (*see also* Morning service)
Communication, 100–4
  in infant schools, 101–4
  in nursery schools, 34–35
  S. Isaacs on, 177–78
  between teachers, 86

Compensatory education, 4–6, 198, 233, 239, 242–44
Continuity, 181, 194, 216–20, 229
  Bernstein on, 197, 199, 206, 208
  Isaacses on, 180–82, 193–94
  preschool and early grades, 2, 5, 6
Corridors, use of:
  in American schools, 249
  in infant schools, 82
  in nursery schools, 22, 24
Critical period, in learning, 2, 229
Curiosity, 170, 173, 183–85, 197, 229, 241
  and language development, 206, 207
  Bernstein on, 201
  Bruner on, 191–92
Curriculum (*see also* Mathematics; Science; Reading; Syllabus; Essentials)
  essentials, 124, 195, 241, 242
  Froebel Institute, 226–27
  prescribed, 233, 250

Dance (*see* Music and Movement)
Day care services (U.S.), 3, 239
Day nurseries, 52–53
Demonstration schools (U.S.), 2, 3
Department of Education and Science, 46
  Board of Education, 148
  inservice courses, 153
  reading approach, 130
  reports, 156
  supervision, 53, 54, 55
  teacher qualification, 149, 151
Deutsch, Martin, 208–9, 240 *note*
Developmental thought, 173–75, 185, 193, 213–14, 226–28, 239–41
Development stages, 171, 180–81
Dewey, John, 165, 170, 184, 187, 234–37
The Dewey School, 235–36
Dewey schools, 236
Dialect, 198–99, 205, 212, 213
Dinner helpers, 75
Discipline, 136–37 (*see also* Aggression; Children's behavior)
Discrepancy (*see* Learning)
Drill, 198, 202–3, 210, 212

Education Act of 1944, 52, 54, 57, 58, 59, 97, 148, 166, 230, 251 (*see also* History)
Educational parks, 246
Educational priority areas, 19, 58, 69
Educationally Sub-Normal, 39 *note*, 40
Elaborated code (*see* Bernstein, Language)
11+ examination, 142, 216
Emotional development, 241
  Bereiter on, 210
  Bruner on, 192
  (*see also* S. Isaacs)
Engelmann, Siegfried, 208, 209–11
English teacher's way, 38–43
Environment, 27, 28, 63, 182 (*see also* Experience)
  adult role in, 224, 225
  in Head Start, 244
  in thinking, 225–29
Environmental studies (*see* Science; Social studies)
Equipment (*see* Materials)
Essentials, 124, 222, 241
  Brearley on, 226–29
  Bruner on, 194–96
Eveline Lowe School, 139, 140–41, 154
Experience, 178–79, 208
  Bruner on, 192
  and language, 222

Facilities:
  nursery schools, 20
  repairs and maintenance, 21, 44
Family grouping, 133, 248
  infant schools, 80–81
  nursery schools, 33–34
Family school, 81, 100
Fantasy (*see* Play)
Fixed points, 94
  and communal life, 97
Follow Through, 6, 242
Formal school, 185–87, 218, 232, 241, 250
Free Day, 90–94
Freud, Anna, 166
Freud, Sigmund, 171, 187
Froebel, Friedrich, 87, 162, 165, 167, 170, 235

Froebel Institute, 91, 110, 153, 172, 195, 226
Froebelian position, 104, 109, 195, 196, 226–27
Funding:
  infant schools, 69
  nursery schools, 57, 58

Garden:
  in infant schools, 68, 125
  in nursery schools, 20–21
  maintenance, 21, 44
Gardner, D. E. M.,
  estimate of informal education, 142–44
  on family grouping, 33, 34
  on free day, 90, 91
  history of nursery and infant schools, 161, 164, 167–68
  on project method, 165–66
  on reading, 77
  on recordkeeping, 112–13
  research, 159
  seminar, 9
  on staffing nursery schools, 54–57, 60, 78
  on teacher education, 152
  on timetable, 90–91
Goddard, Nora, 129–30, 140
Goldsworthy, G. M., 8
Goodlad, John, 232 *note*
Government reports, 156–60, 163–64 (*see also* History)
Gradual procedures, 31–33, 35, 78–80, 248
Griffiths, Ruth, 175, 230
Grouping, small (*see also* Family grouping), 37–38

Hadow Report, 29, 54, 60, 107, 112, 149, 156–58, 161, 163, 164, 166, 169
Handicapped children, 40, 100
Headmistress:
  choice of staff, 71
  freedom, 148, 234
  and implementation, 110
  role, 44–45, 65–66, 71–72
  selection, 45–46
  training, 44–46, 96, 151
  (*see also* Big Hall; Communal life)

Head Start, 3–5, 28, 71, 242–45
Health standards, in nursery schools, 20, 26–27, 55, 75
Health visitor, 18, 59, 75
Hechinger, Fred, 5
Helpfulness (*see* English teacher's way)
History:
  Code of 1902, 163
  Compulsory Education Act, 233
  contrast with U.S., 234, 238, 239
  Education Act of 1918, 148, 161, 164
  Inspectorate report of 1905, 29, 163
  Local Government Act of 1966, 69
  nursery school legislation, 57–58, 161, 164
  payment by results, 162, 163, 234
  role of head, 159, 160
  wartime, 166
Housing, Council estates, 18, 67
Hymes, Dell, 212, 213 (*see also* Linguists)

ILEA, 8, 140
Immigrant children, 18–19, 35, 39 *note*, 101–3
Implementation (*see* English teacher)
In-and-outness:
  Big Hall, 82
  indoor, 88
  in infant schools, 88
  in nursery schools, 29–30
  overflow, 81
Individual differences, 41, 107–8, 173–74, 217 (*see also* Informal education)
Infant schools:
  blocks in, 118
  class organization, 76–81
  entity, definition of, 147
  types, 68–69
Infants School (film), 9, 121
Informal education:
  adaptations for, 217
  Bernstein on, 201–2
  commitment, 70, 199, 221–22
  continuity, 220
  contrast with American primary schools, 233–34
  definition, 10–11, 94–95

Informal Education (*Cont.*):
  idea of, 185
  reexamination, 189–90
  in state conditions, 238
Inservice courses, 153
Inspectorate, 29, 45, 55, 153–56, 158, 163, 234
Institutes of Education, 96, 151–53, 237
Integrated day (*see* Free Day)
Interaction, 177, 194, 210
  (*see also* Communication; S. Isaacs; Social development; Social reciprocity)
IQ, 190, 217–20, 237
Isaacs, Nathan, 171–88, 211
  on continuity, 193–94
  on Dewey, 184
  on environment, 182
  on formal schools, 185–87, 200, 218, 219, 242 *note*
  influence, 9
  on Piaget, 173, 182, 185
Isaacs, Susan, 165, 166, 171–87, 202, 211, 217
  coexistence of disparate functioning, 181, 230
  on continuity, 139, 193, 194
  on fantasy, 175
  on language, 179
  Malting House School, 187
  on Piaget, 171
  on social interchange, 176–78

JMI schools, 7, 69 *note*, 134, 135, 140
Jencks, Christopher, 246
Jensen, Arthur, 219 *note*
Junior schools, 7, 8, 216
  transition to, 92, 137–42, 217

Kindergartens, 4 *note*, 235, 236

Lancaster, Joseph, 162, 233
Language:
  adult role, 179, 210–11, 222–24
    Bernstein on, 197, 205
  elaborated code, 204–6
  experience, 222
  restricted code, 198–206
  social interchange, 224
  S. Isaacs on, 178, 179
  translation, 205

Learning:
assimilation-accommodation-
    reaccommodation, 173–75, 189
beginning points, 107–9
contrast, 194–95
discrepancy, 175–78
disparate functioning, 181, 193, 241
extensions, 181, 194, 225
fantasy, 175–76
S. and N. Isaacs on, 193
spiraling, 193
time, 181, 187, 207, 229–30
unevenness of, 181, 193, 241
(*see also* Curiosity; Continuity; Environment)
Length of schooling:
Nathan Isaacs on, 188
Nuffield on, 187
Linguists, 211–14
on Bereiter-Engelmann, 211, 212
on Bernstein, 211–13
Listening (*see* Interaction; Communication; English teacher's way)
Local Education Authority (LEA) 42, 44, 55, 69, 151, 154, 158
age of transfer, 140, 159
play groups, 59
role in hiring, 45, 71
teacher evaluations, 150
Lochhead, Jewell, 107, 235, 236
London:
city council, 21
county council, 81, 154
school board, 162
schools, 7, 8, 17, 69
London Workers Education Association, 166
Lunch period, 23, 65, 93, 94, 98, 103
(*see also* Communal life)

McMillan, Margaret, 29, 33, 161, 164, 170
McNeill, David, 212 (*see also* Linguists)
Materials:
choice of, 226–27
equipment in Big Hall, 83–85
in infant schools, 114–18
junk, 28, 118
in nursery schools, 21–26, 27–29
(*see also* Environment)

Mathematics, 84, 118–22
manipulative toys, 118
Mather, Sir William, 162
Ministry of Health, 53
Mixed-age grouping (*see* Family grouping)
Montaigne, 170
Montessori, Maria:
influence, 27, 87, 170, 217
methods, 27, 87, 107, 165, 217
Moral education (*see* Morning service)
Morning service, 84, 94, 97–98
Movement:
of children, 36, 87, 100, 111, 133
to children, 36, 71, 101
Moyle, Donald, 132
Music, 21, 36, 84–85
Karl Orff, 117
Music and movement, 64, 65, 84

National Campaign for Nursery Education, 56 *note*, 57, 58
National Child Development Study:
disturbed children, 136
reading, 138
National Union of Teachers, 153
New Town schools, 8, 17, 95, 128
New York State Board of Regents, 4 *note*, 58
NNEB, 8
and age of entry, 78
and infant helper, 73–74
in infant schools, 73
in nursery schools, 25
and scarcity, 55, 56
training, 47–49
Nuffield Foundation, 153, 154, 172, 187, 195, 226
Nuffield Institutes, 123
Nuffield Junior Math, 113, 122
Nuffield Junior Science, 9, 104, 113, 124, 187
Nuffield Teacher's Guides, 92, 110, 129, 157, 183
Nursery classes, 26, 50–51
Nursery School Association of Great Britain and Northern Ireland, 187
at Oxford, 9
on staffing, 55

Nursery School Association of Great Britain and Northern Ireland (*Cont.*):
at Vassar, 2
Nursery schools:
blocks in, 28–29
building design, 19–20
influence, 60
intake, 18–19
location, 18
part-time, 49–50
staffing, 43–49
standards, 26–29, 43, 55, 60–61

Overflow:
class to school, 63, 71, 140–41
teacher supervision, 86, 87
(*see also* In-and-outness)
Owen, Robert, 161, 162, 170, 199, 233

Painting, 115
Parents:
choice of schools, 67
cooperation, 32, 33, 102
Department of Education and Science survey, 58
and gradual procedures, 21, 23, 25, 32, 33
in play groups, 54
role, 166, 177, 178
Payment by results (*see* History)
Peel, E. A., 176, 185
Pestalozzi, 170
Phonics, 131
Physical education (P. E.), 65, 84, 115
Piaget, 119, 171, 173, 185, 191, 195, 202, 211, 220, 226
(*see also* Susan Isaacs; Nathan Isaacs; Froebelian position)
Planning (*see* Teacher, English)
Plan of the Day (*see* Timetable)
Play, 59, 170, 175–76, 192, 210, 240, 241
Play Centres, 152
Play groups, 53–54
Play time (*see* Timetable)
Plowden Report, 7
on age of transfer, 139
on continuity, 139
on educational priority areas, 19

Plowden Report (*Cont.*):
on expansion, 57–59, 216, 231
on family grouping, 81
on free day, 92–93
on in-and-outness, 88
on learning process, 172
on parents, 102
preparation of, 158–59, 216
on staffing, 55–57
Preschool years, research, 229
Preverbal logic, 180–81, 192
Private schools (U.S.), 3, 236, 238, 239
Progression, one-directional, 76, 110
Project method, 165

Rachel McMillan Teachers College, 9, 33, 74
Reading, 126–32, 139
of poetry and stories, 66, 131
Reception class, 77–78
Recordkeeping:
in infant schools, 111–13
in nursery schools, 36
Religious Education (*see* Morning service)
Responsiveness (*see* English teacher's way; Communication)
Restricted code (*see* Bernstein; Language)
Role-playing (*see* Acting)
Rousseau, Jean Jacques, 170

Save the Children Fund, 59
School environment, 182 (*see also* Environment; Experience; Materials)
School keeper, 74
School size:
infant schools, 69–70
nursery schools, 164
Schools Council, 104, 130, 195
Science, 122–26
Simultaneous use, 89, 91
Skills, 65, 93, 106, 109, 119 (*see also* Reading; Mathematics)
Skills period (*see* Timetable)
Social development, 174, 176–78, 194, 210, 217
Social reciprocity (*see also* Interaction), 194

Social studies, 124
Spiraling (*see* Learning)
Staffing:
  infant schools, 71–76
  nursery schools, 43–49
Standards, 234 (*see also* Nursery schools)
Streaming, 217–20
Student help, 44, 74, 150
Suburban schools, 8, 17
Syllabus, 65, 119, 123–24, 148, 232

Tansley, A. E., 132
Teacher, American, 235, 238
Teacher, English:
  direction, 109–11, 133
  education, 46–47, 149–51, 237
  implementation, 109–11, 133
  intervention, 41
  and overflow, 30, 86
  planning, 65, 104–7
  qualification, 151
  remedial, 72
  suggestion, 39, 135
  supply, 72
  unqualified, 73
  (*see also* English teacher's way)
Teacher Centres, 104, 153
Teachers' colleges, 149
Teaching assistants, 4 *note*, 244, 248
  (*see* NNEB)
Tests, 113, 114

Thinking, Froebelian view, 225–29
Time, 207, 229, 230
Timetable:
  activity period, 89, 90, 133
  child's whole day, 93–94
  fixed points, 64–65, 94, 97
  in infant schools, 89
  playtime, 91, 99
  simultaneous use, 89
  skills period, 89, 90, 133
Trust of children, 42, 87, 170, 183, 229

Undifferentiated day (*see* Free Day)
University of London, 8, 9, 166
University Socialist Federation, 166

Visitors, 42, 103
Voluntarism, 246
Vouchers, 246

Watching, child, 106–7, 170, 225 (*see also* Child study)
Water play,
  in infant schools, 126
  in nursery schools, 24
Weather and clothing, 29, 30
Weather station (*see* Science), 125
Welfare helpers, 75
Wendy House, 21, 117, 118, 125
Writing, 128, 129

"Both the English infant school and its model, the English nursery school, are examples of state education that have changed and that possess human dimension, and so they are examples for us of a genuine possibility for change within our own public schools."

Lillian Weber reached this conclusion after a year and a half devoted to observations and analysis of 47 state schools in England. This book, the result of her study, offers a full presentation of the practice and process, the history and theory of informal education in England's primary schools.

Professor Weber discovered that despite large classes in poor neighborhoods and a limited national education budget, the learning in English schools was geared to individual children, and a responsive relationship between children and teachers was fostered. She found that informal schools cultivated the conscious use of the whole school in order to maximize such interaction, and in the free atmosphere, each child could follow his own interests as well as being part of this whole.

Through vivid descriptions of actual episodes, scenes, and schedules for British children up to age eight, Mrs. Weber shows the reader exactly how English informal schooling works. She discusses the curriculum in depth, especially reading, math, and science.